FLY-FISHING COASTAL CUTTHROAT TROUT

Flies, Techniques, Conservation

LES JOHNSON

FLY-FISHING COASTAL CUTTHROAT TROUT

Flies, Techniques, Conservation

LES JOHNSON

Frank
Amato
PORTLAND

About the Author

Les began fishing and hunting in western Washington as a young boy more than sixty years ago with his grandfather and mentor, Edward J. Knight. He has been a writer for more than forty years, concentrating on fishing, fly-tying, hunting and conservation subjects. His articles have appeared in *Field & Stream, Western Outdoors, Saltwater Sportsman, Salmon Trout Steelheader, Fly Rod & Reel, Fly Fishing in Salt Waters* and *Fly Fisherman.* His books include, *The Sea-Run Cutthroat Trout; Fly Fishing for Pacific Salmon* (co-authored with Bruce Ferguson and Pat Trotter), and *Tube Flies* (co-authored with Mark Mandell). Les was founding editor of *Western Fly Tying* magazine which he later expanded into *Fly Fishing & Tying Journal.* In 2000 Les moved temporarily to Jackson, Wyoming to help develop and manage the editorial content for a national fishing and hunting web site, Greatlodge.com

In addition to writing about his fishing adventures, Les has been a tireless advocate for the protection of salmon, steelhead and coastal cutthroat trout. Since 1973 he has lobbied for the welfare of the coastal cutthroat trout in Washington which is now safeguarded on a river-by-river basis and sheltered under catch-and-release regulations in all marine waters. In 2000 The Washington Fly Fishing Club presented him its *Tommy Brayshaw Award* for his continued contributions to conservation efforts and conservation-oriented legislation. In that same year he joined a gathering of like-thinking individuals and helped to found the *Wild Steelhead Coalition,* an advocacy group dedicated to saving wild steelhead. In 2002 he was given the *Dawn Holbrook Memorial Award* from the Northwest Fly Anglers for lifetime achievement in teaching others to grow in the art and science of fly-fishing.

Les lives in Redmond, Washington with his wife and fishing partner, Carol. Their present favorite fishing areas include Washington's central basin lakes, the Coeur'd Alene River in Idaho, and Vancouver Island, British Columbia.

All inquiries should be addressed to:
Frank Amato Publications, Inc. • P.O. Box 82112 • Portland, Oregon 97282
503-653-8108 • www.amatobooks.com

Photography: Les Johnson unless noted
Fly Plate Photography: Jim Schollmeyer
Book Design: Jerry Hutchinson

Cover painting of freshwater coloration of sea-run cutthroat trout by artist Dave Bartholet.
Contact him at P.O. Box 920, Seaside, Oregon 97183, www.davebartholet.com or Bartholet@theoregonshore.com

Softbound ISBN 10: 1-57188-333-9
Softbound ISBN 13: 978-1-57188-333-9
UPC: 0-81127-00165-1
Hardbound ISBN: 1-57188-334-7
UPC: 0-81127-00166-8
Limited Hardbound ISBN: 1-57188-344-4
UPC: 0-81127-00178-1
Printed in Hong Kong
3 5 7 9 10 8 6 4 2

Contents

Dedication

Dedicated to the Memory of Roderick Haig-Brown 1908-1976

I can think of no single person who has done so much for the coastal cutthroat—and ingrained his convictions about this beautiful western trout on those of us who have read his works—than Roderick Haig-Brown. The man wrote with penetrating depth and passion, but in such a straightforward style that his books are easily assimilated and committed to memory. In addition to entertaining me over the years as I've read and re-read his works, Haig-Brown made it clear that the worth of a small, non-commercially valued trout is, in the grand scheme of things, every bit as important as that of Pacific salmon and steelhead. Although many of us in the United States consider Roderick Haig-Brown to be one of our own, since he often fished the Stillaguamish River and other U.S. waters, he was a Canadian whose writing about the coastal cutthroat was largely framed within his beloved Campbell River and its surroundings on Vancouver Island. For this reason I asked Arthur Lingren, British Columbia writer and angling historian to write the following addition to this dedication:

> Roderick Haig-Brown had a profound influence on many North American fly-fishers. Being a city-dweller and not familiar with river terminology I remember poring over Haig-Brown's words in *The Western Angler* when I was a young man just taking up the sport. His writings taught me so much in my early years when I tried anything to catch a fish. Haig-Brown's writings planted the seed that led me to fly-fishing. In his 1951 book Fisherman's Spring in the "Fishing and the Common Man" essay Haig-Brown wrote, "In sport, method is everything" and suggested that the more skill we use to catch our quarry the more satisfying the gratification. He goes on to support his argument that the trout of the west are the fly fishers' fish and should be caught by no other method than fly-fishing. Unfortunately, the regulators of the day paid little heed to his sage advice. A half-century later British Columbia has few fly-fishing-only regulations for its waters. Notwithstanding, his words influenced thousands of others to take up the sport and become fly fishermen and on some British Columbia waters they far out number other gear types. To me and many others he is the master of fly fishing in British Columbia, and many fly-fishers visiting Vancouver Island make the pilgrimage to Campbell River to see where he wrote his great works and to cast a line into the waters he fished.
>
> –Arthur Lingren

Acknowledgements

When embarking upon the writing of this book I knew that it could not come to fruition without participation from a lot of dedicated people who, like me care deeply about the coastal cutthroat trout. Almost without exception I received the participation I requested and am pleased to have included important material from fisheries and academic professionals, the personal insights of valued friends, and the donation of beautiful flies from such broadly experienced contributors. By sharing your knowledge and expertise you have been instrumental in making this a better book.

To begin with this book would never have seen the light of day had it not been for the Sea-Run Cutthroat Symposium held in Reedsport, Oregon on October 12-14, 1995. This incredibly well organized milestone event was spearheaded by James D. Hall of the Department of Fisheries and Wildlife, University of Oregon, the Oregon Chapter of the American Fisheries Society and the Lower Umpqua Flycasters Club. Volunteers included a long list of groups and individuals all of whom worked tirelessly to make it happen. We all owe the leadership and vision of James Hall a big debt of gratitude.

A writer needs an objective sounding board when working on a book and my good friend Preston Singletary was always available to talk me through a tough spot in a chapter or to provide council when I needed it. His knowledge of coastal cutthroat literature and fishing was invaluable as well in helping me chase down hard-to-find pieces of information that I needed in order to fill in blanks that always seem to turn up in the middle of a chapter.

Bob Young, another long-time friend volunteered to compile the index for the book, a thankless job that I was hesitant to take on but one that is critical if a book is to be considered complete. His effort has made the book a better reference volume.

Gene Fassi, alias "Sam Fario", a book dealer and good friend took time to dig up facts I requested on fly tiers. Another well-known book and tackle dealer, Jim Adams of Adams Angling helped me with the history of some of the California flies. Thanks to you both.

British Columbia biologists Ron Ptolemy and Dana Atagi provided valuable data on coastal cutthroat populations in lakes, streams and saltwater areas on Vancouver Island and the North Coast. Allan Costello was my primary resource for the Queen Charlotte Islands. Their hard work added tremendous dimension to this book and cannot be appreciated enough.

Peter Caverhill edited the entire British Columbia chapter with special attention to the Fraser River. Peter proved to be a very patient, if stern critic and an exceedingly wise editor; attributes which were vital to get the chapter even close to where it should be. He made me write the chapter, warts and all, which was exactly what was needed. Then Peter sat down to do a detailed and sensitive edit of the work. Thanks so much Peter.

The chapter on flies filled with beautifully dressed cutthroat patterns could have been the basis for a stand-alone book. The new and different flies developed for coastal cutthroat; the classic patterns; the generosity of the people who took time to tie them; and the eloquently written tier's notes will give us all cause to spend more evenings at the tying bench or to settle into a comfortable chair to pore over the tier's notes at our leisure. All of you have made this chapter of the book very special for me through your efforts and for affording me the opportunity to form a bond with you as fellow fly tiers.

Arthur Lingren wrote the special Roderick Haig-Brown section and tied six of Haig-Brown's most popular flies. This book certainly would not have been nearly so comprehensive without Art's thoughtful essay on Haig-Brown, the man whose marvelous writings should be required reading by every person who ever plans to pick up a fly rod and cast over a coastal cutthroat.

Ron Jenkins, award-winning Montana-based wildlife artist worked long and patiently on the identification illustrations of the coastal cutthroat. These are fine examples of the coastal cutthroat in both fresh- and saltwater coloration, and should be carefully studied by all cutthroat anglers who become taken by this wonderful trout.

Artist John Roberts, another old friend, came up unexpectedly with his fine watercolor portrait of Roderick Haig-Brown that he allowed me to use as an illustration for the Haig-Brown section.

To both of you very talented gentlemen, my sincere thanks.

The technology of modern-day publishing has given us the luxury of punctuating our prose with high-quality photographs. The photos that appear in the book came primarily from those of us who fish together along with others that I contacted. Thank you, Allison Benner, Jerry Gibbs, Brian O'Keefe, Leland Miyawaki, John Roberts, Preston Singletary, Barry Stokes, Keith A. Willits, Bob Young and Glenn Young.

Photos of coastal cutthroat appearing in the identification chapter were provided by another fine artist, British Columbian Loucas Raptis. These photos show the varied physical features displayed by the coastal cutthroat in upper watersheds, lakes, inland streams and rivers open to the sea. Thanks Loucas.

I can't consider the acknowledgements complete without thanking my wife Carol for putting up with all that writing a book entails. Writing, or living with a writer, during the process of putting out a book has never been easy and never will be. Thank you for your patience Carol.

Curt Kraemer, Region 4 biologist for the Washington Department of Fish and Wildlife went the extra mile to provide a tremendous level of support and a wealth of both technical and in-the-field knowledge on coastal cutthroat. Curt read through several of the chapters making astute comments, suggestions and needed corrections. He spent additional time digging up hard to find nuggets of information that fleshed out gaps in my text. Finally, Curt even reluctantly accepted the role of art critic when I asked him to examine the Ron Jenkins sketches of the coastal cutthroat that appear in Identifying the Coastal Cutthroat and to suggest changes to improve the accuracy of the final renderings. There is a lot of Curt Kraemer lightly woven into the text of this book which may not be obvious but truly speaks volumes about his knowledge and love of the coastal cutthroat. Whatever this book may do to improve the quality of life for the coastal cutthroat throughout its range will be due in large measure to the invaluable support of Curt Kraemer. Thank you, Curt.

Of course I cannot forget Frank Amato my friend and publisher for going on forty years. Frank gave me the green light on this book. Needless to say, I really appreciated the counsel of my editor, Kim Koch who was patient to a fault in helping me work through areas of difficulty during the project. To Jerry Hutchinson I am indebted for the excellent design and production of a book that I hope will become a standard reference for a long time.

I make no claims to be an expert on the coastal cutthroat. I am quite simply a writer and fly fisher who has, through the years become closely identified with this amazing trout. I feel uniquely fortunate for my association with the coastal cutthroat and privileged to have been able to work with so many fine caring people in putting the book together. I am a very lucky man.

Les Johnson
April 4, 2004

Foreword

It was by neither skill nor determination that I made my first stumbling acquaintance with the coastal cutthroat trout. As a callow eastern Washington farm boy right out of college, in the fall of 1969 I took a teaching position in Newport, Oregon. Having committed myself to the trenches of the public education system, I soon realized that if I was to maintain some semblance of sanity I had better find an escape valve, some way to get my mind off meddling administrators and screaming kids. What better diversion than the hushed cathedral of a rainforest and the ceaseless sigh of a coastal stream?

After shamelessly eavesdropping on angling-oriented conversations at the local Laundromat (fish stories and clean skivvies), I made a pilgrimage to Lou's Tackle Shop in downtown Newport, where the proprietor confirmed the rumors and hearsay regarding sea-run cutts in the nearby Siletz and Alsea rivers. He then proceeded to sell me a handful of crudely tied Borden Specials and Spruce streamers, which I added to the clump of Muddlers and Renegades already occupying space in my motley fly box. Thus equipped with a smattering of flies, which in those days I thought was a pretty damned regal array, and further bolstered by Lou's parting advice—"look for 'em in the shadows and cutbanks above tidewater"—I drove up the Siletz River corridor on a mission to find maybe a fish or two, but, more to the point, to find the certainty of peace and quiet.

Despite a deep and abiding ignorance, in the very first spot I fished, a jade-green plunge pool immediately below the Old Siletz Highway bridge, I hooked eight cutthroat in rapid succession. As each gleaming, ocean-burnished fish came to hand I shook my head in utter disbelief. Such sleek elegance, such pure unfettered wildness strained credibility. In the terminology of the day: "It was unreal. Totally unreal, man." Of course, in retrospect I realized that it wasn't actually cutthroat I had landed that day on the Siletz; it was my own heart that got swooped up in the net.

No one knows more about the science, not to mention the compulsions, surrounding coastal cutthroat than Les Johnson, and he's written a big, honest book to tell us about it. Rest assured, this rather comprehensive volume does not issue from the dreary hook-and-bullet school of outdoor journalism that has come to dominate the publishing realm. So many fishing books one has the displeasure of reading nowadays are blatantly and unabashedly predatory in context. I'm not referring to predatory here as in a celebration of nature—bloody of tooth and claw—but predatory as in exploitive, an allusion to the cynical how-to/where-to screeds that mine the very resource being regaled.

If you go pawing through *Fly-Fishing Coastal Cutthroat Trout* looking for five ways to rig an indicator with dropper flies, you're going to be —and deserve to be —sorely disappointed. If you pore through this book with the expectation of pinpointing "fishin' holes", you're going to be —and, again, deserve to be —duly frustrated. In short, this is not a guidebook. That does not mean that reading *Fly-Fishing Coastal Cutthroat Trout* won't make you a better fisherman; because it most assuredly will. Increased acuity as an angler, after all, does not come from being spoon-fed glops of easily digestible, Gerber-formula information; it comes from a greater understanding and appreciation of a species and its ecosystem. And that's precisely the driving force behind this book.

Although *Fly-Fishing Coastal Cutthroat Trout* is a detailed examination of a complex and endearing species, aptly described as "the non-conformist of the trout family", Johnson does not let lyricism get in the way of the brutal fact that many cutthroat stocks face a perilous and tenuous existence, if not certain annihilation. Though not formally laid out in sections, Johnson's book basically divides into four parts: 1. the life history and characteristics of coastal cutthroat; 2. the cutthroat's range—a state-by-state and watershed-by-watershed breakdown; 3. a parade of fly patterns (who doesn't love a parade?) which pays colorful homage to the prey; and 4. the methods of presenting the fly in both fresh and salt water by which the gap between fish and fisherman might subsequently narrow, if not occasionally entirely close. Johnson's treatise teaches us, by the intimacy inherent in knowledge, to cherish the species.

But that's not all. *Fly-Fishing Coastal Cutthroat Trout* also functions as a call to arms. The information in this book could be viewed as ordnance, as ammunition for doing battle with greed-mongering extractive industries, corrupt and cowardly politicians, soulless bureaucracies and the vacuous, comatose (legally brain-dead?) public.

What about us noble anglers, all agog at nature's beck, giddily stooping to smell the skunk cabbage? Johnson spares no one, pointedly admitting, "We the sport fishers have to share the blame for the decline in coastal cutthroat stocks throughout much of its realm." We are directly to blame through irresponsible recreational harvest rates and indirectly to blame through lack of political gumption. In my view, sportsmen tend to be strong of tongue and weak of knee. But then I have tendency to get surly and provocative. Johnson, by contrast, adopts the voice of reason and calm indignation.

God knows that Fish and Wildlife departments are not going to storm the Bastille in defense of the lowly (non-commercial) sea-run cutthroat. Until quite recently, the fish and wildlife agencies' response to most every outrage—particularly the decimation of nursery habitat, ala clear-cut logging, and subsequent steep population declines—was to fill the void with truckloads of hatchery-manufactured replicants.

Although there have been few comprehensive, longitudinal stream studies devoted to coastal cutthroat, strong circumstantial evidence suggests that aggressive stocking of hatchery fish, as was carried out in the late 80s/early 90s in Oregon watersheds, had a chilling impact on wild populations. Johnson notes that on the lower Columbia, for example, "catches that once totaled more than 10,000 fish [per year] in the 1970s dwindled to as few as 69 fish in 1994." Finally recognizing this despairing trend, in 1997 the Oregon Department of Fish and Wildlife got the hell out of the hatchery cutthroat business. Addressing cutthroat populations in Washington State, Johnson observes: "Ironically, in spite of, or because of, hatchery supplementation, many coastal cutthroat stocks in Grays Harbor and lower Columbia River tributaries are under consideration for Endangered Species Act (ESA) listing as either threatened or endangered."

The biggest, dirtiest, bloodiest battles, of course, involve habitat. Special interests—logging, ranching, farming, mining, and development—are pleased as punch to let us have the fish as long as they have their way with the fishes' domicile. Johnson warns: "In state and federal management bureaucracies, advocates for commercial harvest, timber sales, real estate development and agri-business operate powerful and well-funded lobbies. Without a unified voice to compete with the business lobby complex our coastal cutthroat trout, particularly the anadromous or sea-run form, will continue to decline throughout its historic range in our Pacific Coast rainforest watersheds."

Lest I give the impression that *Fly-Fishing for Coastal Cutthroat* sounds like a funeral dirge, nothing could be further from the truth. The attitude of this tome is unflaggingly positive and upbeat. Not Pollyannaish, mind you, but not defeatist either. Johnson exhorts us to stand up to the pressures of "progress" in all its perversely coded manifestations, going so far as to state, "I am confident that returning our salmon and steelhead (and cutthroat) stocks to a measure of good health consistent with available habitat can be accomplished." Furthermore, Johnson exults in the resilience of this wonderfully oddball species: "I urge you to go out and meet the coastal cutthroat along the margins of a brackish estuary, well out into the saltwater proper, in the pools of its home river; or in an overlooked pond, or lake or creek that drains the upper reaches of a steep watershed. When you fish for cutthroat, keep in mind that you are stalking a trout that has survived for centuries with very little assistance from man…If we did nothing for the coastal cutthroat other than really protect its habitat, we would go a long way toward ensuring its future health."

Amen to that. And amen to this book.

—Don Roberts
Founding Editor, *Flyfishing the West*
Angry Activist and Angler-at-Large

Roderick Haig-Brown casting for cutthroat on the Gold River, British Columbia - circa 1976.

Introduction

Prior to beginning this new volume on the coastal cut-throat trout, I was surprised at what I found as I leafed through yellowed pages of reference material gathered for the update of "The Sea-Run Cutthroat Trout," published in 1972 (the little booklet with the blue cover). Many of those pages were embellished with additional faded, hand-written notations that I had scribbled in the margins.

The old reference material brought one fact into stark clarity; the fragile environment of the coastal cutthroat, which was already battered unmercifully by excessive timber harvest, overuse of water resources, industrial pollution and land development way back when, is even more heavily degraded nearly three decades later.

In October 1995, however, the Lower Umpqua Flycasters, a fishing club located in Reedsport, Oregon and the Oregon chapter of the American Fisheries Society sponsored the Sea-Run Cutthroat Trout Symposium. Participants from each of the Pacific Coast states and British Columbia presented information on the biology; the status of all Pacific Coast stocks; a case study on the decline of the Umpqua River's anadromous coastal cutthroat and the outlook for restoration and recovery. State and provincial fish and wildlife biologists, university school of fisheries instructors, and experienced laymen from Alaska, California, Oregon, Washington and British Columbia were among the presenters. The papers presented and provocative panel discussions shed new light on the state of the coastal cutthroat throughout its range and established the basis for valuable published proceedings, "Sea-Run Cutthroat Trout: Biology, Management and Future Consideration". More than 200 friends of the coastal cutthroat trout attended the Symposium.

I drew heavily from the information published in the proceedings and from my own notes taken at the Symposium along with other materials gathered during the years since the last update of my original book. I did not significantly revise or edit the information since in each case the way it was presented was logical, easily understood and best suited for each state and province. I also utilized proceedings information from Washington. Since I have done most of my cutthroat fishing in my home state of Washington I was able to incorporate more of my own experience into the Washington chapter.

It will be interesting to see what, if anything, transpires from the dissemination of all this information which could, if utilized give a dramatic boost to the well-being of the coastal cutthroat. The efforts of these dedicated people will first have to serve to get others involved. In state and federal management bureaucracies, advocates for commercial fish harvest, timber sales, real estate development and agri-business operate powerful and well-funded lobbies. Without a unified voice to compete with the business lobby complex our coastal cutthroat trout, particularly the anadromous or sea-run form, will continue to decline throughout its historic range in our Pacific Coast rainforest watersheds.

In 1978, when I updated the first edition of this book, most of us were still huddled under a sheltering umbrella of innocence even though we were already seeing evidence on every front that many of our robust salmon and steelhead runs were beginning to falter. During the past decade we have watched salmon and steelhead runs crash all along the Pacific Coast and we are locked in a monumental struggle to save them. Many races of salmon and steelhead are officially listed as threatened or endangered. Others have already been declared extinct.

Wild salmon and steelhead are so scarce in some watersheds that once-thriving runs have undergone emergency closures even for catch-and-release sport fishing while others remain viable only through massive hatchery programs. I am confident that returning our salmon and steelhead stocks to a measure of good health consistent with available habitat can be accomplished. I also believe that it is going to be a long, arduous process.

The loss of salmon and steelhead fishing opportunities has placed increased pressure on the coastal cutthroat. Just a few decades ago, a lot of West Coast sport anglers considered this wild little cutthroat trout, so abundant in ponds, lakes, creeks, rivers and estuaries, an angling diversion to be pursued only when the salmon and steelhead fishing was slow. Now, with angling opportunities for salmon and steelhead sharply curtailed, the coastal cutthroat is becoming a dedicated target for increasing numbers of sport anglers.

So, how does a trout that rarely reaches more than 20 inches in length during a life span of perhaps eight to twelve years manage to survive, albeit by the skin of its teeth, when larger, seemingly stronger species are unable to escape a deadly downward spiral into endangered status or are going extinct? One very important factor is that the coastal cutthroat can still swim easily through the mesh of most gill nets. Many of the lakes and beaver ponds that hold populations of wild, landlocked coastal cutthroat are often difficult to access, thus are bypassed in favor of more easily reached lakes filled with hatchery-reared rainbow trout. Another point in favor of the relatively small size of the coastal cutthroat lays in the fact that Pacific Coast salmon and steelhead anglers have always been impressed with big fish. We have all dreamed of catching a fifty-pound chinook salmon or a twenty-five-pound steelhead. In the past, these larger, more glamorous members of the Pacific Coast anadromous salmonid family have routinely taken the spotlight away from the cutthroat since they could be pursued by expending roughly the same amount of effort and cash with the prospect of reaping far more impressive Kodak moments and certainly more poundage for the backyard smoker.

My early indoctrination to fishing by my grandfather, Ed Knight, was an experience that every young, neophyte angler would treasure and look back upon with unabashed appreciation. Now, as I move into my seventh decade on old Mother Earth, memories of those times are even more vivid and lessons learned more important.

Walking along a brush-bordered trail on the way to a small, gurgling brook filled with trout was made infinitely more interesting by Grandpa Ed's easily understood verbal vignettes on the flora and fauna around us. He warned me to avoid devil's club that could rip both hip boots and flesh. He pointed out stinging nettles, adding that a bit of black river mud on a nettle sting would help soothe the pain. He noted how real wild blackberries were much sweeter and better tasting in my Grandmother Esther's pies than either Himalaya or Evergreen berries. The latter, he added, were certainly valuable though as protective cover for Rufous-sided towhees, varied thrushes and coveys of quail. In the fall, Grandpa Ed and I would fill his landing net with chanterelle mushrooms picked on the way back from a morning of cutthroat fishing.

From the time I was seven or eight until I was a grown man with a family, he and I fished together for yellow perch, crappie, rainbow and brook trout, steelhead, salmon and of course, cutthroat. To my grandfather every species of fish was important and he enjoyed catching them all. More notably though, he respected every hill and dale; every stand of cedar and spruce; every foot-rutted riverside trail and every clear, gravel-bottomed pool of every river we fished. He felt that we were overusing our natural resources those sixty long years ago. I believe that it was his concern over the condition of what he always referred to as, "the great outdoors" that sticks most vividly in my mind to this day.

Grandpa Ed used just one outfit for all of his trout fishing, a handsome old pre-World War Two 8 1/2-foot Heddon Black Beauty cane fly rod and a Pflueger Medalist reel. With it he took beaver pond brookies, stillwater rainbows and cutthroats. Until the late 1950s his only fly line that I can recall was a silk floater that he kept meticulously clean and dressed. There were no sink-tip or sinking fly lines in those days, and I cannot recall that we ever needed anything but a floating line to handle any situation.

To this day, every time I head out fishing I reflect appreciatively on my good fortune to have been granted so many seasons to cast into lakes and streams from Central California to Southeast Alaska. And, whenever I see a muskrat swimming along the shoreline of a river, watch a big leaf maple sailing its autumn-yellow leaves out on a stiff October breeze, or set up on the strike of a heavy coastal cutthroat, I am subtly reminded of my grandfather.

I now realize that from the very first day that he took me along to fish with him so many years ago, that it was always about more than just the fishing. What my grandfather knew was that by gently awakening me to all of the complexities of my outdoor world, no matter how insignificant some things seemed at the time, that I might eventually become, in small measure at least, one of its stewards.

During the ensuing years I believe that I have slowly grown into the responsibility of watching over the precious elements of nature's mosaic that surround my life-long enthusiasm for fly-fishing. I have never kept records of how many salmon or steelhead or cutthroat I have caught during some sixty years as a sport fisherman, but I am sure that the number would be impressive.

Experiencing a big, wild steelhead making a reel-screaming run against a tightly bowed fly rod is one the more elevated thrills in all of angling. And, the tremendous surge of a big chinook salmon moving off almost effortlessly across a pool bottom with my fly stuck in its jaw will never stop sending chills up my spine because a mint-bright mature chinook, king of all salmon, is blessed with such awesome power. There is no escaping the fact that much of the status attached to being a Pacific Coast angler lies in the tremendous average size of the salmon and steelhead that we seek. I will be the first to admit that years ago I went through a period where large salmon and steelhead were my primary focus, although I don't recall that the prospect of big fish ever tempted me to summarily abdicate my love for coastal cutthroat.

There is no logical comparison that can be made by trying to match the coastal cutthroat up against its larger anadromous kin, the salmon and steelhead, because of the tremendous disparity in size. Such a comparison is meaningless anyway because the fair assessment of a game fish should never be based upon size alone. The philosophy that "only big is good" has without doubt provided yet another measure of salvation for the relatively diminutive cutthroat. Anglers who chant the mantra, "only big is good" rarely set their sights on such a small game fish as the coastal cutthroat.

On the other hand, most serious students of the cutthroat trout have long since transcended the "only big is good" years of their angling lives. It is these people who cultivate a rewarding give and take relationship with this amazing trout and usually, over time become champions of its welfare.

The stewardship provided by these anglers is crucial to the coastal cutthroat's future by virtue of offsetting the lack of attention it has received by fish and wildlife agencies in the United States and Canada. Salmon still command vast commercial value while the steelhead remains at the top of the ladder as a trophy, even at a time when many races of these great fish survive only under the tenuous Federal protection or indefensible levels of hatchery support. This fact makes it all the more important for anglers throughout the coastal cutthroat's range to take up their shields in its behalf.

The enigmatic coastal cutthroat is one of many subspecies or races of cutthroat found throughout the western United States. It ranges from the streams of northern California to Prince William Sound in Alaska. It is still fairly abundant throughout much of coastal British Columbia including streams draining the Queen Charlotte Islands and Vancouver Island. Washington State holds pockets of healthy populations of cutthroat along its coastline and in certain streams that flow into Puget Sound, Grays Harbor and Willapa Harbor. Beaver ponds and a scattering of lakes throughout western Washington still have self-sustaining populations of resident cutthroat.

There are anadromous cutthroat populations in most of the coastal streams of Oregon with fluvial strains in several tributaries that empty into the Willamette and Columbia rivers. Many of Oregon's native cutthroat populations have been depleted by the introduction of hatchery rainbow or cutthroat trout. This practice has been suspended in most rivers during recent years.

In California, the coastal cutthroat once maintained a stronghold from the Smith River south to the Eel River. Today it is still found in all of its historic California waters but in significantly reduced numbers.

Throughout its range there are populations of resident or fluvial coastal cutthroat trout that are doing well in beaver ponds, lagoons and lakes or in streams above impassable barriers such as dams or waterfalls that do not allow the passage of anadromous fish. Other populations of coastal cutthroat remain well established in river systems where all of their migration occurs between tributary creeks and the main stem.

The sea-run is the anadromous or true sea-going form of the coastal cutthroat. Many species of salmon and trout attain the largest body size in their anadromous form. This is not the case with the sea-run cutthroat trout. The record cutthroat of all time taken in fresh water was a 41-pound monster commercially harvested from Pyramid Lake, Nevada in 1925. The Pyramid Lake or Lahontan cutthroat, native to the Lahontan drainage of California and Nevada, was so plentiful that a profitable commercial fishery was established in the late 19th Century.

Decimation from unrestricted commercial fishing pressure and later by extensive water diversion from the Truckee River, Pyramid Lake's only tributary was so efficient that the original subspecies of giants was officially declared extinct in 1938. Today there is still a popular Pyramid Lake sport fishery supported by a hatchery that utilizes Lahontan cutthroat stock captured in other watersheds. However, the hatchery operation has never produced truly large cutthroat even though the Lahontan broodstock used is supposed to be taxonomically identical to the original Pyramid Lake strain.

Even a very large coastal cutthroat does not come close to the length and girth of its colossal cousin, the Lahontan. During the shooting of a segment of a television series, "Fly-Fishing Northwest," that I co-hosted with my friend, Pete Van Gytenbeek for Fox Sport Network, I had the good fortune to hook and land the largest sea-run cutthroat that I have ever laid eyes on in all my years of fishing. It was fully twenty-five inches long and probably weighed nearly six pounds. This beautiful, big cutthroat was recorded on videotape and released alive. I have been told by several anglers since I landed my largest cutthroat that even larger specimens have been taken on many occasions.

There is one tragic similarity that the coastal cutthroat shares with its Lahontan relative. It is highly sensitive to degradation of its habitat. Land-ravaging logging practices, which are still allowed, regardless of what slick public relations campaigns by major timber companies convey to the contrary, have absolutely crushed many important tributary creeks into the earth. Other small but once-productive streams have been slightly less ravaged but incurred damage so extensive that they may never again host significant populations of cutthroat.

Culverts constructed by logging companies; for urban expansion and commercial development, and as part of regional and Federal highway projects have through the years been designed with little or no regard for fish passage. At this writing precious little effort has been made to improve these inefficient passageways although they have been well documented by various environmental groups.

Of course we cannot overlook the importance of an adequate flow of rich, cool, clean water, certainly the most critical element for the cutthroat. Water, as we all have learned over the past several years, has become a multi-billion dollar resource for hydroelectric power, refineries, large scale farming operations and land developers. Historically, lobbies for these insatiable water gluttons have been so powerful and efficient that consideration for the preservation of our anadromous fish runs nearly disappeared from the radar screen.

Only recently have State and Federal bureaucracies grudgingly faced up to the evidence that our anadromous fish runs require a fair share of our water resources in order to escape extinction. When salmon and steelhead runs began to nosedive to a precarious degree, it finally brought the importance of water allocation to light for many citizens who had always thought that our western rivers would flow in endless volume forever with enough to go around for everyone and everything. It is a long overdue awakening. The fight for water rights however, is an old one in the West and it is destined to escalate dramatically during the next several decades because the stakes are so incredibly high. When the showdown that looms clearly on the horizon plays out over water allocation we will find out if the value of our anadromous fish and a forceful grassroots uprising of conservation-minded citizens will be enough to turn back the enormously influential one-two punch of big business and big government.

In other regions of the world where true sea trout exist they are often held in higher esteem than even the exalted Atlantic salmon. Throughout the British Isles, Finland, Sweden and Norway the sea trout is greatly respected and anglers pay handsomely for the opportunity to fish the more productive rivers and coastal beats. Along the eastern seaboard of the United States and Canada programs have been in place for years to rebuild small populations of sea-run brook and brown trout, called salters that share some rivers with Atlantic salmon.

If the coastal cutthroat is ever going to move up the ladder of importance its value as a world-class sea trout will have to be established once and for all by every individual and agency responsible for its welfare. Fish and Wildlife agencies can only make the cutthroat a top priority with the cooperation of politicians who control state and federal budgets. Unfortunately, legislators have done little more than routinely drop the ball in this regard. There is no evidence that treaty Indian tribes will step up to the plate in an effort to protect the coastal cutthroat in the streams under their charter. Industry could be a major factor by reversing the deplorable level of destruction it has wreaked on our environment and our wildlife if it put at least as much effort into conservation and restoration programs as it does into profits and highly polished public relations campaigns.

Our struggle to keep the coastal cutthroat swimming throughout its range is one of saving and restoring habitat. We are going to have to hold onto all viable habitat and recover every possible inch of streams that have been fouled to once again see them flow with clear, pollutant-free water. We still have some fairly strong populations of wild cutthroat and there is habitat throughout its range that is still relatively pristine but we cannot afford to lose another square foot of it. This confrontation, one of conservation entities standing up to profit-making land users will be long and I won't see its outcome in my lifetime. Just as it was for my generation to pick up the shield from those who preceded us, it will be up to those who follow to continue when we leave the field of battle; and make no mistake, it is a battle. However, saving the coastal cutthroat is well worth whatever effort we must expend.

I urge you to go out and meet the coastal cutthroat along the edges of a brackish estuary, well out into the saltwater proper, in the pools of its home river; or in an overlooked pond, or lake or creek that drains the upper reaches of a steep watershed. When you fish for cutthroat, keep in mind that you are stalking a trout that has survived for centuries with very little assistance from man. Once you have met the challenge of taking a coastal cutthroat on the fly you will almost surely be a bit closer to becoming a conservationist on its behalf.

This book covers the coastal cutthroat throughout its range. During my life as a fisherman I have been afforded the good fortune to fish for and catch coastal cutthroat from its southern reaches in the redwood country of California to its northern extreme in the Misty Fjords of Alaska. During all of my cutthroat fishing there has been one thread woven through each and every experience I've enjoyed and each cutthroat that I've hooked. This most dauntless trout always strikes fast and hard to let you know, in no uncertain terms, that the battle has begun.

For the last twenty-five years I have pursued the cutthroat only with a fly rod. This is not in any way shape or form due to disdain for other methods of fishing, although I am convinced that cutthroat deeply hooked on bait are at very high risk in a catch-and-release fishery. I use the fly rod since I find it the most enjoyable method of trout fishing. In my openly prejudiced view, fly-fishing is the most sporting, straightforward and, at times, the most productive way to fish for cutthroat trout.

Once you have caught a cutthroat fairly, on a cast fly you will immediately discover that its strength and grit is nothing short of amazing. And, whether you are walking a cobbled saltwater beach in June, floating down a low, clear coastal river, or casting next to a shaded snarl of down-timber in a conifer-shrouded lowland lake on a rainy April morning, you will find that the feisty coastal cutthroat is almost always ready and willing to take your fly.

Finally, please understand that this is not a guidebook. You will not find information on exactly where to locate coastal cutthroat every day of the year. Neither will you find it filled with area maps. Maps become outdated so it is best that you gather local and regional reference material on a regular basis to support this book. I have attempted to tell you in general terms where the coastal cutthroat lives, what it eats and where you should look for it throughout the season. Wherever you plan to cast a fly for coastal cutthroat be sure to have a current copy of local fishing regulations in your possession. Furthermore, fish management and protection often requires the sudden closure of given lakes or watersheds. Emergency regulations are published in local newspapers or posted on fish and wildlife websites but it is your responsibility to check them out. Ultimately, to get up close and personal with the coastal cutthroat you will have to do your homework, crash through barriers of rosehips, negotiate rain-slick mud trails and spend endless hours tramping along the banks of Pacific slope rivers and saltwater estuaries. You will have to learn to live with the joy of hooking half a dozen beautiful cutthroats one day and not coax up another to your fly during several more trips, and always make sure you are fishing legally. That is how it is with coastal cutthroat. It is how I, all of my angling companions and most other serious anglers developed a relationship with the coastal cutthroat trout. To be right it can happen no other way.

Chapter 1 - Realm of the Coastal Cutthroat

"The coastal cutthroat trout occurs along the Pacific Coast of North America from the lower Eel River in California to Prince William Sound, Alaska in a zone that conforms remarkably closely with the Pacific coast rain forest belt."

—Patrick C. Trotter, PhD
Fishery Science Consultant

A PRIMITIVE TROUT

It seems only fitting that the coastal cutthroat, with lineage dating back to the Pleistocene Epoch and considered to be a primitive trout, should be born in rivers that drain watersheds of the ancient rain forests of the Pacific Coast. From approximately 1.8 million years ago until roughly 11,000 years ago, during the Pleistocene Epoch enormous glaciers pushed inexorably southward stretching across the continent of North America from the Atlantic to the Pacific bringing about tremendous ecological and topological changes. It was the relentless gouging action of these southward moving ice floes, more than a mile thick over what is now Washington State that created much of today's most productive coastal cutthroat habitat.

When the Pleistocene Epoch ended the glaciers retreated northward and the Pacific Ocean flooded the inlets, bays and flats that remained along the California and Oregon coastlines. The most dramatic sculpting of the landscape by these powerful glaciers was the maze of trenches that connected to form a rugged, 1200-mile-long landscape of bays,

intertwining channels and islands that we now know as the Alexander Archipelago of southeast Alaska; the Queen Charlotte Strait and Strait of Georgia that separate mainland British Columbia from the Queen Charlotte archipelago and Vancouver Island. Between Vancouver Island and Washington the Strait of Juan de Fuca was formed, and in Washington the advancing waters of the Pacific flowed into canyons vacated by the receding ice to form the San Juan Islands, Puget Sound and Hood Canal. The habitat created so many thousands of years ago became home to the coastal cutthroat trout and remains so today.

An angler standing in Butte Creek, deep in the California redwoods, swings his fly through a cutthroat run.

In fall, the clear, deep pools of California's Smith River hold coastal cutthroat. The Smith, with its miles of protected watershed, is one of California's most productive sea-run cutthroat streams.

Mike Foster

SURVIVAL OF THE FITTEST

Many of the animals of the Pleistocene Epoch went extinct. Theories are divided as to whether it was from overharvest by human hunters of the time or the tremendous global cooling that took place. It could very well have been the result of both global cooling and man. Other species of plant and animals however survived. A variety of conifer trees, mosses, flowering plants, insects, mollusks, birds and animals survive to this day. Among the survivors is the coastal cutthroat trout.

The coastal cutthroat (*Oncorhynchus clarki clarki*) still populates nearly all of the streams and lakes within the Pacific Coast rainforest belt. This enormous expanse of coastal rain forest extends from the lower Eel River in California to Prince William Sound in Southeast Alaska, a distance of 1800 miles. It occurs inland to the crest of the Cascade Mountain Range in Oregon and Washington and to the Coast Range crest in British Columbia and Southeast Alaska.

Although the coastal cutthroat trout is still entrenched throughout this huge rainforest belt, its numbers have been dwindling for decades, particularly in its southern reaches: the lower Columbia River tributaries, southern Oregon coastal rivers and all rivers flowing from the redwood forest drainages of Northern California. The fact that this little sea trout still exists at all stands as testimony to the powerful lust

Even very tiny creeks, like this one winding its way out through a southern Oregon ocean beach, will provide habitat for several spawning pairs of coastal cutthroat.

for life that beats in the heart of every coastal cutthroat; and sheds a bit more light on why it is such a highly esteemed adversary on the fly rod.

The Coastal Cutthroat's Natural Environment

The coastal cutthroat trout does not live an easy life during the best of times because nature, when reduced to its basic

The upper Hoh River in Olympic National Park remains wild but accessible by foot.
Upper watershed cutthroat in our Pacific Coast parks are still reasonably well protected.

Signs like this one on the Rogue River are in place on most public parks and forests to let people know to protect the habitat and the fish.

elements is an arena kept in balance by the strengths and weaknesses of all its creatures. It is a place where only the strongest, swiftest, most adaptable or those with incredible tenacity, ever die of old age.

The abundance of coastal cutthroat stocks is controlled throughout its realm by a variety of naturally occurring phenomena. Populations rise and fall when affected by floods, fires, droughts and predation in its freshwater envi-

ronment. Periods of unfavorable conditions in the cutthroats' ocean environment, such as changes in ocean temperatures and upwelling events like El Niño, adversely affect stocks of important forage. Herring, anchovies, sardines, squid, and all forms of krill can experience tremendous swings in abundance due to changes in ocean conditions. The anadromous form of coastal cutthroat spends a substantial part of each year in salt water, a period when its growth and health is dependent on the usually rich and diverse menu of forage available both in protected bays and the Pacific Ocean proper.

The Coastal Cutthroat's Unnatural Environment

Man, the ultimate predator, has degraded the freshwater environment of the coastal cutthroat unmercifully for nearly two centuries and is undeniably the driving force in its present state of decline. This is very apparent in Northern California and Southern Oregon where most freshwater habitat degradation is directly attributable to abysmal land and water management policies on private, state, federal and provincial watersheds. Further north in Oregon and through Washington, British Columbia and Alaska the sea-run enjoys larger pockets of acceptable environmental surroundings but still suffers a brutal battering to much of its most suitable habitat from clearcut logging and water pollution.

Although heavily logged, the watersheds and rivers of Prince of Wales Island in Alaska hold strong populations of cutthroat trout.

We sport fishers have to share the blame for the decline in coastal cutthroat stocks throughout much of its realm. Until the last twenty years, recreational catch limits on coastal cutthroat, particularly in the sea-run form, have been unbelievably liberal. In most states and British Columbia this element of the cutthroat's decline is slowly being corrected, in large measure through the efforts of concerned sportsmen who have banded together and lobbied for reduced limits or catch-and-release status for coastal cutthroat. The health and numbers of coastal cutthroat trout have shown an upturn, in some areas dramatic improvement, whenever conservative regulations and seasons have been implemented.

It is crucially important for sport fishers to become involved in protecting the realm of the coastal cutthroat because it simply does not rate highly enough anywhere along its range to be much of a priority with fish-and-wildlife agencies. Whatever you may hear or read to the contrary, the coastal cutthroat trout, since it is not part of the commercial harvest of Pacific anadromous stocks, holds a very low position on the priority lists of agency fish managers.

A good example of success is in Washington State where coastal cutthroat limits were reduced from eight to two trout over 14 inches in the mid-1980s. An additional level of protection was achieved in 1997 when Washington sportsmen lobbied the State Fish and Wildlife Commission for further conservation measures by placing anadromous coastal cutthroat on catch-and-release status in all marine waters of the state. Although there are wild cutthroat stocks in Washington that are in very weak condition, primarily in lower Columbia River tributaries, Pacific Coast and Puget Sound populations of wild anadromous cutthroat have stabilized and even increased through the 1990s and into the new millennium.

State of the Realm

Given the bludgeoning we have administered to the habitat of the coastal cutthroat for the past eight or ten decades, it's a miracle that there are still any of them around at all. It would be folly to believe that the Pacific Rainforest Belt will ever be allowed to lie fallow long enough to recover substantially from the damage inflicted by man. It is simply not economically feasible. Along the Pacific Coast we have been, and will remain, economically tied to timber, water and fish. So, we are largely dependent upon the resolve of the coastal cutthroat, with its enviable track record for survival and must give it a hand wherever we can. If state and provincial bureaucrats along the Pacific Coast ever decide to

Pristine beaches like this one in Washington are becoming more and more rare and must be protected.

Captain Keith Robbins carefully releases a big coastal cutthroat taken on a fly in Puget Sound. All cutthroat must be released unharmed in Washington marine waters.

Anglers set up an autumn camp on Washington's Olympic Penninsula to fish for Sol Duc River Cutthroat.

done all that we can in terms of establishing reduced limits though, our next big battle will be one of taking back some of the lost habitat — and returning it to the coastal cutthroat.

It is incumbent on those of us who live in the realm of the coastal cutthroat to do our best to understand all we can about this amazing little non-conformist. Whether our interest is conservation, sport fishing, or both, understanding the habitat and habits of the coastal cutthroat and the state of its health in every stream where it exists is paramount to its future existence and to the quality of our angling opportunities.

Although the coastal cutthroat displays similar characteristics throughout its realm, it has evolved a bit differently wherever it lives, even in drainages only a few miles apart. So, those of us who share the realm of the coastal cutthroat should first learn about the unique qualities of cutthroat strains in streams near to where we live. It is, after all, the trout closest to home that will receive most of our fishing attention. Learning about the coastal cutthroat indigenous to the ponds, lakes and coastal watersheds that empty into sheltered saltwater fjords or directly into the Pacific Ocean close to our homes is the first step to enjoying it as a fly rod quarry. Once an angler has felt the hammering strike of a coastal cutthroat and fought it fairly on a fly rod, becoming a champion of this great little trout and its fragile realm becomes an easy and natural next step.

offer more than lip service to the enormous potential profit that sport fishing for cutthroat would offer to coastal communities we might witness a lessening of the pathetic genuflecting currently practiced before the CEO's of large timber companies, hydroelectric power combines, insatiable irrigators and commercial fishing lobbies.

For now and into the future we have to continually fight to slow — and one day stop—the overall environmental degradation that has been so rampant throughout the coastal cutthroat's realm. Once we sport anglers have

The Misty Fjords of southeast Alaska are a stronghold for coastal cutthroat due to the rugged terrain and difficulty in accessing the water. Many of the best cutthroat lakes and streams can be reached only by float plane.

Chapter 2 - *Life History of the Coastal Cutthroat*

"I have conducted seven years of research on the sea-run cutthroat trout in Southeast Alaska. I by no means have all the answers when it comes to sea-run cutthroat. They are the true non-conformists of the trout family."

—Darwin E. Jones
Biologist, Alaska Department of Fish and Game

This quote by Darwin E. Jones is taken from my earlier book, *How to Fish for Sea-Run Cutthroat Trout*. Jones, a biologist for the Alaska Fish and Game Department, was right on the money with his statement based on what we knew back then (1978). I was compelled to open this chapter with Jones' quote since it sums up the amazing coastal cutthroat trout so succinctly. After attending the Sea-Run Cutthroat Trout Symposium at Reedsport, Oregon in 1995 I have concluded that Mr. Jones may have actually understated the case with his description of this most enigmatic member of the cutthroat trout family.

The coastal cutthroat's reputation for being the non-conformist of the Pacific salmonids is richly deserved but probably not completely understood by the average angler. In reviewing the history of coastal cutthroat it is important to keep in mind that while this plucky little trout is migratory, it is not consistently migratory and has the ability to thrive in diverse environmental conditions.

Curt Kraemer, biologist with the Washington Department of Fish and Wildlife, has stated that the coastal cutthroat should be classified as a trout of small streams. "Early rearing of coastal cutthroat, up to four or more years — and spawning — all takes place in tributaries smaller than those used by other anadromous fish. Their freshwater homes can be best characterized as 'step across streams', since such streams can often be stepped across without wetting one's feet. Typical anadromous cutthroat water is upstream of the major steelhead and coho spawning areas. There is some overlap, thus the hybridization between steelhead and cutthroat, but cutthroat clearly are more successful in competing with the other fish indigenous to these small streams."

The coastal cutthroat is divided into four distinct life history types:

Resident
Resident coastal cutthroat are those living in small streams usually in the upper reaches of a watershed. Many of these populations are not affected by the influence of anadromous species like coho salmon or steelhead as they are above barriers such as impassable waterfalls or dams. Resident cutthroat that live in these tiny creeks often mature at a considerably smaller size than other coastal cutthroats, although they may be the same age as their kin living in larger rivers or in lakes. This smaller size at maturity can be attributed to a biological adjustment to the confined rearing conditions of small streams. Most small western tributaries are not rich sources of food, which certainly is another factor contributing to the generally diminutive size of adult, resident, small-stream cutthroats.

Fluvial
Fluvial coastal cutthroat trout migrate between small spawning creeks and mainstem rivers. They will in fact worm their way into the very tiniest flows that feed the small creeks in search of safe spawning habitat. After spawning, they drop back to their mainstem home water where they feed and attain most of their growth. Fluvial populations of coastal cutthroat are found in larger rivers like Washington's Snoqualmie, the Willamette system in Oregon, and some of the larger tributaries draining into the Columbia River. Fluvial populations are also found in the upper reaches of rivers in British Columbia. While cutthroat compete most successfully for spawning habitat in small streams, the mainstem water with more abundant food sources is preferred for rearing and growth.

Adfluvial
Adfluvial coastal cutthroat trout are primarily lake-dwellers. In springtime, when the spawning urge surges in the flanks of adfluvial coastal cutthroat, they ascend streams and creeks that drain into the lakes where they live. After spawning, adfluvial cutthroat drop back into the lakes for rearing where they will soon be joined by their progeny.

Among all coastal cutthroat populations, adfluvial members usually reach the largest size, in some lakes growing to 15 pounds or more. This is due, in part at least, to the lack of competition from coho salmon and steelhead, and an abundance of forage fish.

Anadromous
Anadromous cutthroat, the true sea-run cutthroat, is the headliner of the species. The ability of the anadromous cutthroat to spend a part of each year in parent rivers that have direct access to the sea and then move easily into protected estuaries, saltwater bays or the Pacific Ocean has placed them in high regard among fly-fishers. It is during their annual saltwater junket that sea-run cutthroat achieve the bulk of their growth and strength, feeding on a rich diet of sand lance, sculpins, herring, squid and krill. The anadromous cutthroat is a bonafide sea trout in

Summer Feeding Habitat: Rivers, Bays, Estuaries

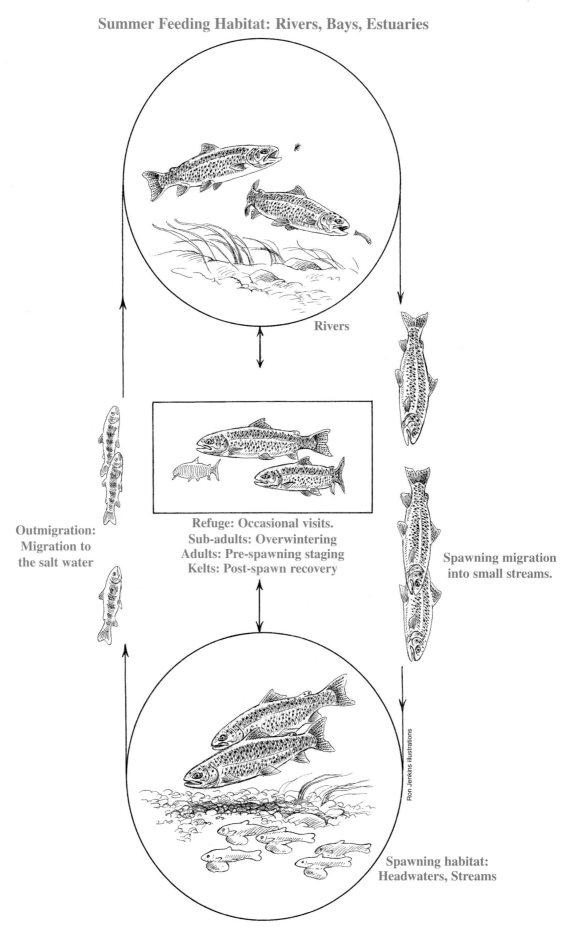

Rivers

Outmigration: Migration to the salt water

Refuge: Occasional visits.
Sub-adults: Overwintering
Adults: Pre-spawning staging
Kelts: Post-spawn recovery

Spawning migration into small streams.

Spawning habitat: Headwaters, Streams

Ron Jenkins illustrations

every respect and deserving of its exalted position in the coastal cutthroat clan.

Up From the Gravel

The coastal cutthroat lives a hardscrabble existence from the moment it struggles free from the security of its gravel sanctuary where it has grown from a fertilized egg to an alevin. Upon clearing the safety of the gravel, the inch-long cutthroat, having used up most of its egg sac, is now called a fry. After a period of orientation it moves tentatively into the flow of its natal stream. In small, upper watershed creeks it can forage quite competitively for food. In larger rivers though it, comes face-to-face with mature resident rainbow trout or young-of-the-year coho salmon that have emerged earlier to stake out ownership of preferred areas of the stream's pools. Cutthroat that spawn in larger streams find that fingerling steelhead are also waiting to bully them, although to a lesser extent than coho. Unable to compete with the larger, socially dominant salmon that control the pools, and steelhead that dominate the riffles, cutthroat fry reluctantly but quickly scurry off into the secondary areas of the stream where feeding is less challenging but not as productive.

The tiny cutthroats get along by feeding primarily on midges with the occasional caddis, stonefly and mayfly nymph providing additional sustenance. Although cutthroat fry do not forage regularly in prime areas of the stream, they do manage to grow steadily as summer approaches. By early July some of the larger juvenile cutthroat, now called parr, will have pushed their way into pools and riffles protected by woody debris and overhanging foliage. Here they find a much more abundant food supply and commence to feed heavily on aquatic insects. With the approach of fall, young cutthroat enjoy the luxury of an additional supplementary food source consisting of mayflies along with ants, grasshoppers, caterpillars and other terrestrial insects that tumble into the water from bank edges and overhanging limbs.

As the first autumn rains progress into the downpours of winter, immature cutthroat are faced with yet another challenge during the early stages of their lives. This is when parent streams can rise until they flow with such volume that during the heaviest winter rains even the tiniest creek becomes a very dangerous place for a small trout to live. Without sufficient cover to break the flow, small cutthroat may simply be swept away and die.

Here again, nature has provided the coastal cutthroat with a built-in sensor. At the first sign of increased stream flows in the fall, young cutthroat begin cruising up and down their river environment in search of deep, dark, protected eddies and undercuts buffered by boulders, root wads, down timber and woody debris that offer a buffer zone from the pounding currents of winter. They will also seek protection in small tributaries where they can wait out the winter flows. The following spring they will find themselves swimming among adult cutthroat that have just completed their spawning cycle, which takes place usually between March and June.

Good habitat in every inch of the cutthroat's home stream is critical to its well being. Whenever streams are scraped clean of woody debris or channeled with riprap for the sake of a riverside lawn or bulkhead, life becomes just a bit more difficult for the coastal cutthroat. If we did nothing for the coastal cutthroat other than really protect its habitat, we would go a long way toward ensuring its future health.

The First Migration

As adult cutthroat forage to recover weight and strength lost during the trauma of spawning, the one-year-old cutthroats, now six to seven inches in length begin swimming with the adults, enjoying the modest but welcome strength in numbers. With their weight and energy sufficiently restored, adult cutthroats embark on their downstream, seaward migration. Their return to saltwater can take place as early as February. More commonly though, the cutthroat's outmigration to salt water occurs from April through June. In British Columbia and Alaska cutthroat outmigration can occur as late as July.

A small percentage of yearling cutthroats will undergo the physiological process of smoltification (the changeover from parr to smolt) at this time and undertake their first venture to salt water with the outmigrating adults. The vast majority of yearling sea-run cutthroat however remain in their natal streams and do not migrate until they are 2 to 4 years old. There is some evidence that the largest sea-run cutthroat, those that grow upward of 18 inches during their lifetime, do not usually migrate as one year olds.

Life in the Salt

Once into the estuaries, cutthroat scatter out for several weeks to several months of high-on-the-hog feeding until it's time for the next spawning run. Both first-year migrators and adults that have spawned at least one time previously may travel together for a time in small pods. Anadromous coastal cutthroat trout are almost never found in large schools and are completely comfortable wandering the salt alone. Wherever cutthroat enjoy the comfort of sheltered salt water, such as Puget Sound in Washington State or the bays and channels of coastal British Columbia, they tend to remain near shore where they feed on pill bugs, mysid shrimp, amphipods, euphausids, sticklebacks and sand lance.

Some anadromous cutthroat rarely venture further from home than the estuary of parent rivers. Larger rivers with wide or braided estuaries and a strong tidal mix to make the water brackish can be very rich feeding areas, and are preferred areas for many migratory cutthroats from spring through fall each year. Some migratory cutthroat can in fact be found in estuarine areas of rivers every month of the year.

Ocean-going cutthroats that move from parent rivers straight into Puget Sound, the waters around Vancouver Island, the Queen Charlotte Islands or the Pacific Ocean proper can become rather adventurous travelers, pushing a considerable distance offshore to feed on small fishes; the primary prey being herring, northern anchovy, kelp greenling, cabezon and rockfishes. There are recorded instances of coastal cutthroat being found off Oregon's Siusilaw River plume more than forty miles offshore and a hundred feet deep traveling alone, apparently quite comfortable and no worse for wear.

Cutthroat will roam and forage through the early days of July and into August at which time they begin moving steadily back toward the estuaries of their natal rivers. Maiden ingeminators will by this time have packed on a lot of muscle from the rich saltwater feeding pastures and grown to a solid foot in length. Older sea-runs may be six to eight years old, weigh up to three pounds and approach the trophy 20-inch mark. By this time milt sacs are growing rapidly in mature males, as are skeins of roe in the bellies of spawning-age henfish.

The majority of sea-runs ascending their home rivers are mature fish ready to spawn for the second, third or even fourth time. Cutthroat that migrated to salt for the first time the previous spring also return to home rivers with the mature adults after having spent perhaps only three or four months in salt water. Younger cutthroats returning to parent rivers for the first time may, or may not have reached spawning maturity.

Return to the River

The first cutthroat to clear the estuaries into the sweet water of their home rivers have almost always spawned at least one time previously. This is one of the enigmatic characteristics of the sea-run cutthroat trout. Whatever the biological reason might be, a vanguard of large sea-run cutthroat push into estuary pools in late May and early June. In many rivers these early arriving cutthroats will be well upstream in their natal rivers by the first week of July.

On a bright day in late June I was fishing the upper Green River, near Auburn, Washington with one of my long-time angling pals, Bob Young. We were working the slot downstream from a high clay bank just below the mouth of Soos Creek. We were fishing for early summer-run steelhead that were reported to be in the river. After more than an hour of casting and changing flies repeatedly we had nothing to show for our effort. Then, while I was distracted by a couple of kingfishers contesting territorial rights to a tree-lined hillside that formed an umbrella over the deep, emerald run, Bob let out a whoop.

"Steelhead!" He yelled. "Wait. It's not a steelhead; it's a sea-run cutthroat." He played and released the fat 15-incher before I could get my camera ready. "It hit a Knudsen Spider," he said holding the black-bodied number 8 spider up for my inspection.

Not long after Bob landed his cutthroat I hooked one on a sparsely dressed McCullough. Mine also looked to be about 15 inches long but managed to spit the barbless hook before I had it close enough for a proper release.

"I have always found sea-run cutthroat in the Green early," I said to Bob. "I've even caught them upstream from here at the Whitney Bridge Hole about this time of year."

The majority of coastal cutthroat enter medium to large rivers between early August and late October with the bulk of the run arriving from the middle of September through early October. After settling into freshwater pools they may wait until mid-November to begin moving into small spawning creeks or tributaries of large rivers due to lack of water volume prior to the onset of the rainy season. In larger rivers from California to Alaska, cutthroat will generally have cleared the estuaries by Thanksgiving holding in deep, quiet upstream pools or under protected cut banks where they continue to ripen sexually prior to spawning.

The Spawning Ritual

Spawning takes place from November through May. Timing for spawning generally occurs earliest for coastal cutthroat in California and Oregon, and progressively later in Washington, British Columbia and Alaska. Throughout the coastal cutthroat's range there will be exceptions to spawning times depending upon the size and flow of its natal stream and the different genetic makeup within the species. Even though mid to late November is usually conceded to be when the last of the sea-run cutthroat arrive in most rivers, a few will wait even longer.

This very late spawning practice takes place in many small creeks that drain directly into the protected salt water of Puget Sound and Hood Canal in Washington and probably some saltwater areas in British Columbia. Such small creeks may not carry enough water volume to allow cutthroat to ascend to the spawning reaches until December through March when winter rains have increased their volume sufficiently. This is substantiated by my angling companions and I who fish along the beaches of Washington and catch large cutthroat with some regularity in December, January and February when we are actually more intent on hooking young, trout-size coho salmon. Anglers who are fishing rivers for winter steelhead also report hooking sexually mature, incidental sea-run cutthroat in December and January.

Nearly all cutthroat streams receive a run of early-returning spawners and others that arrive very late, bracketing the main body of the spawning run. These early and late-run cutthroats lengthen the spawning process by several weeks. Tiny hatching cutthroat that emerge from the gravel over several weeks experience a higher survival rate from predators and a significantly enhanced opportunity to compete with their early-life nemeses the coho salmon and steelhead.

When female cutthroats reach spawning readiness they seek out suitable gravel bottoms, usually in tributaries of large natal streams. A substantial tributary in larger streams may support several pairs of mating cutthroat and have spawning lies more than two feet deep. In small creeks that flow into mainstem rivers, directly into protected saltwater bays or the Pacific Ocean, suitable pools may be barely a foot deep with riffles that carry just enough volume to cover the backs of spawning cutthroat. Overhanging foliage usually shelters the most desirable spots.

In Northern California, mating pairs of coastal cutthroat have been recorded in tiny creeks not more than a foot across where they find impressions in the streambed of sufficient depth for spawning. This fact strongly emphasizes the importance of protecting even seemingly insignificant creeks and adjacent habitat that is utilized by coastal cutthroat.

Digging a depression in its chosen spawning place is tiring for the female cutthroat. Using a vigorous back-and-forth motion with her tail to dislodge gravel, sand and rocks, a spawning bed is eventually groomed to her liking.

Tough Love

While the nest building is taking place, love-struck male cutthroats anxiously awaiting the start of the courting ritual display obvious anxiety as they dart nervously around the pool in the general area of the female. When the female finally settles onto her carefully constructed bed several males may attempt to move in with her. This is when pent-up bucks with milt sacs ready to explode square off in earnest for the honor of sharing her bed, and the battle over gaining the favor of a lady is a dispute they do not take lightly. Engagements between male cutthroats contending over the favor of a female are violent encounters. During the throes of battle, buck cutthroats will bite and lock jaws like bull elk locking horns, while twisting and slamming each other all over the spawning pool. They will often remain joined in combat for more than an hour before the victor can take his place beside the patiently waiting female. The loser, battered but rarely unbowed, leaves in search of another female that has either not yet been spoken for or is paired up with a smaller, less combative male that may be routed with relative ease.

When the male and female cutthroat have settled onto the gravel depression they move close together repeatedly rubbing their flanks against each other in a gentle caress as the moment of spawning approaches. Soon her abdominal muscles send out a series of rippling contractions and the male commences a firm, persistent bumping against her as they hang side-by-side over the gravel facing into the current. The female arches her back, contracting her abdomen to loose the first outpouring of eggs. The male, feeling her contractions, releases his milt to effect fertilization as the eggs settle onto the gravel.

Spawning is usually completed within two days and the new redd is carefully covered over by the female with a layer of fine, protective gravel. At the termination of spawning, thin, spent sea-runs, called kelts, will seek out quiet, protected water to rest for a short time but soon begin feeding actively on nymphs, sculpins, or even on progeny of their old territorial adversaries, the coho salmon and steelhead.

Water temperature throughout the cutthroat's range is the primary factor that dictates the length of time fertilized eggs incubate before evolving into alevins. The term of incubation varies from six to seven weeks. The tiny alevins, remain secure in the sanctuary of their redd, utilizing the last of their yolk sac as nourishment for an additional two weeks before beginning to burrow up through the rocks and sand. They emerge as fry into the hazardous world of their parent stream from March through June and the cycle begins again.

Recovery

Having recouped the strength needed for the trip back to mainstem rivers, lakes or salt water, cutthroats will usually commence their migration in March in small streams and can continue through June in larger systems. During the downstream journey, kelts will be joined again by precocious smolts making their inaugural rearing venture. Anadromous cutthroats hold for a time in estuarine waters, where they begin feeding once again and acclimating to the complete exchange of fresh water to salt water in their bodies. They will stay in the estuaries to gorge on outmigrating chum and pink salmon fry for a time before heading into the Pacific Ocean proper or throughout protected coastal bays and channels. They may roam in small pods of two or three fish but are often found traveling alone. At other times sea-run cutthroat are found feeding with coho salmon of similar body size. Even on their first descent to salt water, cutthroat have the capacity to adjust quickly to whatever conditions they swim into upon leaving the sweet water of natal rivers.

Cutthroat that migrated to salt for the first time the previous spring as yearlings, and returned to home rivers with the mature adults, have spent perhaps only three or four months in salt water and may not have reached spawning maturity. It could be said that they made a practice run of sorts. These immature cutthroat will also migrate back out with recovering adults and smolts after the end of the spawning period. Upon spending a second season in salt water they will return again to natal rivers as mature first-time spawners.

Wandering the Salt

Prior to the Sea-Run Cutthroat Trout Symposium there was a loosely held assumption among some anglers that sea-run cutthroat do not travel far from parent streams during their time in salt water.

In protected bays and channels, such as those found in Washington, British Columbia and Alaska, sea-runs may thrive within a hundred feet of shore in water averaging no more than twenty feet deep, displaying a strong reluctance to cross even a narrow expanse of deep, open water. This does not include the notable documented exceptions of cutthroat that wander great distances offshore.

The Mysterious Spring Run

There is a myth subscribed to by some anglers that sea-run cutthroat ascend rivers in two distinct runs, fall and spring. Studies show however that there is only a single spawning run of sea-run cutthroat along the Pacific Coast, and that is the fall run. It is the cutthroats' fall ascent of rivers that gave it the nickname, "harvest trout."

General spring trout season openings in Pacific Coast rivers have contributed to the "spring run" coastal cutthroat myth. Anglers landing stocked rainbow trout have quite naturally taken significant numbers of hungry coastal cutthroat that are migrating downstream during the spring trout season. A great many anglers do not recognize these "spring" cutthroat as sea-runs even though they may have recovered quite nicely from spawning. Others who recognize the fish as sea-runs determine that since they are caught in the spring, they are part of a "spring run".

Wherever put-and-take spring fisheries for hatchery trout on Pacific Coast rivers coincide with sea-run cutthroat outmigrations, they should be timed to allow recovering downriver fish to clear the estuaries. Better yet, spring fisheries for hatchery trout on migratory cutthroat streams should be stopped altogether. The inadvertent killing of legal-size cutthroat during a hatchery-dependent spring trout fishery, particularly those cutthroat that migrate in their second or third year, decimates the stocks with the highest potential of becoming trophy sea-runs.

Overwintering in Salt Water

A theory exists that certain coastal cutthroat will occasionally skip a spawning run to remain in salt water through the winter and over the following summer. This is an occasional subject for discussion among Washington State anglers.

Fly-anglers have recorded cutthroats taken in salt water during every month of the year in Washington's South Puget Sound and Hood Canal. According to all available data, these are either late-entering fish spawning in small streams and jump-across creeks when winter rains have raised the water levels sufficiently to allow spawning, or kelts that have left small spawning creeks and recovered quickly to begin feeding again in the salt water. Cutthroat that utilize small creeks, like those found throughout South Puget Sound and Hood Canal, for spawning almost surely spend the majority of their lives in salt water because it provides a far richer food source than a small, relatively barren creek.

My friends and I have caught vigorous, coastal cutthroat in South Puget Sound and Hood Canal during every month of the year. Most are less than a foot long, while a few are solid 15- to 20-inchers. The tiddlers are almost certainly immature. Others are obviously late spawners while a few appear to be eccentric individuals that show no evidence of spawning trauma and have spent additional time in the salt, or are very late spring spawners.

In Alaska, cutthroat are sometimes found in salt water late in the season before they either stray into, or purposely seek out, streams with access to coastal lakes where they regularly spend the winter. When the ice leaves in spring they will depart the lakes and move back into salt water to seek out their natal streams for spawning. It has not been confirmed however, that Alaska sea-run cutthroat ever winter over completely in salt water.

In Washington there are no firm data to support speculation that mature cutthroat trout do overwinter in salt water. To this end, biologist Curt Kraemer of the Washington Department of Fish and Wildlife is of the opinion that exceptionally large cutthroats that wander the salt of Washington's North Puget Sound in the winter are more likely to be late spawners rather than overwintering specimens that are skipping a spawning cycle. He further contends that some of the rare extraordinary cutthroats found in North Puget Sound, bruisers in the 22- to 26-inch class may be progeny of cutthroat/steelhead hybridization, a spawning occurrence that has been documented. Curt adds this cautionary footnote to his statement however.

"As everyone who has been involved with coastal cutthroat knows, just when we think we understand them, they seem to escape from the box we attempt to place them in."

Robert J. Behnke, professor emeritus of Fisheries and Conservation at Colorado State University and author of *Trout and Salmon of North America* (The Free Press, 2002), responded to the premise that cutthroat overwinter in salt water during a panel discussion at the Reedsport Sea-run Cutthroat Trout Symposium.

When addressing a statement that sea-run cutthroat winter over for extended periods in salt water, perhaps even more than one year, he said. "If your Puget Sound cutthroat are over-wintering for a year or two or even more, then you should be seeing some pretty big cutthroat, like ten or fifteen pounds."

In *Trout and Salmon of North America,* Dr. Behnke refers to coastal cutthroat trout as "semi-anadromous". Behnke writes that the coastal cutthroat does not roam and spends only two or three months in salt water. In regard to Washington coastal cutthroat his statement is valid for those living in North Puget Sound but does not stand up against the information fly-fishers have gathered over the years in South Puget Sound and Hood Canal where rearing conditions and spawning habitat, as previously stated, are markedly different. The relatively mild winter conditions and well-protected waters of South Puget Sound and Hood Canal are certainly conducive to a cutthroat wintering over in salt water.

Steve Raymond, author of the book, *The Estuary Flyfisher* (Frank Amato Publications, 1996) has studied coastal cutthroat trout for more than thirty years and his findings have convinced him that they do indeed overwinter in South Puget Sound and Hood Canal where nearly all experienced anglers agree that cutthroat spend a good measure of each year in salt water. To verify his conviction, Raymond and his angling companions have documented impressive numbers of cutthroat in the salt throughout the winter months. Many of these fish were in the 10- to 12-inch range and could be early migrators from the previous spring that had not reached spawning maturity. It is also reasonable to believe that these smaller cutthroats could have descended parent streams as smolts and having not reached spawning maturity by fall simply remained in the salt until the following summer. If this should occur they would spend an extra year in the salt and return to natal streams as spawners in autumn. Raymond and his angling companions have also caught large, mature 20- to 22-inch cutthroat in salt water during the winter months that displayed no signs of trauma or spawning color.

The question of whether coastal cutthroat winter over in salt water remains scientifically unsubstantiated. So regardless of what personal observation tells us, we just have to add this conundrum to the long list of mysteries already cloaking the coastal cutthroat.

The True Non-Conformist

Weighing all of the vagaries here certainly validates Darwin Jones' statement that the sea-run coastal cutthroat is indeed "the non-conformist of the trout family". We still have much to learn about coastal cutthroat, and there are a lot of dedicated fisheries biologists in wildlife agencies and university fishery schools that care about this little non-conformist and would like nothing better than to receive the funding needed to study it properly. It will be up to us, the anglers, to keep the pressure on federal, state and provincial legislators to allocate the funds needed to bring such studies into reality. Until such funding is allocated, the mysterious coastal cutthroat, particularly in its sea-run form, is going to have to get along just the way it has for thousands of years—on its grit and tenacity for life.

Chapter 3 - Identifying Coastal Cutthroat Trout

"Many anglers are unable to distinguish cutthroat trout from juvenile or half-pounder steelhead because of close superficial resemblance, and thus may not be aware that they have caught a cutthroat trout."

—Eric R. Gerstung
California Department of Fish and Game

Correct identification of the coastal cutthroat, particularly in its sea-run form, is important on several counts. Upon leaving its river of birth to enter the estuarine and marine environment that it calls home part of each year, the distinctive freshwater markings of the coastal cutthroat give way to its sea-run coloration. The olive back changes to a pale steel blue/green. The flanks brighten from amber to silver with the usually vivid spots less pronounced. Perhaps most importantly, the bright orange slashes under either side of it's jaw often fade to only a slight orange blush.

In its sea-run form, the coastal cutthroat is regularly found swimming with salmon of similar size in the salt waters of Washington, Alaska and British Columbia. This likely occurs in California and Oregon marine waters as well, but there is little saltwater fishing for coastal cutthroat in either of these states to substantiate the statement. Since it takes on a silvery patina during its saltwater period, the sea-run cutthroat is all too often harvested by inexperienced anglers who believe that it's a small chinook or coho salmon.

In Southern Oregon and Northern California the coastal cutthroat ascends rivers at the same time as the famed runs of half-pounder steelhead, which are approximately the same size. Here again, coastal cutthroat have been mistakenly identified and harvested as steelhead by anglers who are not completely familiar with the differences between the two species.

It has always been important for anglers to accurately identify the fish we pursue and catch. Today, though, correct identification is even more essential with so many of the game fish we go after, particularly anadromous species, listed as threatened or endangered and protected under catch-and-release regulations. To make the situation even more serious, there are a whole lot more of us going after game fish like the coastal cutthroat at the very time when runs all along the Pacific Coast survive in varying stages of declining health and continue to lose critical habitat on a regular basis.

If we should mistakenly take a coastal cutthroat from a watershed where the stocks are strong, the error may be minimal. If, on the other hand, we kill a cutthroat that is native to a watershed with weakened wild stocks, the error can have more serious consequences. Being able to correctly identify the coastal cutthroat, in all its forms—resident, fluvial, adfluvial and anadromous—will go a long way to improving its numbers.

A brace of hatchery-stocked cutthroat from an alpine lake in Strathcona Park on Vancouver Island ready for the frying pan of hungry backpackers.

Resident Cowichan River cutthroat pounced on a sizeable hellgramite imitation intended for a big brown trout. Note typical cutthroat slashes under the jaw.

Coastal Cutthroat (freshwater colors)

Coastal Cutthroat

(Oncorhynchus clarki clarki)

The coastal cutthroat trout attains an average adult size of approximately 12- to 20 inches. Weight of the coastal cutthroat will range from 1 to 3 pounds, with exceptional specimens occasionally topping 4 to 5 pounds. In a forage-rich lake environment, coastal cutthroat can grow much larger, often attaining weights of more than 15 pounds.

The maxillary (upper jaw bones) of the coastal cutthroat extend to the rear of the eyes and may extend well beyond the eye. Both the upper and lower jaws have rows of well-developed teeth. There are also teeth on the head and shaft of the vomer (a bone in the upper jaw attached to the maxillary). Two rows of teeth are found on the back of the tongue and two to 20 teeth on the basibranchials (floor of the mouth) which are often difficult to see or are not evident at all in some individual stocks.

Coloration of coastal cutthroat trout varies rather widely throughout its range and even between watersheds within a small geographic area. An important color marking that identifies the cutthroat are the two distinctive orange or red slashes on either side of the lower jaw. Rainbow and brown trout do not have these markings. The intensity of color on the cutthroat's jaw markings may be quite vivid, particularly in freshwater specimens and during spawning. Young cutthroat will have less colorful markings. Cutthroat in salt water or just returning from salt water also display only the merest hint of the distinguishing slashes and some individuals will have no slash marks at all. During spawning, male cutthroat develop a distinct kype on the lower jaw.

In its marine and near-shore environment, the cutthroat is often confused with salmon. The cutthroat can be readily identified in its saltwater environment by quickly counting the anal fin rays. Trout, including cutthroat, always have twelve or fewer rays while salmon always have thirteen or more.

In fresh water, cutthroat are most often confused with rainbow and steelhead trout. In addition to the long jaw length, cutthroat usually have 150-180 scales along the lateral line while the rainbow/steelhead has fewer than 150. In addition, the dorsal fin of the cutthroat is narrower than the rainbow or steelhead, having nine to eleven dorsal rays, typically ten. Rainbow and steelhead trout have ten to thirteen rays with eleven or twelve rays being typical. The pelvic fin of the cutthroat typically has nine rays while rainbow and steelhead typically have ten rays.

The coastal cutthroat in fresh water has a green back and olive to olive/yellow sides with a pale to nearly white belly. It is heavily spotted from nose to tail, from the top of the back and down the sides beyond the lateral line all the way to the belly. In some specimens it may be heavily spotted all the way around the head and along the lower jaw. During spawning, coastal cutthroat will attain a rosy coloration on the cheeks and sides, more pronounced in males than females.

The coastal cutthroat in salt water has a blue to blue/green back and silvery sides. The spots are not as prominent on the sea-run cutthroat but are still clearly visible even with casual observation.

Coastal Cutthroat (saltwater colors)

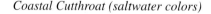

Chapter 4 - Coastal Cutthroat Trout in Alaska

The Alaska Department of Fish and Game's mission is to manage, protect, maintain, and improve the fish, game and aquatic plant resources of Alaska. The primary goals are to ensure that Alaska's renewable fish and wildlife resources and their habitats are conserved and managed on the sustained yield principle, and the use and development of these resources are in the best interest of the economy and well-being of the people of the state.

—Mission Statement
Alaska Department of Fish and Game

Coastal cutthroat trout range through southeast Alaska from rivers and lakes around Ketchikan and on Prince of Wales Island north to Prince William Sound.

The most abundant coastal cutthroat populations occur in the southernmost reaches of the state, which has many more accessible lakes and large rivers better suited to accommodate anadromous fish. Coastal cutthroat particularly the anadromous or sea-run form, are the most abundant trout in southeast Alaska and thus are very important to the sport fishery.

The coastal cutthroat, shrouded in vagaries throughout its range, lives an even more mysterious, wandering existence in the rugged environs of southeast Alaska. Rather than spending the winter in rivers and creeks as they do further south in their range, most anadromous coastal cutthroat of Alaska move into lakes that have access to salt water where they wait out the harsh winters.

Throughout the Misty Fjords in southeast Alaska there are cutthroat lakes and streams that are rarely fished due to difficult access. Many of the prime waters are only reached by float plane.

When spring returns, mature cutthroat are first to emigrate the lakes that afford them winter respite. Young fish rear in small streams and tributaries for the first few years before moving out to salt water and then into lakes. These younger fish probably will spawn the spring following their first wintering over in a lake.

Upon reentering salt water in the spring, mature fish seek out nearby streams for spawning which takes place from March to June. Upon completion of spawning they will return to salt water to recover and forage until autumn, when it's again time to duck into the sanctuary of a lake to wait out another southeast Alaska winter.

Abundance

Studies completed at Eva Lake on Baranof Island and Auke Lake near the city of Juneau show that overwintering populations rarely exceed 2,000 fish and may often be only a few hundred. Since cutthroat trout from several nearby spawning and rearing streams overwinter in Eva and Auke lakes, population size from these individual spawning and rearing streams is probably significantly smaller than the emigrant counts from the lakes. Population records over time are only available for these two lakes in southeast Alaska. In both instances these records indicate that numbers are now higher than in earlier years. No studies have been made on coastal cutthroat spawning or rearing streams near Eva and Auke lakes so comparisons of cutthroat population sizes cannot be made for individual streams.

Weir counts of cutthroat trout emigrating in the spring have been made on a few other systems in Alaska. All of these studies were of short duration, thus a comparison of population growth or decline over several years cannot be made. Investigations of cutthroat trout in Prince William Sound were conducted to determine the effects of the Exxon *Valdez* oil spill. These studies lasted only two years thus provide no accumulative information.

Coastal Cutthroat Sport Fishery in Rivers and Lakes

Coastal cutthroat throughout southeast Alaska are important to sport fishing even when placed against the region's huge runs of salmon. Most of this fishing is over the most abundant populations that occur in the southernmost reaches in the waters on and around Ketchikan and Prince of Wales Island. During the spring of the year, cutthroat lay in wait in the lower reaches of all salmon rivers on the Alaska mainland and most of the many streams on Prince of Wales Island. When huge schools of pink and chum salmon smolts leave their graveled sanctuaries to head downstream for salt water, cutthroat feed voraciously to fatten up after spawning. The Thorne River, the largest stream on Prince of Wales Island has a healthy population of cutthroats that provide an

Dan Lemaich works his fly through a quiet side channel on the Thorne River, Prince of Wales Island, Alaska.

outstanding spring fishery for local and visiting anglers who usually fish the Thorne for steelhead. The outmigration of young salmon usually takes place from late March through June.

The Thorne River fishery can be highly productive for the fly-fisher as the cutthroat lay in wait for swarms of pink and chum salmon fry to emerge from the gravel and begin an immediate downstream migration into Thorne Bay and Clarence Straight. When the fry start downstream, the surface fairly boils with feeding cutthroat as they chop through the hoards of migrating fry. When the frenzy is on, a small fry-imitating pattern cast into the melee will bring strike after strike with the action only slowing when the run of salmon has passed by. Then the angler must wait for the next emergence of salmon which will trigger another feeding spree or work the slow side channels where some of the largest cutthroats occasionally cruise in search of forage. Local anglers generally concentrate on the stretch of Thorne River from just above the Thorne Bay estuary to the bridge a few miles further upstream. There is however good cutthroat water all the way upriver to Thorne Lake.

Staney Creek, a favorite of steelheaders, also holds a fair population of coastal cutthroat. This fishery is even more localized than the Thorne River as visiting anglers look to Staney Creek for the opportunity to fish its steelhead that can hit the 20-pound mark. There is fairly easy access to Staney Creek from the road to the estuary, a distance of more than a mile.

There are myriad cutthroat streams and lakes in the Tongass National Forest on the southeast Alaska mainland that are fished regularly by local anglers. Many of these are above barriers, and are home to resident and adfluvial populations in addition to anadromous runs. Many of the lakes in the Tongass are best reached by float plane. There are float planes for hire in Ketchikan.

Coastal Cutthroat in Salt Water

There is ample protected water to fish for coastal cutthroat in salt water in Southeast Alaska and it is utilized by sport fishers. With so much rugged and well-protected water available, fishing for coastal cutthroat trout in the salt water in Southeast Alaska has the potential to be outstanding. Most recent records available indicate that cutthroat taken by saltwater sport anglers make up 22 percent of the total cutthroat trout sport catch. The Petersburg/Wrangell area consistently puts out a major proportion of the harvest from salt water. This area has many locations where anglers can cast to coastal cutthroat that are milling and feeding in intertidal zones.

There is little long-term saltwater harvest information available for cutthroat since statewide catch estimates were not begun until 1990. Catch increased from a low in 1991 to a high in 1993 and then dropped again in 1994. The percentage of the catch that was harvested in southeastern Alaska

Herb Hall battles a cutthroat in a Misty Fjords creek as guide Sid Cook looks on.

decreased from 51.2 percent in 1991 to 15.5 percent in 1994. This dramatic decrease was in part due to new regulatory restrictions that went into effect during this period. No pronounced decline in harvest was observed in Prince William Sound.

Regulatory Management

Management regulations southeastern Alaska were revised in 1994 to provide additional protection for coastal cutthroat trout. The core element of these new regulations were a 12-inch minimum size limit and a 10-month freshwater bait ban (November 15-September 15) with a bag limit of two trout. The 12-inch minimum size protects approximately 85 percent of all coastal cutthroats until they have the opportunity to spawn at least once. While the bait ban reduces mortality of released fish, trophy and high use systems have even more restrictive regulations.

Regulations for the Prince William Sound area do not provide either size or bait restrictions as of this writing. They do however provide for a closed season from April 15 through June 14 with a limit of two cutthroat trout per day in some areas and five trout per day with only one over 10-inches in other areas.

Most lakes in which mixed-stocked aggregations of coastal cutthroat spend the winter seldom have more than a 2,000 trout emigration annually, and individual stream populations are much smaller. The 22 percent of total harvest that came from salt water in 1994 indicates that anadromous fish contribute a significant portion of the total catch of cutthroat trout. Weir counts at Lake Eva and Auke Lake indicate that these populations are at a high level, while anecdotal information indicates some small lake populations have diminished in two or three years after angler access was developed.

Statewide harvest surveys show that the portion of the catch retained has been decreasing in southeastern Alaska since 1991. There was a substantial decrease in retention of cutthroat trout in Southeast in 1994, when the minimum size was limit and reduced bag limits were adopted. The retention rate for cutthroat trout in Prince William Sound, which has different regulations, has been quite stable and did not show a decrease in 1994.

Conclusion

While the coastal cutthroat trout is a popular sport fish with local anglers and does receive some attention from others visiting Alaska, it has been spared the heavy fishing pressure that exists elsewhere in its range. For this reason and in light of rather strict harvest regulations in place, it appears that the coastal cutthroat will continue to provide a good sport fishery in the future. Another important factor in the good condition of coastal cutthroat populations in Alaska is that many of the lakes and rivers in which they reside are not easily reached due to heavily timbered watersheds and the brush busting involved in order to reach many of the lakes. Alaska remains the Last Frontier of the United States and the coastal cutthroat certainly benefits from its thick cloak of protective habitat.

Dan Lemaich releases a coastal cutthroat.

Chapter 5 - Coastal Cutthroat Trout in California

The Mission of the Department of Fish and Game is to manage California's diverse fish, wildlife, and plant resources and the habitats upon which they depend, for their ecological values and for their use and enjoyment of the public.
—Mission Statement
California Department of Fish and Game

The State of California at one time, two hundred years or so ago, must have been as near to Utopia as any place could be. Southern California had an untapped wealth of oil filling its belly; could boast year-around warm temperatures; and the Pacific Ocean was filled with halibut, sea bass, yellowtail and tuna.

Central California had a huge, pristine estuary; the San Francisco Bay fed by the Sacramento and San Joaquin rivers. These big rivers and their numerous tributaries teemed with seemingly endless runs of salmon and steelhead that migrated in from the Pacific Ocean nearly every month of the year. Commercial fisheries soon developed in San Francisco Bay and along the Pacific coast from Monterey to Bodega Bay to harvest and process the rich lode of the nearby Pacific waters.

In 1849, the mineral-rich tributaries of California's mighty Sacramento River and its tributaries were swarmed over by armies of gold miners whose search for rich strikes left streambeds all through the Sacramento Valley scoured and scarred. Once superb salmon and steelhead spawning gravel was deposited on the banks to form mile after mile of tailing piles that leached a deadly cocktail of toxicity back into the streams.

A clear, deep cutthroat pool on California's lower Smith River.

Along the Pacific coast, from just north of San Francisco to the Oregon border, there were many more clean, swift streams alive with salmon and steelhead. Commercial fisheries sprang up south to Moro Bay and north to Eureka bringing prosperity to nearly every little coastal hamlet with a safe harbor for boat moorage and processing plants.

Vast stands of giant redwood trees that filled lush watersheds provided yet another bonanza ripe for the taking along the Northern California coast. Logging the enormous redwoods destroyed watersheds, which resulted in the silting over of spawning gravel in coastal rivers and their tributaries. While some of these watersheds have recovered sufficiently from the ravages of logging to support a vestige of their once-robust populations of salmon and steelhead, none have been restored adequately to ever see runs of fish anything like the piscatorial treasures that ascended them in the past. Today, California's entire cornucopia of natural resources is still suffering the ongoing aftershocks of being pumped, dug, plowed, dredged, netted, cut, dammed — or diverted to Los Angeles.

Another item in the treasure trove that ranged from the Eel River north along the vast redwood rainforests to the Smith River was the coastal cutthroat trout. Despite the most diligent efforts of man to exploit every last iota of California's natural resources, the coastal cutthroat has managed to cling tenaciously to life and still occupies most of its historic habitat throughout the northern reaches of the Golden State.

Coastal cutthroat never attained the popularity of the salmon, steelhead, or any of the heavy-shouldered resident trout populations among California anglers. Although they enjoyed healthy numbers during their peak years, coastal cutthroat did not boast huge populations, even in larger North Coast rivers like the Smith, Klamath, Mad or Eel, all of which once received substantial runs of highly sought after salmon and steelhead.

Coastal cutthroat found Redwood Creek and other small main-stem streams, tributaries of larger rivers, brackish water estuaries and saltwater lagoons — where there was less competition from salmon and steelhead — more to their liking. It is in these smaller Northern California rivers that the beleaguered populations of California coastal cutthroat still maintain their tenuous fight for existence.

Mistaken Identity

Over the years, thousands of cutthroat that ascended California rivers were mistakenly killed as half-pounder steelhead. This was certainly the case during the salad days of the Klamath River half-pounder steelhead fishery. The proof was inadvertently published in *Field & Stream* and *Western Outdoors* magazines.

In the late 1960s, long before I began writing the first little blue pocket-size volume on the sea-run cutthroat, I read an article in *Field & Stream* about half-pounder fishing on

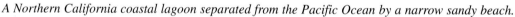

A Northern California coastal lagoon separated from the Pacific Ocean by a narrow sandy beach.

Carlo Borgio

the Klamath River out of Happy Camp Lodge. A black-and-white lead photo showed three anglers and a guide posing beside a Happy Camp river sled with an obscene stringer of half-pounder steelhead stretched out along its gunwale. The next page had a close-up photo of four half-pounders, one of which was clearly a large coastal cutthroat. The same photos appeared illustrating a different article some time later in *Western Outdoors*.

Eric R. Gerstung, California Fish and Game, noted the inability of anglers to identify sea-run cutthroat in his paper, "Status of Coastal Cutthroat Trout in California," which was included in the 1995 Reedsport Sea-run Cutthroat Symposium proceedings. In his paper, he wrote: "Many anglers are unable to distinguish cutthroat trout from juvenile or half-pounder steelhead because of close superficial resemblance, and thus may not be aware that they have caught a sea-run cutthroat trout."

Coastal or Sea-Run Cutthroat?
The life history of the coastal cutthroat trout in California is complicated and not completely understood. Studies published in 1954 by J. W. DeWitt indicated that coastal cutthroats north of the Mad River are anadromous. Others have argued that California coastal cutthroat may only migrate downstream as far as the brackish or saltwater estuaries of streams or lagoons and do not actually enter the Pacific Ocean. This would indicate that they are not truly anadromous. Other cutthroat may reside in large rivers and enter smaller tributaries for spawning thus they are essentially river dwellers. Still others spend their entire lives in parent freshwater streams and lagoons and are actually resident coastal cutthroat.

Gerstung stated in his paper that he suspects some of the larger cutthroat found in the Smith, Klamath and Little rivers may utilize the Pacific Ocean waters for part of the year. He also contends that resident coastal cutthroat could reach the same large size by feeding on the abundant juvenile salmonids in those rivers. Since he had no scale sample analysis to confirm ocean growth, Gerstung used the term "coastal" cutthroat rather than "sea-run" cutthroat in most of his report.

Habitat
About ten percent of California coastal cutthroat habitat that occurs in relatively unaltered drainages, primarily within the boundaries of state parks and national forest wilderness areas. At least one-third of these lands have suffered channel aggregation from natural causes associated with floods and landslides. Channelization, siltation, loss of bank vegetation and flow reduction have degraded another ten percent, nearly all of which is associated with agricultural development. Most of this damage is found along the Smith, Klamath and Eel river deltas and Humboldt Bay lowlands. Loss of overhead stream canopy cover, instream cover and sedation from intense logging has also taken a severe toll on cutthroat habitat throughout Northern California.

Estuarine habitat throughout northwestern California has been severely damaged from channelization, sedimentation, dredging, blockage of side channels and loss of large woody debris and other instream cover. The Smith River and Redwood Creek estuaries have suffered severe damage while the Klamath and Little River estuaries have fared somewhat better. Overall coastal cutthroat habitat throughout Northern California is recovering faster in some places than in others. Steep drainages that were logged of old-growth redwood back when stream protection was of little concern are recovering very slowly. Conversely, watersheds of gentle, stable incline have recovered more rapidly.

Population Status of California Coastal Cutthroat
There is not a lot of hard data available on the population densities of coastal cutthroat along the Northern California coast. All information received from local residents and old newspaper accounts suggest that cutthroat were historically much more abundant throughout their California range than they are today.

In the December 1925 issue of Pacific Sportsman magazine, Game Warden A.D. Lee wrote, "From now through the winter the Smith River and lower branches of the Klamath will be full of cut-throat trout which invariably follow the salmon when they come to spawn."

Although coastal cutthroat were in severe decline from logging degradation from the 1920s through the 1940s, record storms and floods took an additional toll on cutthroat stocks in 1964 and 1965. Since 1970 cutthroat populations have improved as streamside habitat has begun to recover. Observations indicate that since the early 1980s coastal cutthroat stocks have been stable in Northern California streams. This information has been corroborated by data obtained from trapping, seining and diving surveys made on the Smith River, Redwood Creek and the Klamath River estuary during the last several years.

Eel River Drainage
It is estimated that cutthroat trout inhabit approximately 20 miles of tributary habitat in the Eel River drainage. They have been found in Strong Creek, a tributary of the lower Eel River and in Fox Creek, a tributary of the Van Duzen River, which is a major tributary of the Eel. Cutthroats are also found in five tiny streams that flow into Salt River Slough in the Eel River Delta. Prior to 1960, cutthroat trout were occasionally taken from the main estuary of the Eel River. It has been concluded that they were never abundant in the Eel River Estuary. All cutthroat in the Eel River Delta tributaries are now considered to be resident, and no other salmonids have been observed there for several years.

Humboldt Bay Tributaries
Coastal cutthroat are rarely observed in Humboldt Bay, but do occur in several reasonably healthy tributaries, including brackish tidal reaches where they are occasionally taken by anglers. Cutthroat occur in low numbers where other salmonids are present, but in much larger numbers in some headwater streams, such as Janes Creek, where no other salmonids are present.

Humboldt Bay streams are showing signs of recovery in some areas and are becoming increasingly degraded by logging and urbanization in others. The expansion of Humboldt Bay National Wildlife Refuge may result in the restoration of some tidal areas and marshland habitat. This could be beneficial to coastal cutthroat trout provided current logging operations do not cause excessive damage, reversing any possible benefits to the streams. At this time fishing for coastal cutthroat is difficult since public access is minimal. There is foot access permitted on some lumber company property.

Mad River Drainage

The Mad River drainage has been severely degraded by years of being logged time after time. The lower river has been partially channelized to accommodate agricultural development, and during the summer water is diverted from the river for municipal and industrial use. This does not bode well for coastal cutthroat trout that are known to inhabit the Mad for about eleven miles upstream from the Pacific Ocean. They have been sighted in the lower mainstem and nine tributaries.

The Mad River has only limited public land in the lower river. Legal access is restricted in large part to road crossings, levee banks and on some lumber company property. There is

Deep, canopied pools provide excellent habitat on many Northern California rivers and creeks.

a boat launch located on the upper Mad River estuary. Mad River cutthroat exist in very limited numbers and their small size indicates that they are probably not anadromous.

Little River Drainage

Little River, the drainage just north of the Mad River, flows directly into the Pacific Ocean. Surveys show that at least 24 miles of river habitat is suitable for coastal cutthroat trout. The heaviest concentrations of juvenile cutthroat in Little River occur in the headwater tributaries where there is minimal competition from juvenile salmon and steelhead. In the mainstem and larger tributaries, juvenile steelhead are very abundant which is detrimental to coastal cutthroat rearing success.

Modest numbers of cutthroat migrate downstream toward the estuary from April through June. Anglers targeting cutthroat in the spring and early summer have taken mature fish up to 16 inches long, some of which could be anadromous.

Little River runs through a lot of private land with the exception of Little River State Park. Although much of the lower river is private and posted, considerable public fishing takes place. There is some access allowed by written permit on the remainder of the drainage, owned at this time by Louisiana Pacific Lumber Company. Although the Little River drainage was logged between 1900 and 1930, and is being logged again, cutthroat populations are considered to be relatively strong.

Redwood Creek Drainage

Redwood Creek once boasted a hearty population of sea-run cutthroat and provided a very popular fishery. Old National Park Service photos show anglers with fine catches of large cutthroat trout taken from the Redwood Creek estuary. Anglers who fished Redwood Creek in 1897 indicated that in some years there appeared to be as many cutthroat trout migrants as there were steelhead. The fishery became so popular that a skiff rental service was established in the estuary.

Between 1950 and 1978, widespread logging of old-growth redwood, primarily by clearcutting and tractor yarding, devastated the habitat in and around Redwood Creek. The overwhelming habitat degradation caused a nearly complete crash of the sea-run cutthroat population.

Devastating winter storms in 1964 and 1965 caused large landslides, road and culvert failures and major skid road erosion. Instream cover was lost and tributaries were clogged with silt and logjams. Additional storms hit the coast in 1972, further damaging streamside and estuarine habitat. Repeated downstream flooding caused by upstream habitat destruction was curtailed by implementation of a flood-control project, which channelized the lower three miles of the river. Levees were extended into the estuary, drastically reducing its size and productivity as a nursery for juvenile migratory cutthroat and other salmonids. The Redwood Creek estuary, strangled by the grip of the flood-control levee, now holds a very minimal population of cutthroat trout.

Coastal cutthroat are still found in the Redwood Creek mainstem and fourteen tributaries from Coyote Creek downstream to the estuary. Cutthroat are also present in the Prairie Creek drainage where they have been observed in ten tributaries.

There have been attempts made to recover the estuary of Redwood Creek. Continuation of this project is dependent upon funding from Congress and the cooperation of landowners whose properties are adjacent to Redwood Creek.

Klamath River Drainage

Coastal cutthroat trout have been observed more than 60 miles from the ocean in the Klamath River drainage in Horse Linto Creek, a tributary of the Trinity River. As of 1990, reproducing populations of coastal cutthroat have been observed in 23 Klamath River tributaries and are known to occupy nearly a hundred miles of suitable habitat. Cutthroats are regularly observed in the lower five miles of the Klamath and are taken at times by anglers as far upstream as Tectah Creek.

Like most other Northern California drainages, the Klamath River has been seriously degraded, primarily by intense logging which has clogged many streams with debris and filled pools with silt. The damage has been intensified over the years by the winter storms of 1964-65. Studies by both the U.S. Fish and Wildlife Service and the Yurok Tribe indicate that cutthroat populations are relatively low. The contribution of these cutthroat to the lower Klamath River however is significant since studies have shown that downstream juvenile migrants annually number in the thousands. The largest populations of coastal cutthroat are found in Blue, Tarup and Ah Pah creeks. These fish are probably destined for the Klamath River estuary. Fishing opportunity is limited since about 90 percent of the lower Klamath River tributaries are on private timber company land.

The Klamath River estuary remains in reasonably good condition and produces a fair number of cutthroat trout according to creel counts taken from steelhead anglers along the estuary and lower river tributaries. In the summer and fall of 1994 there were an estimated 263 coastal cutthroat landed. There could have been additional cutthroat landed that were not recorded and others that were almost certainly caught and erroneously counted as half-pounder steelhead.

There have been studies made as far back as 1940 indicating that Klamath River coastal cutthroat, like half-pounder steelhead, do not migrate much further than the estuary, rarely nosing very far out into the Pacific Ocean. More recent information shows that a winter spawning migration does occur in lower-river tributaries, although there is no verification that these cutthroat have ever been in the ocean even though they take on the silvery appearance of a sea-run cutthroat. Others have stated that estuarine cutthroat will also take on the silver sides of a true sea-run cutthroat.

The coastal cutthroat could have significant value to California anglers, but there is a lot of work to be done to understand and properly care for them. Scale sample studies must be analyzed to determine the question of anadromy, and additional life history data are needed to determine migratory patterns of Klamath River cutthroat.

Smith River Drainage

The Smith River produces coastal cutthroat trout throughout its main stem, its three forks and 47 tributaries. There is estimated to be more than 230 miles of habitat either available to, or occupied by, coastal cutthroat trout in the Smith River drainage. It is very likely that they also occur in many additional tributaries that have not yet been surveyed.

Coastal cutthroat average about 60 fish per mile in sections of the Smith River where they compete with other salmonids. Cutthroat living above impassable barriers where there is no competition from other salmonids, have densities sometimes exceeding 300 per mile. Cutthroat larger than 8 or 9 inches are rarely found in small tributary streams, except when spawners are present. Larger cutthroat up to 19 inches generally live in the estuary, main stem and larger tributaries. Snorkeling studies since 1991 show that the total population of cutthroat in the lower Smith River and its tributaries is around 1100 fish. The largest numbers of coastal cutthroat are found in the Smith during the late summer and fall months.

A study in 1977 indicated that at least three different life cycle patterns occur within the coastal cutthroat population in the Smith River. These are; resident; stream dwellers and sea-run forms. Those considered to be anadromous were typically 12 to 18 inches long, silvery in color and more wary of divers than resident cutthroat.

The Smith River watershed has suffered degradation similar to other north coast California rivers. The pools in the estuary, once deep and clear, have become partially filled with silt and gravel. Agricultural development has increased bank erosion. Levees and gates have cut off many productive oxbows and sloughs. Erosion from extensive logging aggraded the Siskiyou Fork, South Fork and other large tributaries, including Hurdy Gurdy and Jones creeks.

There is a chance for the Smith to recover however since much of its watershed lies within national forests and

This nice sea-run cutthroat was taken from Stone Lagoon in Northern California.

national and state parks which have more than 70 percent of the available cutthroat habitat. Additionally, the Smith River, including its forks and major tributaries, are part of both the State and National Wild and Scenic River Systems. This ensures that any additional water development will be prohibited.

Smith River has a long and storied history of producing some of the largest chinook salmon and winter steelhead found on the entire Pacific Coast. It also carries a limited population of coastal cutthroat that push up into the trophy 18-inch range. This certainly makes the Smith River coastal cutthroat worthy of increased stewardship.

Small Coastal Drainages

There are nineteen small streams between the Mad River and the Oregon border that hold populations of coastal cutthroat trout. Many of these small streams offer minimal angling opportunity since they run through private land. Blocked culverts and logjams limit most of these to resident cutthroat although they do drain into the Pacific Ocean. Where there is no competition from other salmonids, these little streams hold relatively good populations of cutthroat. Upper watershed logging methods are improving and harvest is more carefully regulated. However, unless there is adequate access allowed, these little streams will not add significantly to the California anglers' fishing opportunities.

Coastal Lagoons

Cutthroat trout inhabit five lakes and lagoons along the northern California coast with a total of more than 4500 acres. Coastal lagoons do not include those that become temporarily blocked in late summer such as Redwood Creek nor do they include sloughs found in the Smith River and Eel River deltas.

The largest lagoon combining the Lake Earl and Lake Talawa complex north of Crescent City holds a fishable population of very tenacious coastal cutthroat. This could be a much more productive sport fishery if it weren't for the rather dismal regard for spawning tributaries and water-level management. The sandbar between Lake Talawa and the Pacific Ocean is artificially breached every spring at the request of property owners to lower the lake and surrounding groundwater table. This drives cutthroat searching for cooler water into the channel between the two lakes where they become heavily concentrated and highly vulnerable to anglers.

Big Lagoon also holds a fair population of cutthroat trout. It is not a productive fishery although there has been some habitat improvement of primary spawning tributaries made during the past several years. Veteran anglers who understand Big Lagoon and know its most productive areas do enjoy good catches of cutthroat.

Stone Lagoon north of Big Lagoon carries only a small population of cutthroat. It has been artificially breached allowing some cutthroat to migrate and others to succumb to disease.

Freshwater Lagoon, immediately north of Stone Lagoon once supported a small population of cutthroat. It was chemically treated to kill fish affected by parasites and restocked with bass. A few cutthroat may still exist in Freshwater Lagoon.

Angling access to coastal cutthroat water in California is generally good. The coastal cutthroat of California has managed to survive in most of its historic habitat throughout the state, although in reduced numbers. In 1991 the American Fisheries Society declared California stocks of sea-run (coastal) cutthroat stocks of "special concern". It is also possible that the Endangered Species Act could identify specific populations of California coastal cutthroat for protection.

Conclusion

Whatever measures may be required to maintain the coastal cutthroat in California will be well worth the effort. Better yet, increased numbers of coastal cutthroat would provide a big boost to anglers who fish northern California in the spring and summer, a time when salmon and steelhead fishing is slow. The gold that was mined is gone forever. The oil that was pumped from the ground is history. But the trees, the water and the coastal cutthroat can be restored as part of California's heritage. And anything this good that can be made to happen, should happen.

California coastal lagoons hold varying populations of sea-run cutthroat depending on the condition of the water and surrounding habitat.

Chapter 6 - Coastal Cutthroat Trout in Oregon

Our mission is to protect and enhance Oregon's fish and wildlife and their habitat for use and enjoyment by present and future generations.

—Mission Statement
Oregon Department of Fish and Wildlife

The coastal cutthroat trout holds a hallowed place in the annals of Oregon fishing history. On the fabled Rogue and Umpqua rivers the coastal cutthroat was fished for by anglers that included noted authors, dignitaries and sportsmen from around the world. Famous fly tiers Polly Rosborough and Al Knudson forged their storied reputations around patterns they originated for cutthroat trout in the rivers of Southern Oregon. More importantly though, the coastal cutthroat throughout its range in Oregon offers the average local angler potentially world-class fishing in spectacular and storied settings at hometown prices.

Distribution of the Coastal Cutthroat in Oregon

Oregon is home to all four types of coastal cutthroat trout; resident, lake dwellers, river dweller and sea-run. Coastal cutthroat trout are found in Oregon in nearly all streams that flow into the Willamette River. They are indigenous to literally thousands of small creeks that run down through evergreen and oak-studded canyons to reach larger tributaries that flow in from east and west feeding the Willamette System that drains this huge watershed before running into the lower Columbia River.

Resident and migratory cutthroat are present in Columbia River tributaries downstream of the Hood River. Anadromous, true sea-run cutthroat, are found in lower Columbia tributaries downstream from the mouth of the Willamette River.

On the Pacific Coast cutthroat inhabit almost every evergreen canopied river that drains into the Pacific Ocean

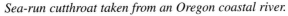

Sea-run cutthroat taken from an Oregon coastal river.

from the mighty Columbia River estuary to the tiny Winchuck River that cuts through the ocean beach near the California border.

Resident coastal cutthroat are widespread throughout Oregon and are believed to be the most populous trout in headwater tributaries and small streams along the Pacific coast that enter directly into the ocean. River dwelling populations exist in larger coastal river systems. Lake dwelling cutthroat are found in isolated coastal lakes and in non-isolated lowland lakes that have outlets to the Pacific Ocean.

Multiple age classes of resident cutthroat reside throughout the drainages of most Oregon coastal streams. Such wide distribution indicates that overall, cutthroat are in good condition throughout their range in Oregon. It is not certain however if those trout observed in tributary streams downstream from migration barriers are juvenile sea-runs, in-stream migratory, or resident fish.

Resident coastal cutthroat populations in Oregon have battled through the same ordeals as their kin in every other state and province on the Pacific Coast. Rivers and lakes have suffered bank damage, siltation, culvert blockages from clear cut logging practices, road building and development. Environmental challenges notwithstanding, coastal cutthroat in all forms appear to be doing pretty well throughout their Oregon range. Studies conducted by Oregon Department of Fish and Wildlife in 1993 showed that the cutthroat is consistently the gamefish with the widest distribution.

This is not to suggest that Oregon's resident coastal cutthroat took all those years of destructive habitat hits without suffering population losses. The effects of timber harvesting on small coastal tributary streams was examined in the Alsea Watershed Study. It was found that Needle Branch, which had been clear cut without buffers in 1966 showed a decline to about one-third of its original population prior to being logged. Needle Branch remained depressed for 25 years before recovering in the 1990s. Other cutthroat streams have suffered the same decline as Needle Branch after intense logging of their watersheds.

Studies on several Coquille River basin coastal cutthroat populations indicated that there is a very high level of diversity within the basin. Diversity can be rather easily explained by natural physical barriers such as waterfalls. In other populations however, there was a high level of genetic diversity even though there were few if any physical barriers.

Coastal Cutthroat River Systems

Fluvial populations of coastal cutthroat are found the Nehalem, Nestucca, Wilson, Yaquina, Siletz, Alsea, Coquille, North Umpqua and Rogue river systems. There are probably other coastal streams that hold fluvial cutthroat as well.

Oregon coastal rivers that hold wild populations of fluvial cutthroat have also been planted with hatchery rainbow and cutthroat trout since the early 1980s. The effect of these plantings on native cutthroat is not known. To avoid further possible harm to native cutthroat, such plantings in streams holding wild cutthroat have been discontinued.

Several isolated adfluvial populations of cutthroat are found in natural lakes above barriers to anadromous fish. Grassy Lake (North Nehalem River) and Buttermilk Lake (Yaquina River) are examples of lakes that hold adfluvial populations of cutthroat. Above barrier cutthroat populations are generally considered to be healthy since they have not been influenced by releases of hatchery trout and are lightly fished. Slide and Klickitat lakes have been monitored every spring for several years and show consistently stable catches for sport anglers.

Lake-dwelling cutthroat populations are also thought to be present in low-elevation lakes along the Pacific Coast that have outlets to the ocean. In these lakes sea-run cutthroat are also present. Lakes thought to hold both forms of coastal cutthroat include; Devils, Sutton, Mercer, Siltcoos, Tahkenitch, Tenmile and Floras. These fish have also been exposed to hatchery fish releases. The effect of hatchery introduced cutthroat on wild fluvial or anadromous cutthroat has not been studied.

Pacific Coast Cutthroat Rivers

All Oregon coastal rivers that do not have upstream barriers in their lower reaches (cascades, waterfalls, and dams) hold populations of anadromous or true sea-run cutthroat trout. Most of the mainstem rivers also hold populations of coastal cutthroat in their tributaries.

Primary coastal river basins holding cutthroat populations include the Nehalem, Nestucca, Yaquina, Alsea,

Glenn Young holds up a nice Oregon cutthroat.

Siuslaw, Umpqua, Coos, Coquille, Rogue and Chetco. Smaller coastal rivers and tributaries holding cutthroat are the Miami, Kilchis, Tillamook, Salmon, Siletz, Beaver, Yachats, Smith, Floras, Sixes, Elk, Pistol and Winchuck.

The practice of planting hatchery sea-run cutthroat into coastal Oregon rivers has been carried out by the Oregon Department of Fish and Wildlife for many years. In recent years however all such plantings have been switched to releases only into lakes. The effect of heavy releases of hatchery sea-run cutthroat on wild fish is unknown as there have been no studies on the effects of hatchery cutthroat stockings on wild populations. Since 1997 however, all plantings have been discontinued in Oregon rivers known to hold anadromous coastal cutthroat trout. This is a good move and should be the rule for all rivers holding wild coastal cutthroat populations.

Umpqua River
Coastal cutthroat trout are as ingrained in the history of the famed Umpqua River as are its legendary wild summer steelhead. This river and its magnificent fish have been written about since the days of Zane Grey and it is still a river commanding annual pilgrimages by anglers around the world. Unfortunately, the Umpqua River cutthroat has fallen on hard times in recent years with all of its wild populations in severe decline. In 1995 there was a year-around angling closure placed on a large part of the Umpqua Basin known to hold cutthroat trout. It was thought that some of this decline was caused by the stocking of Alsea River hatchery cutthroat, a program that had been in place from 1961-1976. This program has since been discontinued. However, wild stocks have shown no signs of recovery since supplementation of Alsea River hatchery cutthroat was stopped. Continued decline may also be in part due to habitat degradation, predation by smallmouth bass and competition from shad and other exotic species.

In an effort to stem further decline the Oregon Department of Fish and Wildlife has placed all Umpqua River fluvial or anadromous cutthroat under 12-inches in length on catch-and-release status. Despite the non-retention ruling, counts over Winchester Dam on the Umpqua River have continued to fall. Wild coastal cutthroat throughout the Umpqua River system are presently considered to be near extinction. The Umpqua River is being carefully monitored by ODFW in an ongoing effort to stop the downward spiral and nurse its depleted wild coastal cutthroat stocks back to health.

Alsea River
The Alsea River basin was, just a few years ago, showcased as one of the premier sea-run cutthroat rivers along the Oregon coast, boasting wonderful fishing, enhanced by a very prolific hatchery program. The downside to this great fishing was that the plantings of hatchery cutthroat smolts competed heavily with wild cutthroat. For this reason the program was discontinued. In spite of stopping hatchery plantings, wild anadromous cutthroat have not rebounded

according to creel counts and are considered to be in a continuing state of decline.

Fluvial and resident wild cutthroat on the other hand appear to be healthy throughout the Alsea River drainage. There are no hard data on resident cutthroat trout abundance in the Alsea basin but creel counts indicate that populations do not appear to be in significant decline.

Siuslaw River
Sea-run cutthroat in the Siuslaw River basin are in decline. Resident coastal cutthroat populations, however are considered to be in relatively healthy condition although there are no long-term data available to substantiate this opinion by ODFW.

Wilson River
Snorkeling surveys on twelve standard resting pools in the Wilson River have been made nearly every year since 1965. From 1965 through 1970 there was an average of 10.7 coastal cutthroat trout counted per pool. From 1990 through 1996 there was an average count of 1.7 cutthroat per pool. This rate of decline is considered to be about the same for the Alsea and Siuslaw systems.

Lower Columbia River Tributaries
Historically, coastal cutthroat were present in all lower Columbia River tributaries from the mouth of the Columbia east to Hood River. The abundance of cutthroat in the lower Columbia has declined significantly in recent years with catches that once totaled more than 10,000 fish in the 1970s dwindling to as few as 69 fish in 1994. Since the disastrously low numbers registered in 1994, wild coastal cutthroat have been placed on catch-and-release status in all Columbia River tributaries.

Lower Columbia River tributaries were also stocked heavily with legal-size hatchery fish through the years. Up to 15,000 cutthroat were annually released in to the Lewis and Clark River alone.

Other Columbia River tributaries receiving liberal hatchery plantings included the Klaskanine River, Big Creek, Gnat Creek and Scappoose Creek. All releases into the Lewis and Clark have been discontinued and all other releases have been confined to lakes that have no access to tributary rivers.

Many of the lower Columbia River tributaries downstream of the Willamette River confluence run through privately held timberlands. While cutthroat trout population densities in these tributaries have not been studied, it is thought that abundance has diminished over the years due to the habitat degradation that goes along with commercial logging and related land and water use.

Sandy River Drainage
The lower Sandy River once hosted a small population of sea-run cutthroat trout numbering only 20 to 30 fish that entered the river each fall. None enter the river now, a fact confirmed by angler comments. According to creel samples,

no large cutthroat trout have been counted upstream of Marmot Dam since 1977.

Since 1997 Oregon sport fishing regulations have allowed the killing of wild trout only in the lower mainstem Sandy River and all its tributaries below Brightman Bridge. Above Brightman Bridge all wild trout must be released. All hatchery trout releases into streams within the Sandy River drainage were stopped beginning in 1995. Whether this action will ever bring the small wild cutthroat population back to good health will not be know for years to come. A run that numbers less than fifty cutthroats should never be opened to a kill fishery anywhere on the Sandy River.

Bull Run River

This major tributary of the Sandy River is thought to have once been a significant producer of coastal cutthroat. Water development projects by the City of Portland in the 1900s eventually blocked all passageways with impassable dams. Resident cutthroat populations still exist in healthy numbers in the tributaries and reservoirs of the Bull Run basin and in tributaries of the Upper Sandy River. These areas have in effect become sanctuaries for coastal cutthroat since no public access is allowed on most of the property operated by the City of Portland Water Bureau. There may be an isolated adfluvial population of cutthroat in Bull Run Lake but it is also closed to the public.

The Columbia Gorge

At one time populations of sea-run cutthroat trout inhabited several streams in the Columbia Gorge. At one time Latourell, Bridal Veil, Multnomah, Oneonta, Horsetail, McCord, Moffett, Tanner, Eagle and Herman creeks held cutthroat below impassable barriers. Cutthroat in the Columbia Gorge are not studied on a regular basis and there is concern that passageways at hatchery diversion dams on Eagle and Tanner creeks is inhibiting the upstream migration of cutthroat.

Hood River Drainage

The Hood River drainage is no longer an important coastal cutthroat fishery. Anadromous cutthroat have not been seen or collected at Powderdale Dam since 1993. Additionally, Punchbowl Falls on Hood River's West Fork sets in place at least a partial or seasonal barrier to migration. This area is on the eastern border of coastal cutthroat habitat thus probably never did hold significant populations of the anadromous form.

Hatchery coastal cutthroat smolts have been introduced into the Hood River in the past. There was a planting in 1955, from 1974 to 1978 and from 1985 to1987. Numbers of smolts stocked ranged from around 500 upward to 33,000. These stockings have surfaced little evidence of establishing a sea-run cutthroat population in the drainage.

Fifteen Mile Creek Drainage

Coastal cutthroat trout are found in Fifteenmile Creek Drainage but not in large numbers. Fivemile Creek also holds a small population of cutthroat and there may be a few in Eightmile Creek as well. None of these watersheds are thought to provide particularly productive fisheries.

Willamette River System

There are populations of fluvial, adfluvial and resident coastal cutthroat trout distributed through the Willamette River mainstem and its vast system of tributaries upstream of Willamette Falls. There are no anadromous cutthroat in the Willamette River system above Willamette Falls near Oregon City.

The Willamette watershed stretches from Portland, its confluence with the Columbia, to Cottage Grove to the south, and east to the Cascade crest. Coastal cutthroat are the only native trout present throughout all the Coast Range tributaries. The Willamette River system, draining an immense geographical area, has the potential to be one of the truly great resident and in-river migratory cutthroat trout fisheries on the entire West Coast.

Clackamas River

The Clackamas River, a major tributary of the Willamette at one time held strong populations of coastal cutthroat. It is not known how far up the Clackamas River anadromous coastal cutthroat migrated but construction of Casadero Dam near Estacada blocked all upstream fish migrations from 1917 through 1939. Additionally, no coastal cutthroat have passed the North Fork Dam since 1958. Dams and pollution have caused a significant decline in Clackamas River cutthroat populations. Huge plantings of pre-smolt coho salmon into the lower tributaries during the 1970s and through the early 1980s was another detriment to wild cutthroat, a practice that was discontinued in the early 1990s. Deep, Clear and Eagle creeks in the lower Clackamas River are thought to be the most viable spawning areas for remaining cutthroat in the system.

Resident coastal cutthroat are still abundant in the lower Clackamas River tributaries. Although there is an overlap with resident rainbow trout and juvenile steelhead, cutthroat trout populations are holding up well and are dominate in steep, primary tributaries.

Coast Range Rivers

Coastal cutthroat are the only native trout indigenous to Coast Range tributaries of the Willamette River. Tualatin, Yamhill, Rickreall, Luckiamute, Marys and Long Tom rivers all hold fishable populations of coastal cutthroat. The Oregon Department of Fish and Wildlife at one time stocked brook trout into the Willamette's Coast Range tributaries in an effort to increase sport fishing opportunity. As of this writing, rainbow trout are still released into Yamhill, Rickreall and Luckiamute rivers. This is a practice worthy of review as rainbow trout introductions are almost always detrimental to native coastal cutthroat populations.

The lower reaches of most Willamette River Coast Range tributaries are populated by fluvial cutthroat. These smaller rivers and their even smaller tributaries in turn provide spawning habitat for cutthroat from the mainstem Willamette River. In the headwaters of Coast Range rivers resident cutthroat are dominant due to impassable barriers or because of the limited habitat in the watersheds of upper tributaries.

Long Tom River

Upper Long Tom River was formed in 1941 when Fern Ridge Dam was completed. Construction of Fern Ridge Dam trapped a population of cutthroat that now reside in Fern Ridge Reservoir. Cutthroat that reside below Fern Ridge Dam are blocked from upstream migration by Fern Ridge Dam and cannot migrate downstream to the Willamette due to blockages by impassable irrigation dams built on the lower reaches of the river.

Prior to completion of Fern Ridge Dam the coastal cutthroat population in the upper section of Long Tom River was fluvial. Since being trapped above the barrier of Fern Ridge Dam these fluvial cutthroat have become adfluvial, making upstream spawning runs during the late summer and fall at which time they take on a silvery hue similar to that of sea-run cutthroat. The relatively abundant food sources in the lake have allowed the Fern Ridge cutthroat to produce some large specimens that regularly exceed a foot in length. Other cutthroat high in the watershed of Long Tom River are fluvial, living out their lies within the confines of small parent tributary creeks, often maturing at less than eight inches in length.

Only two major fluvial cutthroat populations from Coast Range tributaries have been monitored on a regular basis (Long Tom and Marys rivers) but it is believed that many if not all are generally in decline. This probable decline is based on the fact that there has been a long history of habitat degradation resulting from agricultural expansion and urban development throughout the Willamette Valley. Since 1994 catch-and-release regulations have been in place for all wild trout in the Willamette River from the McKenzie River confluence downstream to the town of Harrisburg. This measure is intended to slow the decline. Catch-and-release regulations alone however are not going to reverse the downward trend. The decline of cutthroat populations in Coast Range streams is likely to continue in direct proportion to the ongoing loss of habitat that is almost a certainty.

East Side Willamette River Tributaries

Populations of fluvial cutthroat trout occur in most streams draining from the Cascade Mountains into the Willamette River. The primary exception is the McKenzie River where a fairly strong adfluvial population is present.

Molalla, Santiam and Calapooia Rivers

Upper tributaries of the Molalla, Santiam and Calapooia rivers hold good populations of resident coastal cutthroat. The lower reaches of these streams however are nurseries for juvenile steelhead and resident rainbow trout, both of which are known to dominate coastal cutthroat. Crabtree Creek, is the single exception, contributing good numbers of fluvial coastal cutthroat trout to the lower South and mainstem Santiam systems.

McKenzie River

The lower twenty miles or so of the McKenzie River has a strong population of fluvial cutthroat trout. There is good spawning habitat in Mohawk River and Camp Creek, which also provide good early rearing conditions. The fairly low gradient of this section of the McKenzie is the type of habitat in which coastal cutthroat thrive and compete very well, in fact having an advantage over resident rainbow trout. Studies made since 1988 show that the lower McKenzie's coastal cutthroat population is increasing.

Upper McKenzie and Middle Fork Willamette Rivers

In both of these drainages wild coastal cutthroat trout are present primarily in small tributary streams and headwater areas. Many of these small streams flow through private land and National Forest timberlands. On private land and throughout the National Forest, road building, logging, and the altering of stream habitat has served to reduce cutthroat populations.

North Fork of the Middle Fork Willamette River

The North Fork has been monitored regularly since the 1970s. Surveys made in twenty pools by snorkeling have shown that both rainbow trout and coastal cutthroat populations have remained stable and healthy with good numbers ranging from 8 to more than 12 inches in length.

The adventuresome angler will find that all of the Willamette's eastside tributaries hold isolated populations of fluvial coastal cutthroat above impassable barriers, primarily dams. These populations are considered relatively healthy although they are not checked on a regular basis.

Cascade Mountain Lakes

Mountain lakes throughout the Clackamas, Santiam, McKenzie and Middle Fork Willamette River sub-basins hold good populations of wild, lake dwelling coastal cutthroat trout. In some of these lakes cutthroat populations remain well isolated from introduced stocks of rainbow and brook trout. In others introduced rainbow and brook trout have become serious competitors with native coastal cutthroat.

Donaca, Pamelia, Moose, Gordon, Bingham, Elk, Fish, Hidden and Windfall lakes are thought to hold only wild, coastal cutthroat trout. Marion, Lava, Whitewater, Riggs, Clear, Nash, and Middle and Lower Horse lakes have received plantings of rainbow and brook trout.

Cutthroat stocking programs are in place on only two Cascade mountain lakes. Twin Lake receives broodstock developed from a westslope cutthroat trout in eastern Washington. Hackleman is planted with broodstock developed from coastal cutthroat native to the upper McKenzie River drainage.

Management Objectives

The Oregon Department of Fish and Wildlife has not ignored the decline of coastal cutthroat populations in Oregon, particularly the anadromous form. Management objectives have been offered by Oregon Department of Fish and Wildlife and adopted by the Oregon Fish and Wildlife Commission to monitor cutthroat abundance and health throughout Oregon. It is critical that these management objectives are implemented and carried through since Oregon coastal cutthroat have been listed as "sensitive" under the Endangers Species Act. Additionally, the National Marine Fisheries Service has proposed that all Oregon coastal cutthroat in the Umpqua River basin below natural barriers be declared "endangered".

The plan to build a recovery program for coastal cutthroat trout throughout Oregon includes well-defined objectives for the Willamette, Yaquina, Tenmile and Coos river basins. Plans are also progressing for the Rogue, Coquille, Umpqua, Siuslaw, Alsea, Salmon, Nehalem, Sandy, Hood and Fifteenmile river basins. Genetic samples of cutthroat trout have been collected and are being analyzed for the Hood, Fifteenmile, Sandy, Upper Willamette, Coquille, Elk, Umpqua and several other basins along the Pacific Coast in cooperation with the NMFS.

Monitoring is in place on the Hood River at Powerdale Dam; in Willamette River tributaries including the Mohawk, McKenzie, North Fork, Long Tom and Marys rivers; on the North Umpqua River at Winchester Dam — and on the Rogue River at Elk Creek Dam. Native cutthroat trout brookstocks for the Cascade Mountain Lakes Stocking Program are being developed from Hackleman Creek and Pamelia Lake stocks.

Testing for resistance to Ceratomyxa shasta has been conducted on several Willamette basin coastal cutthroat stocks and further testing is proposed for additional stocks. Life history studies on North Umpqua River cutthroat have been in place for several years and are ongoing in cooperation with NMFS.

Since 1994 stocking of hatchery anadromous cutthroat has been discontinued in all lower Columbia River tributaries, mainstem and North Fork Nehalem River, Tillamook Bay tributaries, Nestucca River, Scholfield Creek and Smith River (Umpqua River tributary). Since 1996 the stocking of anadromous cutthroat in the Siusilaw, Alsea and Salmon rivers has been discontinued. Catch-and-release regulations for all trout angling in coastal streams holding populations of sea-run cutthroat were implemented in 1997.

The future of the coastal cutthroat in Oregon lies not only with the efforts of ODFW but with concerned sportsmen who want the health of this great western trout restored. It is going to take a lot of effort and significant funding to make it happen. The cutthroat trout is part of Oregon's fishing heritage. This heritage should not be viewed lightly in a historical sense or looked upon as unimportant as an essential cog in Oregon's sport fishery in the present — and for years to come.

Conclusions

The terms abundance and decline in regard to coastal cutthroat populations in Oregon can be misconstrued and should be kept in perspective. Decline from historical numbers is consistent throughout the range of the coastal cutthroat. It is not exclusive to Oregon. Conversely, abundance only refers to the estimated number of cutthroat in a river, lake or watershed, not that cutthroats are around in vast numbers.

The truth of the matter is that coastal cutthroats still provide a popular sport fishery throughout Oregon and should continue to do so for decades to come for it is not a trout that lacks champions. Cooperation of the ODFW, sportsmen, residential landowners, water users, the logging industry, land developers and a turnaround of the industrial complex's environmental practices will be required to maintain and improve the status of the coastal cutthroat. This level of cooperation, as we all know, does not come about easily.

Brian Thielicke prepares to release a hefty Oregon cutthroat.

Chapter 7 - *Coastal Cutthroat Trout in Washington*

Sound stewardship of fish and wildlife.

—Mission Statement
Washington Department of Fish and Wildlife

The multitude of rivers and vast expanses of protected salt water throughout Puget Sound and Hood Canal in Washington is where the coastal cutthroat trout really takes on all the trappings of a genuine sea trout. From Budd Inlet at the southern extreme near the State Capitol of Olympia, north to the Strait of Juan de Fuca, Puget Sound and Hood Canal to the west are a network of deep trenches, shallow inlets and wide bays that surround a labyrinth of islands; perfect habitat for the coastal cutthroat.

Further enhancing this amazing natural habitat, Puget Sound is fed by a wealth of large rivers and literally hundreds of small creeks. Hood Canal is a similarly rich combination of salt water with streams tumbling in from the east slope of the Olympic Mountains and the Mason County Peninsula.

The anadromous coastal cutthroat of Washington is made up of two predominant run-timing groups; early returning and late returning. These two runs are determined by stream size and marine access. Cutthroat entering large rivers often show up as early as late June or early July and will remain resident through fall spawning and not leave the river until the following spring as late as April or May. Cutthroat that spawn in small creeks flowing directly into Puget Sound or Hood Canal will duck in from January through April when winter rains swell flows, spawn, and be back out into the marine environment within days.

All forms of coastal cutthroat are found throughout Southwest Washington in above barrier reaches of coastal river systems, in lower Columbia River tributaries, in beaver

Who says sea-run cutthroat can't jump? This frisky 15-incher took Bob Young's entire fly line out of the water with this leap.

Preston Singletary

ponds, lowland lakes and sub-basin lakes on the slopes of the Cascade and Olympic Mountains. Some of the largest coastal cutthroat trout in Washington are thought to reside in Lake Washington and other large lakes that have viable spawning streams.

Freshwater Habitat, Rivers

Coastal cutthroat in Washington, like cutthroat all along the Pacific Coast, have been adversely affected by severe habitat degradation to low gradient areas and upper watersheds. Years of land-raping logging practices, road building, destruction of riparian areas and channeling of streams have all played a part in reducing viable habitat for the coastal cutthroat in a long list of rivers and tributaries. In addition, environmentally slipshod agricultural practices, and industrial and residential land development have caused sedimentation of spawning areas. Loss of protective cover and woody in-stream debris are the result, which combine to increase water temperatures and decrease water volume and quality.

Healthy populations of coastal cutthroat reside in upper watersheds and in above barrier stretches of coastal rivers. These are populations that live something of a scaled-down life, reaching maturity at a considerably smaller size than other resident, river-dwelling or sea-run cutthroat that enjoy more expansive and food-rich environs. These small streams primarily provide fishing opportunity for hikers and backpackers.

Freshwater Habitat, Lakes

Self-sustaining populations of coastal cutthroat are found in coastal beaver ponds and small natural lakes, particularly those fed by small streams that facilitate spawning. When these bastions of wild cutthroat receive introductions of brook, brown or rainbow trout, the wild cutthroat almost always suffer a decline.

Despite all of the environmental degradation there are still numerous lakes scattered throughout western Washington that either hold self-sustaining populations of wild cutthroat, or are planted from time to time with hatchery cutthroat. It would seem prudent for the Washington Department of Fish and Wildlife to work on restoring wild coastal cutthroat populations rather than introducing brook or brown trout into waters that previously held only cutthroat. In this age of genetically engineered trout, exotic species such as tiger trout, or super-fast growing triploid rainbows, the importance of stewardship of native species like the coastal cutthroat appears to have been, if not lost, surely misplaced.

Marine Habitat

Marine habitat is generally healthy throughout Puget Sound although wherever degradation has occurred due to agricultural, aquaculture, real estate development and industrial pollution, coastal cutthroat populations have suffered. This is particularly critical in estuarine areas, vitally important to

Bob Young (left) and Leland Miyawaki take a break on the beach during a morning of saltwater cutthroat fishing.

Preston Singletary

the growth of outbound smolts and as habitat for much of the year for some adult cutthroat populations, providing both a rich feeding ground and protective cover. Degradation of estuarine areas reduces water quality, has an adverse affect on available food supplies, can alter water temperatures and may introduce exotic organisms to an estuary. These factors in combination brew an environmentally deadly mix that can drastically reduce the quality of life during the cutthroat's estuarine period.

Hatchery Stocking

Attempts to develop hatchery programs for anadromous cutthroat began in the 1940s. In most instances these have been small-scale programs involving selected stocks in various parts of the state. These hatchery efforts were intended to increase opportunity for recreational anglers. At this time the only cutthroat populations receiving hatchery support are those in Grays Harbor rivers and in lower Columbia tributaries. Ironically, in spite of, or because of, hatchery supplementation, many coastal cutthroat stocks in Grays Harbor and lower Columbia River tributaries are under consideration for Endangered Species Act (ESA) listing as either threatened or endangered.

The stocking of steelhead has also been in place in Washington for several decades. Many of these programs have released steelhead into streams that also hold wild coastal cutthroat stocks. One result of such planting programs that has been documented in several river systems is that hybridization occurs which can be damaging to the genetic integrity of wild cutthroat.

Coho salmon plantings in Washington rivers have also been detrimental to young cutthroat since coho are the dominant species due to earlier emergence thus larger body size. Coho salmon push cutthroat into marginal areas of a stream.

Whenever juvenile cutthroat are displaced from the prime areas of a rearing stream where food and cover are abundant, their growth rate, health and mortality are adversely affected. Competition with juvenile salmon and steelhead within a completely natural population is a daunting enough challenge for young cutthroat without the addition of hatchery salmon and steelhead supplementation.

Status and Trends of Cutthroat in Washington

Geographic areas for making coastal cutthroat stock assessments are; (1) North Puget Sound; (2) South Puget Sound (including Hood Canal and the eastern Strait of Juan de Fuca); (3) North Coast (including the western Strait of Juan de Fuca and Pacific Coast north of Grays Harbor; (4) South Coast (including Grays Harbor and Willapa Bay; and lower Columbia River (including tributaries). Fisheries for cutthroat occur in streams and estuaries throughout western Washington and are important in certain marine areas of Puget Sound as well. With several major exceptions Studies made by Washington Fish and Wildlife Department biologists indicate that overall,

stocks of cutthroat have either declined or remained stable since the last status review in 1980.

In 1997 Washington Fish and Wildlife placed coastal cutthroat throughout the marine waters of Puget Sound and Hood Canal on catch-and-release status. Cutthroat stocks from different rivers tend to mix in Puget Sound. Catch-and-release was implemented to protect weak stocks from being further decimated. It has proven to be a winner for the cutthroat and the anglers. According to many dedicated cutthroat fishermen, coastal cutthroat fishing throughout Puget Sound has improved every year since the catch-and-release regulation was set in place.

North Puget Sound Rivers

Coastal cutthroat in North Puget Sound are found primarily in large streams that drain directly into the marine environment. Although cutthroat stocks in this region have been studied since the early 1980s, the work has not covered the long-term status of specific stocks. Most of the data that were collected came about from limited WDFW hook-and-line surveys in the mainstem Stillaguamish River beginning in 1978. Standardized surveys have been conducted since 1991. Data show that stocks appear to have improved in the Stillaguamish River system since 1978.

Hatchery introductions of anadromous coastal cutthroat have not occurred in the Stillaguamish and other North Puget Sound streams since the mid-1980s.

Nooksack River

The Nooksack River system is large, extending from Bellingham Bay nearly to the Canadian border and east to the Cascade Range. Anadromous coastal cutthroat are found in the mainstem Nooksack River and its north south and middle forks. Although the Nooksack is not considered to be a great sea-run cutthroat stream it does provide a sport fishery, mostly for local anglers, from late August through early November.

Skagit River

The Skagit River system is large by any measure, stretching well into British Columbia and encompassing the Baker, Cascade and Sauk rivers as primary tributaries. Although the Skagit River built its reputation on its runs of big chinook salmon and winter steelhead, it does hold a strong population of coastal cutthroat, particularly in its lower reaches downstream from Mount Vernon. Local anglers fish much of the lower mainstem and the north and south forks from small boats. Cutthroat show in the lower Skagit as early as July with the best fishing reported to be in September and October.

Sauk River

Better known as a steelhead and Dolly Varden river, the Sauk does host a small population of coastal cutthroat. Its primary tributaries, the Suiattle and White Chuck also have modest populations of cutthroat. Not many anglers in

Washington fish the Sauk River system for cutthroat, instead zeroing in on its wild steelhead and large numbers of hefty bull trout.

Stillaguamish River

There is probably not a single river on the West Coast, including Oregon's Umpqua that has a longer or more storied history as a sea-run cutthroat fishery than the Stillaguamish River, or Stilly as it is affectionately referred to by most Washington anglers. Of fairly low gradient and blessed with dark undercut banks, root wads, woody debris and overhanging vegetation, the Stilly offers miles of classic habitat for coastal cutthroat trout. Although the Stilly is not believed to hold historic numbers of coastal cutthroat, its population is considered to be very healthy.

Cutthroat are scattered throughout the mainstem Stillaguamish in fishable numbers from Arlington downstream to the estuary in late June. By September there are cutthroat in the famous North Fork Stillaguamish from Arlington upstream beyond Old Fortson Mill. The less renowned South Fork Stillaguamish is something of a sleeper that also holds a good population of coastal cutthroat that can be fished from the forks, at Arlington, upstream to Granite Falls. The Stillaguamish gives up trophy cutthroat in the 18-26 inch class every year.

Snohomish River System

The Snohomish is a big and slow moving river formed from the confluence of the Skykomish and Snoqualmie rivers near

*Author prepares to release a chunky
Stillaguamish River cutthroat.*

State Highway 522, west of the town of Monroe. The Snohomish River flows rather lazily for about 17 miles, braiding its way for the last few miles before flowing into Port Gardener just north of Everett.

Local anglers who understand the big, lumbering Snohomish do pretty well from August through early October on sea-run cutthroat moving through on their way to the Skykomish and Snoqualmie rivers.

Skykomish River

The Skykomish River is born on the west slope of the Cascade Mountains. The Sky as it is called picks up flow from the Beckler, Tye, Wallace and Sultan rivers plus a wealth of smaller streams as it plunges through roaring rapids interspersed with long beautiful runs that are coveted by steelhead anglers. This is not however the type of water that appeals to coastal cutthroat. The Sky does receive a scattering of sea-run cutthroat in the fall primarily in its lower reaches from Monroe to its confluence with the Snoqualmie River but is not considered to be a great cutthroat stream.

Snoqualmie River

From its confluence, upstream for twenty miles to the base of Snoqualmie Falls, the Snoqualmie River has a lot of good cutthroat water. Although the Snoqualmie and many of its vital little tributaries have been degraded severely in places by dairy farms and real estate development, it still receives a good run of coastal cutthroat, some of which show up in late August.

The Snoqualmie does not garner the attention of cutthroat anglers that the Stillaguamish River enjoys but it is a productive cutthroat stream that a lot of fishermen would prefer to keep under wraps. With summer-run steelhead the anadromous fish of choice from June through October in the Snoqualmie, not many folks concentrate on cutthroat.

Cutthroat can be found throughout the Snoqualmie River but the best stretches are from Fall City to the mouth of the Tolt River and from the town of Duvall to the confluence with the Snohomish. There is bank access along both stretches but most serious cutthroat anglers prefer to float these stretches. From Duvall to the mouth the Snoqualmie is very slow, often requiring a lot of rowing to reach the takeout. A small outboard is recommended.

Green River

The Green River heads in the Cascade Mountains and flows down through the Kent Valley for nearly thirty miles, to the town of Tukwila where it becomes the Duwamish River before flowing into Seattle's Elliot Bay. The Green is another stream that meanders through farm fields from Eagle Gorge Bridge to the town of Auburn where it becomes lost for several miles in a jungle of industrial parks and shopping malls through the town of Kent and into south Seattle. Industrialization has degraded much of the lower Green river from Auburn downstream to Elliot Bay. This degradation of the lower river and its vital estuarine area has caused a decline in its once fairly abundant coastal cutthroat stocks.

Above the town of Auburn and upstream to Flaming Geyser Park the Green is still in reasonably good shape and begins receiving cutthroat in June. Some of these cutthroat may be stream dwellers rather than sea-runs which could account for the still relatively healthy populations in the upper reaches of the river. The upper Green River is served by a well-maintained road, and Flaming Geyser Park provides an excellent riverside spot for lunch during a day of fishing.

North Puget Sound Saltwater

During the last several years there has been renewed interest in fishing for cutthroat along the beaches of Puget Sound. This is in part due to a resident coho salmon program initiated by the Washington Department of Fish and Wildlife in the early 1970s. As interest and angler success grew in fishing for coho salmon from the beaches of Puget Sound, incidental cutthroat became an ever increasing part of the catch. As interest in beach fishing increased anglers have ranged further, investigating one Puget Sound beach after another; fished at waterfront state and county parks and have invariably found cutthroat eager to take their flies — sometimes when salmon would not.

North Puget Sound cutthroat are primarily born and reared in large rivers such as the Skagit, Stillaguamish and Snohomish systems. They tend to enter parent streams as early as June and are usually well into upstream spawning reaches by early October. Large stream coastal cutthroat will often remain in their river environs until May when they migrate back down to the estuaries. Some large river cutthroat will travel several miles from parent rivers while others may never leave the estuaries. Since large river cutthroat are often in the river system from July through the following May, they offer somewhat limited opportunity to the saltwater fly caster.

During the summer months however, literally any accessible beach on the shores of North Puget Sound can provide good cutthroat fishing from time to time. A few favorite spots include Kayak Point, Picnic Point, Golden Gardens, Lincoln Park, Agate Pass, Eglon, Point No Point and the beaches of Whidbey Island among many others.

South Puget Sound Rivers

Cutthroat in South Puget Sound live in a highly diverse range of habitat. Most cutthroat streams in this area are smaller than North Puget Sound Rivers and enter directly into the marine environment. Cutthroat in South Puget Sound enter small parent rivers and creeks late in the season with some of the tiniest watersheds receiving no more than a few dozen spawning adults. The two largest rivers in South Puget Sound, the Puyallup and Nisqually host small populations of cutthroat.

The lower Puyallup is heavily industrialized and has suffered severe degradation largely from industrial pollution. The Puyallup flows into Commencement Bay which holds the distinction of having made it onto the Environmental Protection Agency Super Fund list as one of the most polluted estuaries on the Pacific Coast.

The Nisqually River has a small population of anadromous coastal cutthroat but does not receive much attention from anglers. The Nisqually, managed by the Nisqually Tribe, flows through the pristine Nisqually Delta before emptying into south Puget Sound.

Deschutes River

Washington's Deschutes River lacks the hoopla afforded the great Oregon Deschutes River but does have its own claim to fame as an excellent coastal cutthroat stream. Each autumn sea-run cutthroat enter Capitol Lake in the southernmost end of Puget Sound, climb the Tumwater Falls fish ladder and are in the Deschutes River. Sea-run cutthroat move through the clear pools all the way to Deschutes Falls, an impassable barrier to further upstream migration. Above Deschutes Falls there is a fair population of resident cutthroat.

South Puget Sound Saltwater north end

South Puget Sound cutthroat range from the west side of Vashon Island to Budd Inlet near Olympia. Since the vast

This beautiful cutthroat is about to be netted.

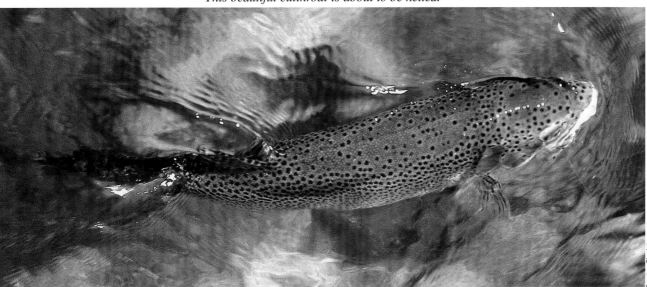

Preston Singletary

majority of South Sound sea-run cutthroat are small stream spawners they enter their tiny parent waters very late in the season and emerge quite soon after spawning. It is not unusual to catch prime, fat cutthroat as late as February that have not yet moved into spawning creeks. After spawning they will very quickly return to the salt, as there is not sufficient food in their parent creeks to facilitate recovery from the trauma of spawning. Cutthroat kelts feed eagerly, fill out quickly and are regularly caught along saltwater beaches of South Puget Sound as early as March.

This late-entering, early-emerging trait of small stream coastal cutthroats makes them available to salt water fly casters year-around. In addition, there is mile after mile of protected bays and passages throughout South Puget Sound making it a Mecca for small boat anglers. A few favorite spots include; Olalla, the Tacoma Narrows, Point Fosdick, Purdy, Wauna, Penrose Point State Park, Kopachuck State Park, Sunrise Beach and Colvos Passage from the mouth of Gig Harbor to Lisabuela Park, among many others.

Hood Canal

Slicing to the southwest at the eastern edge of the Strait of Juan de Fuca, Hood Canal is a large, hook-shaped inlet that bounds the Mason County Peninsula. Fed by the Quilcene, Dosewallups, Duckabush, Hamma Hamma, Dewatto,

Carol Ferrera with her first sea-run cutthroat trout. This fat 17-incher hit a Reverse Spider.

Tahuya, Skokomish, and Union rivers, plus countless more small creeks, Hood Canal was once a paradise for sea-run cutthroat. It has the potential to be a great cutthroat fishery again and has displayed signs of improvement since catch-and-release regulations were implemented in 1997.

The lower reaches of all Hood Canal rivers are of gentle gradient with deep undercut pools, canopies of cover and an abundance of woody debris which is perfect habitat for anadromous coastal cutthroat. Once they reach into the east slope of the Olympic Mountains which border Olympic National Park and the Olympic National Forest, these same streams and creeks become steep and rugged, some with impassable barriers and home to isolated populations of resident cutthroat.

Since about 1985, runs of chum salmon into Hood Canal have been liberally supplemented by hatcheries which has resulted in exceedingly heavy returns into Hood Canal rivers in the late autumn. While these runs have been a boon to the commercial and tribal fisheries, and to a lesser extent boosted the sport fishery, it is a certainty that such a heavy load on the limited and fragile spawning beds of small Hood Canal rivers have adversely affected cutthroat.

In 1976 broodstock of late-arriving cutthroats was successfully developed from wild sea-run cutthroat trout by biologists Jim Johnston and Stewart Mercer for use in Hood Canal to supplement wild stocks. The program was expanded to Puget Sound but ultimately discontinued due to poor adult returns. No hatchery releases of cutthroat trout presently occur in Hood Canal and none are planned.

The Washington Department of Fish and Wildlife estimates that Hood Canal probably holds a mix of healthy and depressed stocks of coastal cutthroat. If the Hood Canal cutthroat's environment is left to heal the fish will almost surely return in reasonable numbers provided they can adapt to the rigors of working around the runs of chum salmon. Since they are slow growers though, we should expect Hood Canal cutthroat fishing to make a long and steady return to health. In the meantime, the fishing can still be good along the cobbled beaches and unsullied estuaries of Hood Canal, from early spring through late autumn.

Eastern Strait of Juan de Fuca

From Port Townsend, around Point Wilson and west past Discovery Bay there are several small streams that hold populations of wild sea-run cutthroat. Beyond Dungeness Spit and along the main Strait of Juan de Fuca to the huge Elwha River there are miles of beaches fed by small rivers and creeks, many with at least modest populations of wild coastal cutthroat. These are cutthroat that probably remain very close to parent estuaries and are lightly fished by a rather small cadre of local anglers, many of whom focus primarily on salmon and steelhead.

Some of the smaller creeks feeding directly into the Strait of Juan de Fuca are on Olympic National Forest land that has been heavily logged for decades. Logging practices have not been closely monitored and it is a fact that many of the smaller cutthroat creeks have become degraded by siltation, the result of clearcutting logging. Poorly designed roads are another cause of cutthroat decline, often built with culverts that either hinder or stop passage of migratory fish altogether.

North Coast and Western Strait of Juan de Fuca

Coastal cutthroat stocks are considered to be stable during the past several years from west of the Elwha River out to Cape Flattery.

Lyre River

The Lyre runs only a scant five or six miles from its source in Crescent Lake to its confluence in the Strait of Juan de Fuca. The Lyre produces a few cutthroat each fall.

West and East Twin River

Just west of the town of Joyce the East and West Twin rivers drain into the Strait of Juan de Fuca not more than a quarter mile apart. Both of these streams hold small populations of wild sea-run cutthroat.

Waatch River

Just south of Cape Flattery the Waatch River flows through the Makah Indian Reservation to enter Mukkaw Bay. The Waatch is under Makah jurisdiction and holds a population of cutthroat in the lower reaches right down to the estuary most of the summer.

Sooes River

Entering Mukkaw Bay from the south arm, the Sooes River holds wild cutthroat trout. Like the Waatch, the Sooes is managed by the Makah Tribe.

Quillayute River System

The Quillayute River is a wide, slow river that travels only a few miles from its source with the Sol Duc and Bogachiel rivers to the Pacific Ocean. The Quillayute is very likely an important rearing area for migratory cutthroat trout from both the Sol Duc and Bogachiel rivers. Although Quillayute cutthroats can enjoy the protection of the estuary, there are a lot of cutthroat that crash through the surf every spring to spend a few months roaming the Pacific Ocean.

Sol Duc River

The Sol Duc River is a large tributary of the Quillayute and it receives the vanguard of its migratory cutthroat by mid-August. It is a bit of an anomaly as a cutthroat river as it carries a good flow and has a lot of white water not usually considered friendly to cutthroat. Summer-run steelheaders using small flies in the clear Sol Duc summer flows regularly find cutthroat all the way up to the confluence of Bear Creek, a distance of more than ten river miles.

Bogachiel River

Although the Bogachiel or Bogey as it is called, is not best known as a sea-run cutthroat river, it does offer excellent stretches of slow water scattered with root wads, woody

Preston and Carol working through a prime cutthroat run.

debris, downtimber and canopies of vegetation over deep dark holes along its banks. Cutthroat are found from the Bogey's confluence with the Quillayute River to well above the Highway 101 bridge. There is small stream degradation in the upper reaches from clearcut logging but overall the cutthroat population in the Bogachiel is considered to be healthy.

Calawah River
This tributary stream enters the Bogachiel River just north of the town of Forks. The Calawah produces a small number of sea-run cutthroat each fall in its lower reaches.

Hoh River
The Hoh has a strong population of sea-run cutthroat trout, which includes some trophy-size specimens. Cutthroat probably spend a fair part of their lives in the lower river which has excellent habitat from Highway 101 bridge downstream to where it pounds out through the beach into the Pacific Ocean. Hoh River cutthroats cross the beach at Oil City in the late spring into the Pacific where they roam and feed until late summer.

The upper Hoh River from Highway 101 well beyond the National Park Visitor Center probably holds more Dolly Varden than it does coastal cutthroats There is degradation from logging in the Olympic National Forest, bordering the middle stretch of river, which primarily affects feeder streams. In general though, the Hoh has excellent habitat throughout its vast watershed, extending into its headwaters in Olympic National Park. There is some bank access in the lower river but the entire upper Hoh is bordered by an 18-mile blacktop road from Highway 101 to the National Park Visitor Center and by a well-worn foot trail for another several miles into the park. Run off from Olympic Mountain glaciers keep the Hoh running gray and cloudy for much of the summer which does not help the fly fisher.

Queets River
Coastal cutthroat are found throughout the Queets River from its confluence with the Pacific Ocean into its upper reaches inside of Olympic National Park. Primarily a local fishery, the Queets does produce some large cutthroat. The river is served by a good trail. The best fishing is mid August through October.

Clearwater River
This major tributary of the Queets River has a population of cutthroat but is not heavily fished. The lower end of the Clearwater, downstream from the gauging station is littered with root wads, downtimber and excellent overhead cover which is prime habitat for cutthroat.

Quinault River and Lake Quinault
The lower twenty miles of the Quinault River, from the outflow at Lake Quinault to its estuary at the community of Taholah runs through Quinault Tribal land. It is not fished regularly for cutthroat except by tribal members. Most of the cutthroats in the lower Quinault River are sea-run fish some of which may remain close to the estuary while others will travel into the Pacific Ocean some distance.

The upper river, from Olympic National Park to its entry into Lake Quinault is fished primarily by local anglers from mid-summer through October. Upper river cutthroat drop down into Lake Quinault in the spring after spawning where there is a popular troll sport fishery. Most of the cutthroat caught in the lake each spring are kelts that have not completely recovered from their spawning ordeal. Some upper Quinault River cutthroats live in Lake Quinault through the summer and early autumn where there is good forage. Others that are anadromous continue downstream through the lower Quinault River to salt water.

South Coast including Grays Harbor and Willapa Bay
Grays Harbor and Willapa Bay are important coastal cutthroat areas that are in obvious trouble. Each of these large estuaries on the south coast of Washington is fed by several rivers and countless small creeks, all of which are potentially productive coastal cutthroat trout habitat. Coastal cutthroat populations throughout the Grays Harbor and Willapa Bay river systems are however in a state of decline.

Most of the rivers and creeks flowing from the hills surrounding these two major Washington estuaries have been severely degraded for several decades, primarily from extensive logging which has adversely affected coastal cutthroat populations. Grays Harbor streams are supported by significant plantings of hatchery fish. Willapa Bay cutthroat are estimated to be in a bit better shape, maintaining sustainable numbers without the support of hatchery supplementation.

Since both Grays Harbor and Willapa Bay range from being nearly pure salt water at high tide, to brackish at low tide, cutthroats that migrate from tributaries to spend time in either estuary can be considered anadromous.

Grays Harbor
The primary artery into Grays Harbor is the Chehalis River. A big, slow-moving watercourse, the Chehalis heads from a gathering of creeks on the east slope of the Willapa Hills and meanders for more than sixty miles; east, then north and finally west into Grays Harbor at the city of Aberdeen. On its way, the Chehalis picks up flow from the Newaukum, Skookumchuck, Black, Satsop and Wynoochie rivers. The north side of Grays Harbor is fed by the Humptulips and Hoquiam rivers. The South Arm of Grays Harbor receives flow from the Johns and Elk rivers. All of these rivers host runs of wild coastal cutthroat. Although Grays Harbor is a large, navigable estuary that surely holds anadromous cutthroats through the summer, most of the cutthroat fishing occurs on its many rivers.

Chehalis River
The lower Chehalis River is better known for its salmon and sturgeon fishing than cutthroat. The tributaries of the Chehalis do however have fair populations of coastal cutthroat at least

Chapter 8 - Coastal Cutthroat Trout in British Columbia

BC Fisheries in partnership with British Columbians will: Work to protect, restore and manage our fish populations and aquatic ecosystems; Lead the development and diversification of the fisheries; and, Manage the fisheries and to provide economic, environmental and social benefits for all British Columbians.

Mission Statement

BC Fisheries Management Branch

One of the most popular trout fisheries in British Columbia is for coastal cutthroat trout primarily in the mountain watersheds and marine areas of the western coastline. More specifically coastal cutthroat are found in the waters of Vancouver Island, Lower Mainland, Queen Charlotte Islands and the North Coast including the Skeena River drainage.

Coastal cutthroat populations throughout British Columbia exist in a state of constant risk, receiving considerably less attention and care by both the British Columbia and Federal fisheries management agencies than either the more dominant salmon or steelhead. Sea-run cutthroat in British Columbia were included in a larger investigation of salmonid population status undertaken by the North Pacific International Chapter of the American Fisheries Society in 1996. This study included anadromous stocks of chinook, chum, coho, pink and sockeye salmon as well as steelhead and anadromous coastal cutthroat trout. The study used escapement numbers to determine populations. Since escapement numbers were not available for most coastal cutthroat stocks estimates were made by local management personnel.

The study results showed that coastal cutthroat stocks throughout British Columbia, as elsewhere along the Pacific Coast, range from healthy to depressed to threatened with some populations declared extinct. The decline in coastal cutthroat stocks can be largely attributed to the progress of man. Clearcut logging practices have degraded watersheds and rivers; habitat has been lost to urban and commercial development; the encroachment of people has increased water diversion and caused low summer flows; and the cutthroat's inability to compete with salmon, steelhead and other species such as rainbow and brook trout cannot be overlooked. An effort to minimize the impact of habitat loss has been implemented, primarily by placing coastal cutthroat on catch-and-release status in selected rivers and marine areas. Still, all in all, the coastal cutthroat trout, a resilient rascal, is doing pretty well in British Columbia and remains at the top of the list as a gamefish among many dedicated fly fishers.

A coastal cutthroat smolt stocking program has been in place on Vancouver Island and the Lower Mainland of British Columbia for many years. Vancouver Island stocks several waters with sea-run cutthroat including the Gorge Waterway in Victoria. In the Lower Mainland, the primary

A beautiful, big-shouldered Vancouver Island sea-run cutthroat. Chances of catching a trophy like this are better than average on many Vancouver Island streams and estuaries.

stocking program is focused on the Fraser River with the Brunette River, Stave River, Alouette River, De Bouville Slough, Nicomen Slough, Harrison River and Hope-Camp Slough receiving fish on a regular basis. All of these hatchery cutthroats are the progeny of Fraser River broodstock.

There have been concerns that hatchery produced cutthroat may have a harmful impact on native fish. At this time these concerns are being studied. The purpose of hatchery support is not to augment natural production but to provide a harvestable cutthroat for the sport fishery.

When and Where to Fish for Coastal Cutthroat

In British Columbia the coastal cutthroat can be fished nearly every month of the year depending upon current regulations and weather. This chapter will tell you where to find coastal cutthroat throughout British Columbia. They are found in lake and certain rivers year around. In streams open to marine water they can be found along beaches and the mouths of estuaries through the summer and into Autumn. By late summer sea-run cutthroats are entering parent streams and will continue to do so until October with some fisheries not coming on until winter. Figuring out the fishery is a major part of the game because just when you think you have them figured out the coastal cutthroat of British Columbia will surprise you. And British Columbia is so big, with so much unexplored water that the coastal cutthroat can become a lifetime adventure for any fly fisher who loves pursuing a trout that provides a never-ending challenge with every new year. Fishing for the magnificent coastal cutthroat never becomes a sport that one can become blasé about. There is a great deal to learn. Fortunately there are a lot of fly fishers in British Columbia who already fish cutthroat and will usually help a newcomer out. There are also excellent fly shops throughout BC where all the right stuff can be purchased — and there are some outstanding fishing clubs whose ranks are well endowed with cutthroat anglers. Joining a fishing club will not only put you in touch with cutthroat anglers, it will get you involved in important conservation issues and projects aimed at keeping the cutthroat around forever.

Coastal Cutthroat Fishing by Region

Anglers pursue coastal cutthroat throughout western British Columbia river systems along the shoreline of the mainland, Vancouver Island and the Queen Charlotte Islands. There is also a sport fishery in a great many lakes. Although coastal cutthroat are commonly referred to as sea-run or anadromous, it is not easy to establish just which stocks are actually resident (live in upper watersheds in above-barrier streams); fluvial (live between small creeks and mainstem rivers); adfluvial (primarily lake-dwellers that spawn in feeder streams); or anadromous (sea-runs that migrate to marine waters). These different stocks of coastal cutthroat trout may overlap within a given watershed or river system.

Vancouver Island

The streams and lakes of Vancouver Island once abounded with coastal cutthroat trout. While some still do contain healthy numbers, some stocks have declined during the past several years from the adverse effects of large scale logging, urbanization, agricultural impacts and other habitat degradation. However, populations remain strong enough in many Vancouver Island streams and lakes to provide a robust sport fishery. Continued monitoring of wild stocks combined with restricted bag limits and catch-and-release regulations where it is called for should be a major factor in continued rebuilding of coastal cutthroat in most Vancouver Island watersheds.

Rivers

Anadromous cutthroat are found in nearly every river on Vancouver Island. Some of the more popular streams are: Sooke-DeMamiel, Muir, Kirby, San Juan, Nitinat, Pachina, Sarita, Somass, Consinka, Ritherdon, Kaouk, Strandby, Nahwitti, Salmon, Mohan, Campbell, Simms, Willow, Oyster, Nile, Big Qualicum, Little Qualicum, Chemainus, Cowichan, Koksilah, Colquitz, Sandhill and Craigflower.

On the Queen Charlotte Islands, fly-fishers may view fascinating First Nation artifacts. The Haida Indian burial logs are near the remains of a village on Graham Island.

Small Streams and Headwater Creeks

Resident coastal cutthroat are located above barriers on many small streams and creeks throughout Vancouver Island. As in other headwater areas of the cutthroat's range, these fish generally attain modest size at maturity and are not found in abundance. Small stream resident cutthroat do, however provide a good fishery for backpackers, day hikers and youngsters in places where a fly can be easily cast or dapped along the surface.

Lakes

It is in Vancouver Island's largest lakes that trophy-class coastal cutthroats are found. It is not uncommon to hear about individual fish upwards of 10 pounds being taken every season. During the spring when resident lake cutthroat are cruising the shallows there is potential for hooking some of these big bruisers on the fly.

Lakes that are known to hold good populations of coastal cutthroat, together with some large fish include: Cowichan Lake, Como Lake, Great Central Lake, Sproat Lake, Upper and Lower Campbell lakes, Buttle Lake, Nimpkish Lake, and Woss Lake. High counts of spawners and sightings of large fish occur in May and June in natal tributaries to Buttle and Upper Campbell lakes such as Elk River and Thelwood Creek.

Vancouver Island has numerous small lakes that support both hatchery and wild stocks of coastal cutthroat. Examples include: Misty Lake in the Keogh River system and Doobah Lake near Nitinat. Most Vancouver Island lakes are biologically low in productivity; hence they often support large numbers of smaller fish wherever there is sufficient stream habitat for spawning.

Dave Lock, veteran saltwater fly-fisher and tier, readies a nice Vancouver Island cutthroat for release.

Salt Water

There is excellent cutthroat fishing and ample access along the beaches and estuaries of Vancouver Island and this is a sport fishery that is growing in popularity annually. These estuarine areas include all of the major Vancouver Island rivers already listed. In addition to major river estuaries nearly any stream flowing directly into saltwater is worth a good effort with the fly. Other areas that provide good salt-water fly fishing include: Gorge Waterway and Esquimalt Lagoon, near Victoria; Bazan Bay, south of Sydney near the ferry terminal to Anacortes; Island View Beach, near Saanichton near the end of Island View Road; Fulford Harbor, near Duncan; Sooke Basin, at Sooke; Baynes Sound streams, and Willow Point south of Campbell River. On the less populated and considerably more remote west side of Vancouver Island are several estuaries worth checking out including; Kaouk River northwest of Zeballos and Cypre River near Tofino. Fly fishers have taken large coastal cutthroat from the estuarine areas everywhere along the Vancouver Island coast with some husky specimens weighing up to six pounds.

Lower Mainland

The Lower Mainland region of British Columbia encompasses the southwest portion of the Province. Coastal cutthroat anglers in the metropolitan Vancouver area are within easy striking distance of rivers and lakes throughout the Lower Mainland, most of which are served by highways or good secondary roads. The Lower Mainland stretches northward along the coast, including two ferry hops (across Howe Sound and Saltery Bay). It then extends still further north but the main road terminates at the little town of Lund. North of Lund there are many islands, bays and deep fiords that can only be reached by boat or aircraft.

The Lower Mainland boundary extends southeasterly from the coast to just east of Chilliwack. The British Columbia/United States border forms the southern boundary line of the Lower Mainland. Near the town of Hope the Fraser river plunges down from the north bringing with it the flow of several streams, including the famous Thompson River so highly revered for its run of large, powerful fall steelhead. From Hope the Fraser courses directly west, cutting right through metropolitan Vancouver to reach its confluence with the Strait of Georgia. Coastal cutthroat can be found in downtown Vancouver although this highly industrialized and urbanized lower stretch of the Fraser does not lend itself to fly-fishing. Reaching the more attractive waters upstream of Vancouver where the scenery and the cutthroat fishing really gets good is not difficult, since the river is paralleled by Trans-Canada Highway 1 all the way to Hope. Along the way short junkets off the highway on secondary and unimproved roads put you onto the Fraser.

Coastal Rivers

Along the Pacific Coast north of Vancouver, good populations of coastal cutthroat are present in the Vancouver River and the much larger Powell River. These and other rivers in the area all the way to the town of Lund are served by secondary and unimproved roads that can be negotiated nicely via pickup truck or SUV. The secondary road ends at Lund. Remote areas north of Lund are also served by separated and isolated systems of logging roads. A multitude of rivers enter a maze of bays and inlets north of Lund. The Toba, Southgate and Homathko, rivers are but a few that flow into the bays north of Lund

Rather than set out on a cavalier thrust into any of these backcountry fishing areas, it would be prudent to research the many bays and inlets carefully as passage into such a wild area either by water or logging road should be looked upon as a modern day wilderness adventure for coastal cutthroat. Such an excursion would open up a potentially outstanding coastal cutthroat fishery for anyone with an unfulfilled spirit of adventure.

Squamish River System

From Lion's Bay, Highway 99 takes the cutthroat angler north 30 miles to the town of Squamish and the Squamish River. The Squamish; major river in this area, gains volume from its primary tributaries; the Elaho, Ashla, Cheakamus and Mamquam rivers and myriad smaller creeks before flowing into Howe Sound just north of the Fraser River estuary. The Squamish River is served by a good road beyond the confluence of the Cheakamus where a logging road continues along the river providing another 30 miles of good access.

The Squamish River watershed has been badly degraded by logging practices that have stripped its steep watershed of trees leaving it vulnerable to spring flooding which has silted valuable spawning areas. At this writing the Squamish River system is not considered to be productive for coastal cutthroat trout.

The Fraser River System

The magnificent Fraser River and it tributaries hosts an excellent population of wild and hatchery coastal cutthroat from its mouth at Steveson to the town of Hope at the lower end of the Fraser River Canyon. Finding cutthroats is not easy though because the Fraser changes from year to year. Spring spates may relocate the Fraser's many braids and side channels giving cutthroats entirely new places to roam and feed. Downstream from the town of Hope the channel of the Fraser becomes very complex with islands that further break up the flows and provide countless soft areas in the current that will hold cutthroats. This ever-changing character of the Fraser allows schools of cutthroat to cruise the mainstem, the lower ends of its major tributaries, small feeder creeks and side channels at will. Given their wandering nature, an angler may enjoy a banner day of fishing at a favorite spot one day and find the same place completely barren of cutthroat the next. Some Fraser River fly anglers have affectionately nicknamed Fraser River cutthroats "gypsies" in light of their penchant to be constantly moving from known fishing spots into new areas whenever there is a change in the river's flow.

Coastal cutthroats that call the Fraser River system home exhibit a variety of life history patterns. These are not well understood but certainly reflect the diversity of habitat of the mainstem and large and small tributary streams including access to a nearby estuarine and ocean environment.

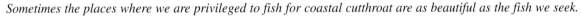

Sometimes the places where we are privileged to fish for coastal cutthroat are as beautiful as the fish we seek.

Barry Stokes

Cutthroat that utilize the Fraser as a primary freshwater environment are, to one degree or another, migratory in nature with a segment of the population being sea-runs that move various distances along the salt water margins of the Strait of Georgia. Cutthroats that prefer life in Fraser's many tributaries are more likely to be roaming residents that spend periods in the mainstem and rarely, if ever move downstream into brackish or estuarine water. The headwater creeks that flow into the Fraser's scores of tributary streams host populations of resident coastal cutthroat that probably use only the tributary waters or do not migrate at all.

Fraser River Fishing Seasons
Winter
Flows are generally low and the river runs clear with backwaters, bays, channels and bars clearly defined. There are not a lot of forage fish around; juvenile salmonids have migrated to the Strait of Georgia and beyond and resident bait fish are in hiding. Warm days brings about hatches of midges, small stoneflies and mayflies all of which will interest a cutthroat if no meatier opportunities are available. The river is generally not crowded since there is no salmon fishing going on in the winter. However, heavy rains can raise and muddy the Fraser during the winter months.

Spring
When spring arrives the Fraser comes alive with millions of pink and chum salmon fry; coho, chinook, sockeye and steelhead smolts that begin itching to head downstream to the salt. Resident minnows like sticklebacks become active and cutthroat are ready to partake of these more substantial food items. Fry-feeding cutthroat can be finicky though so matching the hatch with one's minnow patterns is paramount to cashing in on a great fly-fishing opportunity.

Late Spring/Early Summer
This is the time when the Fraser and its tributaries go into spring freshet. The main Fraser becomes very high and dirty during this period inundating physical features. This is not the best season for coastal cutthroat.

Summer
The river may remain high well into the summer but the bars are usually beginning to show. If the Fraser is open to retention of sockeye salmon it will be very crowded, limiting opportunities for the cutthroat fly fisher.

Fall
The Fraser cools, clears and drops at this time but runs of late-arriving salmon are in progress. If there is a kill-season announced for salmon you can expect serious crowding. If there is not a kill-season on salmon the cutthroat fishing can be very good as the river will be devoid of other anglers. By November salmon runs have pretty well gone through allowing excellent access and angling opportunity for the cutthroat fly fisher.

Fraser River Estuary
The estuary section of the Fraser River splits into two arms, North and South. Here the Fraser enters the Strait of Georgia through tough access for the angler as much of the property is privately owned and is highly industrialized with manufacturing facilities, retail services and an ever-growing number of luxury hotels to serve the nearby Vancouver International Airport and charter flights out of the South Terminal. In addition to heavy shipping traffic, the Fraser River estuary is still employed to anchor huge log rafts reminiscent of times early in the Twentieth Century when the huge, conifer-rich water shed was being cut and enormous log rafts were floated downstream to the river mouth every spring for delivery to sawmills along the British Columbia coast.

North Arm
There is a boat launch on the North Arm of the Fraser at Richmond Marina near McDonald Beach. However, with heavy shipping traffic, poor water quality and a shoreline that is congested with log booms and commercial venues, the North Arm is not a highly desirable fishing area for the coastal cutthroat.

South Arm
From the estuary past Woodward Reach, upstream beyond Ladner Reach and Gravesend Reach the South Arm of the Fraser fairly bristles with navigational buoys to assist the boat traffic that moves through on a steady basis. There are boat launches on the South Arm at Ladner Reach between George Massey Tunnel and the Alex Fraser Bridge. There are also launches at Pitt Meadows and Skyline Marina. There is another at Deas Island and one on each side of Pattulla Bridge. The South Arm launches are primarily used by anglers headed for the Strait of Georgia to fish for salmon.

Tom Johannesen releasing a prime 18-inch Harrison cutthroat in early March. The cutthroat fell to a small fry pattern on a Ghost Tip fly line.

As fishing areas the North and South arms are so tremendously congested and with water quality so poor that they are not looked upon seriously by fly-fishers seeking good spots for coastal cutthroat. However, there are surely anadromous coastal cutthroat moving back and forth through the North and South arms nearly every month of the year.

New Westminster to Pitt River

Upstream from the junction of the North and South arms the Fraser River begins to open up with a showing of good bars that provide river access. These bars are not prime spots for the cutthroat fly-fisher but can be productive year around.

A few possible cutthroat fishing spots along the New Westminster/Pitt River stretch of the Fraser include; Brownsville Bar downstream from Pattillo Bridge; Richie, Gypsum and Dock bars along Queen's Reach, upstream from Pattillo Bridge on the south side of the river; Leader Bar, downstream from the mouth of the Coquitlam River and Coquitlam River Bar at the mouth of the Coquitlam River. Further upstream on the Pitt River a ramp on the east end of the Lougheed Highway Bridge provides access to good cutthroat fishing from the bridge stanchions downstream to Douglas Island in the main channel of the Fraser.

Port Hammond to Mission

At Port Hammond the Fraser becomes distinctly more recognizable as a fisherman's river. The shoreline is less populated and there are several popular angling access points between Port Hammond and Mission. Coastal cutthroat are found through this reach of the Fraser every month of the year. This stretch is also great for the angler who owns a seaworthy skiff with a reliable outboard. The big, powerful Fraser does not lend itself to rowing.

Downstream from McMillan Island, Derby Reach Park (Allard Crescent Park), on the river's south bank, offers the cutthroat fly-fisher picnic and camping facilities, making it a nice spot for a weekend outing. There is a handy boat ramp located at MacKay Avenue adjacent to River Road.

At Fort Langley, Fort Langley Marine Park Bar provides access from the south side of McMillan Island. There is a boat ramp at Fort Langley Park Bar and another further upstream along River Reach just across from the east end of McMillan Island.

Upstream from McMillan Island, Nathan Creek Bar at the mouth of Nathan Creek offers cutthroat fishing from the south shore of the Fraser. A short distance further upstream, just west of Nathan Slough and Crescent Island, Two-Bit Bar provides additional fishing access to this stretch of the Fraser.

Near the mouth of the Stave River which empties into the Fraser from the north shore, near the community of Ruskin, anglers find good cutthroat fishing at Ruskin Bar. At the east end of Crescent Island, Duncan Bar provides fishing access from the south side of the Fraser River.

Mission to Chilliwack

It is at the town of Mission, the uppermost rush and ebb of tidal influence, that the Fraser is known as the "gravel reach" and where the truly superb fly-fishing for coastal cutthroat begins.

At the east end of Matsqui Island, Mission Bar and Mission Bridge Bar there is productive coastal cutthroat fishing. On the north side of the river, west of the Mission Railway Bridge there is a public boat ramp.

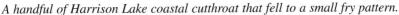

A handful of Harrison Lake coastal cutthroat that fell to a small fry pattern.

Tom Johannsen

This far up the Fraser River with so many streams feeding in from both the north and south shore, there is probably a scattering of resident and mainstem roaming stocks of cutthroat in the waters around Chilliwack along with sea-runs. It is an easy distance for sea-run cutthroat to migrate to the salt and back but it is also an area that provides good habitat for those cutthroats that prefer to remain in fresh water.

For all its confusing twists and turns, the Mission-to-Chilliwack stretch of the Fraser has a lot of access points that will put the cutthroat fly-fisher onto some outstanding water that tends to hold coastal cutthroat year around.

Dewdney Park Bar and Strawberry Island Bar located at the west and east end of Strawberry Island respectively, are popular cutthroat spots among local anglers. A ramp at Dewdney Nature Park allows the boat angler to probe further along the main Fraser and into Nicomen Slough.

On the south side, upstream across from Strawberry Island, the short Sumas River, joined by the popular Vedder River, enters the Fraser. The Vedder offers good cutthroat fishing during the spring when fry are moving downstream and again in August when cutthroats show up. This fishery is primarily utilized by boat anglers working bait. It is not a

Brian Nyberg with a beautiful sea-run cutthroat taken and released while fishing a Gulf Island beach. Note the economical stripping basket.

commonly used area by cutthroat fly-fishers. Fly-fishing from a boat is however a good way to test such places and should not be discounted.

Chilliwack to Hope
This stretch of the Fraser River is complex, very interesting — and would take the novice cutthroat fly-fisher the longest time to learn as it is an ever-changing maze. In this the upper reach of the Fraser, there are more islands, braids, dead-end sloughs, secondary channels and rough, two-track access roads than one could ever imagine. I had the good fortune of fishing the area with my long-time angling companion, Bruce Ferguson a few years ago. Fortunately we were fishing under the guidance of Cliff Olson, a Fraser River veteran and member of the Osprey Flyfishers of British Columbia. We enjoyed a marvelous day of fly-fishing for pink and sockeye salmon but would not have ever found our way around the labyrinth of channels without the experience and guidance of Cliff, a very gracious host.

Jesperson Bar, located downstream from Greyell Slough is best known as a salmon and steelhead spot. However, local anglers find that the cutthroats also begin biting in this area in the fall and continue to take flies well into the winter. Across the Fraser at the mouth of Pumphouse Slough Bar, cutthroat fishing is rated as very good from autumn through winter and into the spring. Just downstream from the mouth of Pumphouse Slough, Tunnel's Bar, at the base of Mount Woodside, is another access favored by cutthroat fly-fishers.

First Nation Lands on the Fraser
The lower Fraser River, from Hope downstream to its mouth, is the traditional home and fishing grounds of many First Nation groups. A significant amount of the lands adjacent to the Fraser and its tributaries are within First Nation "reserves" or under land claims debate. Angler access through these lands may, or may not be available, depending upon the policies of individual First Nation bands. Anglers need to be aware that access conditions can change and as with any private property, no trespassing signs need to be respected.

Herrling Island
An exit off of Trans-Canada Highway 1 on the Fraser's south side takes the angler over a bridge, under a railroad bridge and across a gravel bar (that is sometimes covered with water) onto Herrling Island, a favorite fishing location among coastal cutthroat flyfishers. The roads on Herrling Island are primarily two-tracks that can be tough to negotiate without benefit of a four-wheel-drive vehicle. Catermole Slough along the south shore of Herrling Island is considered to be one of the better stretches of the Fraser River for coastal cutthroat trout. There are several places along the Herrling Island shore where a cartop boat or other craft can be launched.

Above Herrling Island anglers find fair to good cutthroat fishing through the fall and winter and on the north side of the Fraser upstream from Maria Slough, yet another good cutthroat spot. Further upstream on the north side of the Fraser, Ruby Creek Bar draws a fair number of cutthroat anglers, also during the fall and winter. Landstrom Bar is the last spot below Hope that attracts cutthroat anglers although it is better known for its excellent salmon fishing.

Pitt River/Pitt Lake

The lower Pitt River flows south out of Pitt Lake to meet the Fraser River just east of Port Coquitlam. Anglers concentrate their attention on the lower Pitt River primarily in the vicinity of the Alouette River, De Bouville Slough and the outlet of the large lake near Widgeon Slough. A boat and motor can be used to advantage for exploring this area as it is large. At Grant Narrows, which is at the lake outlet, there is another boat ramp.

Up Pitt Lake a short distance, Goose Island also produces good cutthroat fishing from the northern tip of Grant Channel to the point bar off of Goose Island. Most veteran anglers concentrate their attention on the deep, outside drop-off of Grant Channel where baitfish hold in abundance.

From Williams Landing up the east shore of Pitt Lake, past Osprey Creek to Gurney Creek fishing is rated as fair. From Gurney Creek to Cactus Point cutthroat fishing improves significantly.

Pitt Lake is one of the world's very few large, tidally-influenced freshwater lakes. Tidal rise and fall can be seen all the way to the upper end of the lake. The vast mudflat at the south end of Pitt Lake is called a "reverse delta" because muddy spring water flows in from the Fraser depositing sediment as the turbid waters slow. Pitt Lake can also be very treacherous when wind and tide combine to make it extremely rough. A steep shoreline makes an emergency landing during a storm extremely hazardous. All this considered Pitt Lake is an interesting place to chase cutthroat, particularly at the mouths of the many streams that enter along its shoreline and at the upper end where the Upper Pitt River and Red Slough enter.

Harrison River/Harrison Lake

The Harrison River watershed is one of the largest tributaries and includes two large lakes with interconnecting rivers. It is a salmonid producing queen bee of a river that hosts five species of salmon, steelhead, Dolly Varden/bull trout, and coastal cutthroat trout. Harrison Lake is the largest lake in the system and one that many anglers find intimidating because it is so large. For this reason they pass it by to fish smaller streams and rivers that seem to be of a more manageable size. Nevertheless, the Harrison River system can be very rewarding and worth any time spent poring over maps, reading guide books and exploring its many facets.

Cutthroat trout fishing gets good very quickly right at the narrow throat of the Harrison River outlet. The very popular Kilby Provincial Park on the east shore of the Harrison River outlet offers a picnic area, overnight camping and a boat ramp. There is good fishing in the vicinity of the park and downstream from the railroad bridge to the Harrison-Fraser confluence.

Upstream from Kilby Park finding cutthroat becomes a searching game as there is a lot of river between the park and the outlet of Harrison Lake. In this stretch fishing from a boat offers definite advantages. Locations worth trying are at the Lougheed Highway bridge, French Creek, the braids at the mouth of the Chehalis River, the junction of Morris Slough and the outlet of the big lake.

Lower Mainland Lakes

Many of the lakes on the Lower Mainland and near the Fraser River hold populations of coastal cutthroat. There are also lakes that hold self-sustaining populations of wild cutthroat.

A beautiful, fat sea-run cutthroat from Vancouver Island. Note the prominent golden "harvest" colors and red slash on the throat, typical of cutthroat.

Wherever the cutthroats are self-sustaining and are not in competition with rainbows they grow to good size and provide excellent fly-fishing from spring through early summer. There is also a rainbow trout stocking program which is restricted to a limited number of urban area lakes and ponds.

Most, if not all of the larger lakes that are tributary to the Fraser River hold varied forms of coastal cutthroat trout. Many of these Fraser system cutthroats migrate either between river and lake, or downstream to marine waters.

Large and small lakes along the Sechelt Peninsula and Powell River have populations of coastal cutthroat. Some of the larger lakes also have forage fish such as kokanee salmon. Such rich forage can result in some exceptionally large cutthroat. Powell Lake, Ruby Lake and some of the other lakes around the town of Powell River fall into this category. Generally, it is safe to say that some of the very largest coastal cutthroats awaiting the fly fisher are probably swimming in British Columbia lakes.

Queen Charlotte Islands

Coastal cutthroat trout populations on Queen Charlotte Islands waters are generally healthy and lightly fished. As the more popular steelhead receives increased pressure though and becomes more difficult to catch the cutthroat is sure to receive additional attention from sport fishers.

Habitat degradation is probably the number one issue affecting the health of coastal cutthroat populations wherever they exist in the Queen Charlottes. The aftermath of clearcut logging is a major culprit as these area eventually slide into the valley bottoms after being cut, silting feeder and spawning creeks.

Coastal cutthroat trout in Queen Charlotte Islands streams and lakes probably receive some of the lightest pressure of any stocks in British Columbia. In large measure sport fishing for coastal cutthroat trout is primarily a local pursuit due to the lack of easy, inexpensive access to the Queen Charlottes. The visiting fly fisher can reach the Queen Charlotte Islands via air service out of Vancouver and by ferry or air from Prince Rupert.

The Queen Charlotte Islands archipelago, located some 60 nautical miles off the north British Columbia coast west of Prince Rupert consists of 1884 islands rising from sea level to mountains reaching upward 2600 feet. Covering more than 3800 square miles, the Queen Charlotte Islands economoy is driven by logging, mining, commercial fishing and tourism. There are salmon fishing charter services located at Masset, Port Clements, Queen Charlotte City, Sandspit, and Rose Harbor. A few guide services and lodges also attract steelhead fishermen but coastal cutthroat rarely even appear in much of the Queen Charlotte Island sportfishing information that I have seen.

Fly-anglers who have fished the Queen Charlotte Islands for coastal cutthroat are generally impressed with the quality of the fishing and in certain waters, by the large size of the genuinely exceptional specimens they catch. Coloration of Queen Charlottes coastal cutthroat ranges from the silver flanked sea-run to the olive and gold stocks that reside in rivers and lakes, to those that choose dark bogs and black-bottomed streams as home and are nearly all black around the head, lower jaws and well down onto the flanks. One characteristic that Queen Charlotte Islands cutthroat share with their kin from northern British Columbia mainland to the Eel River in California is their inherent instinct to climb all over a well-placed fly.

Rivers

Distribution of coastal cutthroat trout in the Queen Charlotte Islands is restricted to the northeast lowland regions of Graham Island with resident and all migratory cutthroat forms represented. The topography of the northeast lowlands is unique, consisting of a series of plateaus:

Hecate Lowlands

I have looked down at the Hecate Lowlands many times on helicopter rides to Langara Island. The area is only a bit above sea level and is ribboned with dark, slow moving, low gradient streams, some of which spill unhurriedly from black-bottomed lakes that appear from the air to be bogs rather than lakes. Cutthroats inhabit this area but most are thought to be resident only and not anadromous even though they have direct access to the sea.

Skidegate Plateau

Located above Hecate Plateau, Skidegate Plateau is home to both rainbow and coastal cutthroat trout. A limited amount of hybridization has been detected between rainbows and cutthroats wherever the two species co-exist. Very little sport fishing is attempted in this area, by visiting anglers at least.

Range Area

This part of the mountainous west coast includes most of Morseby Island. Streams throughout the Range Area are mostly high gradient, fast-flowing and turbulent, the type of water that cutthroat have never been prone to populate. Most of the trout all through this area are resident rainbows and steelhead.

Fly-fishers seeking cutthroats of good size and in good numbers usually begin with the larger Queen Charlottes rivers; the Yakoun, Tlell, Copper, Deena, and Honna. Cutthroat move into these streams in the fall but can be found hanging around the estuaries almost any month of the year.

The Tlell River and creeks that empty into Hecate Strait, on the east side of Graham Island, are very popular with fly fishers looking for the anadromous cutthroats that show up in September and October. These cutthroats, along with equally hefty sea-runs that show up to ascend the Oneanda River are very large and strong, in some cases rivaling steelhead in length and girth.

Small Streams and Headwater Creeks

Smaller streams such as Datlaman Creek and its tributaries lace the Queen Charlottes and can offer some excellent fishing but mostly for diminutive, non-migratory cutthroats. The black-bottom streams of Hecate Plateau should not be overlooked either as the cutthroats that cruise these dark environs would seem to be blessed with rare coloration. Since many of these small streams flow only a short distance before entering saltwater they could host some sea-run cutthroat in addition to resident populations.

Lakes

Lake-dwelling populations of cutthroat trout are abundant throughout the northeast lowlands of Graham Island. Lakes in the lowland regions that host coastal cutthroat trout include; Ain Lake that enters Masset Inlet, Mayer, Yakoun, Skidegate, and Mosquito lakes. Generally the cutthroat that live in these lowland lakes are aggressive and will readily take a fly. There is also good dry fly fishing at times. In general, all the Queen Charlotte Islands lowland lakes hold healthy populations of cutthroat trout, most of which are residents.

There is some speculation that the coastal cutthroat trout that live in murky, black-bottomed lakes and streams may also have eye pigmentation that allows them to see quite well in the reduced light. Large, resident cutthroats in particular that are taken from these waters often display very dark flanks with heads that are black from the top of the skull to the jawbone with vivid red slashes along each side of the gills. These distinctive cutthroats will be high on my list next time I can arrange a trip to the Queen Charlotte Islands.

Salt Water

Very little information is available on saltwater fishing opportunities on the beaches and estuaries of the Queen Charlotte Islands. For one thing there is so much fishing available in lakes and streams that anglers have little need to pursue cutthroats in the salt. Secondly, the long tidal runouts make estuary fishing less appealing with low tide turns that could be nearly a mile offshore. I have, however seen rock outcroppings and tide rips along the Queen Charlottes coastline that I would love to investigate with a fly rod as they certainly appear to be fishy places.

Fly-fishing around the mouths of rivers and creeks, particularly during high tide turns does attract anglers. This estuary fishing is about as close to actual open-ocean, saltwater fly-fishing that one will find in the Queen Charlotte Islands.

North Coast

Most of the coastal watersheds of British Columbia's North Coast hold cutthroat trout but they are less common further north until they reach the northernmost boundary of their range in Southeast Alaska. North Coast cutthroat are primarily anadromous where they exist in watersheds open to marine waters. Populations of cutthroat in North Coast waters, particularly in the Bella Coola, lower Skeena River tributaries and Douglas Channel are thought to be some of the healthiest stocks in British Columbia but many are so remote that they have not been inventoried so little is actually known about them.

Cutthroat populations are generally restricted to the coastal watersheds of the North Coast. Distribution and abundance of coastal cutthroat is considerably less in the interior portions of North Coast watersheds such as the Skeena, Nass and Taku.

Sea-run cutthroat are most common throughout the North Coast but moving toward the interior reaches of its watersheds there are increasing numbers of stocks that utilize only mainstem and tributary rivers. Since the majority of sport fishing pressure throughout the region is concentrated on salmon and steelhead, coastal cutthroat stocks are probably not heavily fished, being left to the relatively few dedicated anglers who concentrate on them. On the interior reaches of the Skeena and Nass watersheds by far the most popular autumn sport fishing is for steelhead and salmon. Cutthroat inhabit the coastal reaches of these watersheds. The Kitimat River hosts a spring run of steelhead and salmon. Some cutthroat are certainly taken incidentally during this fishery but are not regularly targeted. Throughout the North Coast steelhead, salmon and coastal cutthroat sport fisheries are considered to be mutually exclusive. The following are a small sampling of the vast number of good coastal cutthroat fishing waters in the North Region.

Streams

The Kitimat, Lakelse, Kasiks, and Bella Coola river systems and their tributaries all hold healthy populations of coastal cutthroat trout. Good cutthroat fishing is also found throughout the Skeena sloughs.

Lakes

The provincial fishery agency stocks cutthroat in some area lakes including Helen, Round, Llama, Vallee and Dunalter in the Bulkley watershed. Areas that hold widespread populations of wild cutthroat include the Lakelse, Bulkley and Babine watersheds. Some smaller interior lakes also have natural populations of cutthroat.

Yellowhead Route 16 cuts through the Northern interior from Prince George to Prince Rupert and provides secondary highway and road access to remote backcountry lakes and tributary rivers all along the way. Many of these waters hold excellent populations of coastal cutthroat trout. Near Terrace, Yellowhead Route 16 tracks the Skeena River to its confluence with the Pacific Ocean at Prince Rupert. Secondary Highway 37 cuts off to Kitimat to put the adventuresome fly fisher into another cornucopia of cutthroat rivers and lakes.

Anyone planning to explore the North Coast and interior watersheds of British Columbia for cutthroat trout will need more than this chapter for guidance. There are many books on British Columbia fishing by talented writers: all of which tell you a lot but none of which tell you everything that you will need to know. In addition to the excellent selection of reference books available, good maps and current fishing regulations will further thicken your coastal cutthroat adventurer's portfolio. The Internet can also be a very good source of information. I employ the Internet regularly in my work. For me however it will never replace an evening in a comfortable chair with a touch of fine Scotch and a good reference book. Regardless of the work that would be involved, the prospect of finding new, possibly untouched coastal cutthroat water in this day and age, certainly makes it a quest worthy of any serious fly fisher's time.

The Northern Region of British Columbia may very well be the last great trout fishing frontier in North America with its immense network of rivers and wealth of untapped lakes that harbor large, wild coastal cutthroat trout. Its expanse, topography and fishing possibilities boggle the mind. It is a fly-fisher's wonderland by any modern standard.

Chapter 9 - *Coastal Cutthroat Flies*

"After some thirty years of fishing, during which I have tried most methods, I am satisfied that to catch a fish which might have been caught on the fly, in any other way is a waste of fish, a waste of sport and denial of a high experience."

Roderick Haig-Brown
Fisherman's Spring

I believe that fly-fishing has been the primary driver in the resurgence of fishing for coastal cutthroat trout over the past several years although I hold no concrete evidence to support my opinion. I'm sure that there has also been an increase among anglers using light spinning gear to cast tiny spoons and spinners whom also ply their skills on cutthroat waters. Fly-fishing for coastal cutthroat trout though has literally exploded during the past decade.

Today we have the luxury of selecting from an array of technologically advanced rods, reels and lines that staggers the imagination. Tackle has not been critical though because in all due respect we did very nicely with the functional, albeit more staid tackle available to us fifty years ago. I will further argue that much of the increased interest and upsurge of success in coastal cutthroat fishing during the past several years can be attributed in significant measure to the fly tiers who have melded their observations into fly patterns developed specifically to entice this unique trout, mainly in estuarine and salt water. New flies to tempt coastal cutthroat in freshwater have not enjoyed the renaissance of estuary and saltwater patterns probably due to the fact that so many of our classic freshwater cutthroat trout patterns are still employed very successfully in coastal lagoons, lakes, rivers, beaver ponds and tiny headwater streams.

I also contend that most fly development for Pacific Coast river fishing is dedicated in large measure to enticing steelhead; to a lesser extent salmon and lastly, coastal cutthroat trout. The preponderance of stillwater patterns developed have been targeted primarily at rainbow, brown, brook and inland cutthroat trout (westslope, Snake River, Yellowstone, etc.).

This uncluttered box of streamers, bucktails and krill imitations are all that Dan Lemaich carries during a fishing tide. A talented and innovative tier, Dan constantly experiments with realistic and attractor patterns.

In addition, trout flies that work well for other species of trout in fresh water are equally attractive to coastal cutthroat throughout their range. Mayfly, chironomid, damselfly and scud imitations are all standards in the fly boxes of anglers who prowl brassy-bottomed western lakes and beaver ponds in search of big, amber-flanked coastal cutthroats. Veteran anglers who fish coastal streams have long known that a properly presented Adams, PMD, Blue-Winged Olive or Elk Hair Caddis is very effective on anadromous cutthroat and a Royal Wulff searching its way along under a sunshade of willows will bring just about any respectable cutthroat charging from cover to strike. Dry flies are in fact, at times more appetizing to cutthroat than even the most reliable wet flies late in the season.

In estuary and salt water fly fishing there have been dramatic developments because there are so many more anglers now probing the salt for cutthroat. This increase in saltwater anglers has resulted in additional attention being placed on fly patterns. Forage-imitating flies that have been created for use in brackish and salt water exemplify the surge of creative energy that has pushed the anadromous coastal cutthroat fishery to new heights. Most of the lifelike krill, baitfish and attractor patterns that appear in these pages were developed by tiers in Washington and British Columbia. Some of this tying interest has been a spin-off from the burgeoning fly fishery for coho salmon along the hundreds of miles of protected beaches around Washington's Puget Sound and British Columbia's marine waters.

New patterns designed to take Pacific salmon, predominantly coho, have proven to be equally effective for cutthroat trout. This should come as no surprise since coastal cutthroat in saltwater cruise within easy casting range along the very same beaches as salmon, foraging on the same baitfish and crustaceans. Other flies intended specifically for cutthroat have in turn, proven to be very effective for taking salmon.

The flies that grace the pages of this chapter reflect the ingenuity, creativity and tying acumen of fly tiers all along the Pacific Coast. The skillful blending of traditional materials with the vast and ever-growing selection of synthetics has resulted in some strikingly beautiful and realistic flies.

While the expertise of many Pacific Coast tiers is immediately apparent upon inspecting some of the new patterns we now enjoy, it is not tying skill alone that has brought us the superb and growing selection of flies we now have available. In fact, many tiers who dress outstanding fly patterns are not necessarily highly skilled craftsmen. There is one crucial element though, that is sometimes overlooked when it comes to the creation of all the productive flies we now enjoy for fishing coastal cutthroat, particularly sea-runs. This connecting thread is observation — and observation is every bit as important in creating a working fly as the ability to attach materials to a hook skillfully.

The person who ties flies that consistently arouse the cutthroat to strike in its marine environment has much in common with the freshwater tier who dresses flies that regularly trigger the strike response in brook, brown, rainbow, or river-dwelling coastal cutthroat trout. In both arenas, success often lies in matching-the-hatch. The successful stillwater angler for example requires a proper selection of callibaetis or midges. A spring creek specialist strives to create the perfect scud. The angler on a freestone river needs the right Pale Morning Dun, caddis or stonefly.

It is no less essential for the Pacific Coast saltwater cutthroat trout angler to have a selection of sand lance, euphausid and herring patterns that accurately imitate the primary forage of the coastal cutthroat. While the cutthroat angler's observations may result in a highly detailed imitation of a baitfish or krill, they may also be reflected in a basic impressionistic shape, a touch of well placed flash, or just a pinch of color creatively incorporated into a pattern.

In praising the efforts of today's tiers, it is apparent that they have respected the foundation of fly tying development that was laid down in the 1930s, 1940s and 1950s by adventurous anglers who probed freshwater streams, brackish reaches of rivers and continued on into the Pacific salt. Anglers relatively new to coastal cutthroat fishing may cast jaded eyes upon flies such as Letcher Lambuth's Candlefish, Roderick Haig-Brown's Silver Brown, or Clarence Shoff's Polar Shrimp; sweeping them aside as old hat or out of date. I personally find a special pleasure in tying and fishing with traditional patterns that carry so much rich history. They are, we should remember, the solidly positioned cornerstones of West Coast fly tying upon which we are privileged to build.

I am still completely comfortable with the prospect of going after coho in the Strait of Juan de Fuca with the tried-and-true Lambuth Candlefish. I would feel equally ready for action from estuary to upper-river pools with a Silver Brown. And, I doubt if there is a self-respecting coastal cutthroat from California to Alaska that could not be coaxed into taking a swat at the reliable old Polar Shrimp. I still employ all of these patterns in my cutthroat fishing and go to them regularly.

The Reverse Spider is one of the most popular coastal cutthroat flies in Washington. It is primarily used for fresh water, but it has its moments in salt water as well.

Fly tying is an evolutionary process and not much in the craft is really new. We have hooks in astonishing variety, marvelous tying tools (many of which I have never learned to use) and no end of natural and synthetic materials. New space age materials have in fact served to both celebrate and bastardize our fly tying craft as we started incorporating the seemingly limitless array of gaudy, shimmering stuff that continues to show up on the pegs of fly shop shelves and in our flies. Fortunately, astute and insightful fly tiers have learned to integrate these new materials into their fly patterns wherever there is a genuine improvement as a result rather than allowing the material to overpower the craft.

With excellent fly-tying classes readily available through tackle shops and clubs, we no longer struggle alone under weak light dressing hooks while studying Roy *Patrick's Tie Your Own Flies* and *Pacific Northwest Fly Patterns* or Noll's *Guide To Trout Flies And How To Tie Them*. However, most of us who go back far enough to remember those days have managed to become reasonably proficient fly tiers.

With all the present day hyperbole we should be forever thankful for the leadership of our pioneer West Coast tiers whose tying skills at the vise provided the groundwork that

Leland Miyawaki searches his fly box for just the right surface popper. Leland fishes for cutthroat along the beaches of Puget Sound using his popper exclusively.

our flies are measured by today. Fly tying is a valuable tradition that provides a priceless visual chapter in the history of fly-fishing. Being such, the chronicles and craft of fly-tying should be respected, embraced, and made use of as a constant reference; then passed along to our children and grandchildren.

The fly patterns in this chapter represent everything practical that was submitted for fishing coastal cutthroat. Wherever possible the flies that appear in this chapter have been tied by the originators, or by tiers who have consented to research and contribute flies originated by other tiers. In addition, I have taken the liberty of sprinkling in a selection of my own favorite patterns developed by past masters of coastal cutthroat fly tying because they remain viable cutthroat flies to this day. The people who designed and tied these old favorites should be remembered. Some of these patterns are from my original cutthroat book along with others that have been added because they continue the historical thread that I hold important to the spirit of fly-fishing in general and coastal cutthroat fishing specifically.

I am particularly pleased with the tier's notes, so well written by fly contributors. The tier's notes are concise short courses (and some not so short) in fly tying theory and fishing techniques, historical vignettes or just fishing stories that provide a valuable new dimension to coastal cutthroat fishing and fly-tying for our immediate orientation and enjoyment. To this end I was compelled to include a selection of flies from Roderick Haig-Brown. The flies, chosen and tied by Arthur Lingren, are listed alphabetically with the patterns of all other contributors, which is, I believe, the way Roderick Haig-Brown would have preferred. Art wrote the following about his selection of Haig-Brown flies.

"It was on the waters of the Campbell back in the 1930's that Haig-Brown developed his early cutthroat trout patterns. Fashioned after salmon fry, the Silver Brown and Silver Lady were two of his earliest creations. After World War II they were followed by the Humpback and General Fry imitation. In the 1960s he added the Mysid and Asellus as he continued to experiment in tidal estuaries close by his Campbell River home."

Coastal Cutthroat Fly Patterns

The patterns listed are broken down alphabetically into two groups; freshwater, and estuary, and saltwater–and by state and province. A few of the patterns, as stated in the tier's notes, cross the line and have proven to be productive in just about any venue of the coastal cutthroat. Many older dressings were in fact routinely used in both fresh and salt water. It is my hope, along with all the contributors to this chapter that the flies herein will serve to whet your fly-tying appetite and bring about even more great flies in a continuing tribute to the coastal cutthroat trout.

The name and home town of each contributor is at the bottom of the tier's notes. If a contributor has additional patterns in this chapter the name only is listed. The classic patterns that I chose to add and tied include tier's notes. My name is listed as the tier.

Bobbie Dunn

Originator:	Peter Schwab
Tier:	Gene Fassi
Hook:	Partridge S2, size 6-8
Thread:	Sue Burgess 6/0, black
Tail:	Red bucktail
Body:	Copper wire, .020 for size 6, .018 for size 8. Body is finished with clear lacquer
Rib:	None
Hackle:	None
Wing:	White bucktail overlaid with red dyed brown bucktail

Tier's Note: "This is an old pattern that was first tied in 1928 by Peter Schwab for use on the Eel River. Although it is difficult to cast with its wire body, the Bobby Dunn has a good reputation for getting down into the deeper holes in northern California rivers." -Gene Fassi, San Rafael, California

Carmichael Spider

Originator:	Unknown
Tier:	Gene Fassi
Hook:	Partridge S2, size 6
Thread:	Sue Burgess, 6/0 black
Tail:	Red hackle fibers
Body:	Yellow yarn
Rib:	Oval silver tinsel
Hackle:	Mallard flank or pheasant rump feather

Tier's Note: "This is another vintage California pattern that has continued to be effective through the years." -Gene Fassi

Carson

Originator:	Sumner Carson
Tier:	Les Johnson
Hook:	Mustad 3906B, or equivalent size 4-8
Thread:	Danville 6/0, black
Tail:	Red hackle fibers
Butt:	Dark green chenille
Body:	Red or fluorescent red chenille
Hackle:	Brown hen hackle, three or four turns.
Wing:	White polar bear, calf tail, arctic fox or bucktail

Tier's Note: "Jim Adams, proprietor of Adams Angling in Berkeley, California informed me that the Carson, a beautiful married-wing offshoot of the Royal Coachman, was originated in about 1935 by California tier, Sumner Carson. The pattern went through several modifications during its years of popularity on the Northern California coast. The simplified version of the Carson shown here was a favorite of California writer and cane rod-builder, Claude Krieder. Although less ornate than the original, the Carson variation by Krieder is touted to be very effective on Northern California coastal cutthroat from the Eel to the Smith River" -Les Johnson

Mike's Sign

Originator:	Mike Foster
Tier:	Mike Foster
Hook:	TUE salmon hook, size 4-10
Thread:	Gudebrod orange or fluorescent orange, 3/0
Tag:	Oval gold tinsel, small
Tail:	Bright orange hackle fibers
Body:	Rear half, bright orange Danville Fuzzy Yarn. Front half, Peacock herl.
Rib:	Fine gold tinsel
Hackle:	Dark furnace, four turns
Wing:	Dark elk with light tips

Tier's Note:" I first tied this pattern for *Fly Tyer* magazine in 1981. Shortly after Mike's Sign was published a friend of mine used it to take cutthroat from the Smith River. I have since used it from California to southeast Alaska on cutthroat." -Mike Foster

Mohair Leech

Originator:	Randall Kaufmann
Tier:	Carlo Borgio
Hook:	Tiemco 200, size 8-10
Thread:	Black 6/0
Body:	Black Krystal Flash and 4 to 6 strands of black mohair
Beadhead:	Optional

Tier's Note: "I tried the Mohair Leech in several colors for coastal cutthroat in the Northern California lagoons before settling on black which has been by far the most consistent producer. I fish it with slow strips and pauses. I really enjoy looking for coastal cutthroat and have found them to be fairly abundant in tributaries of the Klamath and Trinity rivers and many headwater creeks in Northern California." -Carlo Borgio, Rhonert Park, California

Momar Leech

Originator:	Mike Foster
Tier:	Mike Foster
Hook:	Mustad 9672 or 9671. Dai-Riki 070, size 6-8
Thread:	Gudebrod or Danville 6/0 brown
Tail:	Thick bunch of brown marabou
Body:	Brown mohair (with orange and gold highlights)
Rib:	Copper wire
Hackle:	Picked out mohair

Tier's Note: "I experienced success on cutthroat in Northern California lagoons with both marabou and mohair so decided to combine the two into a single fly. Results have been good and I now use it regularly on sea-run cutthroat". -Mike Foster, Miranda, California

Sea Shrimp

Originator:	Don Harger
Tier:	Gene Fassi
Hook:	Partridge S2, size 6-8
Thread:	Sue Burgess 6/0 black
Body:	Orange wool
Hackle:	orange saddle, four turns, palmered body length and clipped on top
Wing:	Brown bucktail dyed orange, half body-length

Tier's Note: "The Sea Shrimp is used in tidal water and has been equally successful on cutthroat and steelhead. It is at its best in very clear water." -Gene Fassi

Silver Hilton

Originator:	Lloyd Silvius
Tier:	Michael Fong
Hook:	Perfect bend, size 8-12
Thread:	Black, 3/0
Tail:	Mallard flank
Body:	Black chenille
Rib:	Silver tinsel
Hackle:	Grizzly (gray)
Wing:	Grizzly hackle points

Tier's Note: "According to Jim Adams of Berkeley, California, Lloyd Silvius created the Silver Hilton around 1950. Lloyd resided in Eureka and was a protégé of Jim Pray, a tier famed for his optic patterns. I have used the Silver Hilton for sea-run cutthroat successfully in the Smith River and Stone Lagoon in northern California. I have also caught steelhead with it in rivers throughout the west". -Michael Fong, San Francisco, California

Oregon - Fresh Water

Atomic Prawn

Originator:	Keith Burkhart
Tier:	Keith Burkhart
Hook:	Eagle Claw 1197B, size 6-8
Thread:	UNI-Thread 6/0, fire orange
Tail:	Hot orange calf, tied down over hook bend
Body:	Hot orange Ice Chenille
Shellback:	Cream Swiss straw
Hackle:	Hot orange saddle
Eyes:	5/32" Nickel Real Eyes

Tier's Note: "I developed the Atomic Prawn to imitate a shrimp. With the eyes the fly rides upside down when retrieved and with the tail tied down to the bend of the hook the fly will swim from side to side. The fly works best when fished on a short sink-tip line of 5 to 7 feet. Casting close to the bank on tide-affected sections of coastal rivers, with the sink tip allows the fly to follow the contours of the bank into prime cutthroat habitat." -Keith Burkhart, Salem, Oregon

Bloody Nose

Originator:	Brian O'Keefe
Tier:	Brian O'Keefe
Hook:	2XL, down eye streamer
Thread:	Monocord, any color
Tail:	Rabbit strip, cream or buff
Body:	Diamond Braid, gold
Wing:	Rabbit strip tied at head skin side up and pulled back to tie off at hook bend
Head:	Brass bead

Tier's Note: "I've taken sea-run cutthroat up to 20-inches at Port Townsend while waiting for the Keystone Ferry. It also scored well on a trip to Southeast Alaska and along the beaches of Vancouver Island. It is a good producer in Oregon's coastal rivers as well." -Brian O'Keefe, Gates, Oregon

Borden Special

Originator:	Robert Borden
Tier:	Robert Borden
Hook:	1X long, size 4-6
Thread:	Black 6/0
Tail:	Yellow and hot pink hackle fibers
Body:	Fluorescent hot pink rabbit dubbing
Rib:	Medium silver tinsel, four turns
Wing:	White kid goat
Hackle:	Pink (7-8 turns) in front of yellow (5-5 turns) in front of wing

Tier's Note: "I originated this fly in 1961 for use on central Oregon coastal cutthroat. It has also proven to be a great pattern on sea-run cutthroat on Vancouver Island and around Gibsons, British Columbia on the Sunshine Coast." -Robert Borden, Monroe, Oregon

Claude's Favorite

Originator:	Robin L. Kaup
Tier:	Robin L. Kaup
Hook:	Mustad 3906, size 4-8
Thread:	Black 6/0
Tail:	Red and yellow hackle fibers
Body:	Rear third; hot pink chenille, middle third: flat gold tinsel, front third: one wrap, hot pink chenille
Hackle:	Red and yellow saddle, mixed
Wing:	White calf tail

Tier's Note: "While attending college in Albany, Oregon in 1975 I met Claude, head custodian at the school. We discovered a mutual love of fishing and he invited me to troll for cutthroats with him at the Alsea River tidewater area. Claude enjoyed trolling with a Ford Fender and worms. However, the second time we went, I took my fly rod. The cutthroat responded so well that Claude gave up his Ford Fenders in favor of the fly.

One of our trips to the Alsea was crowded with trollers when we came upon a school of cutthroat so thick that several would attack my fly at the same time. I took my fly away from the smaller fish so the larger cutts could grab it. Claude began netting so recklessly that I soon realized he was knocking the trout from my hook rather than netting them for the ice box. It was the last year of the ten-fish limit (at that time they still had a hatchery program).

We fished often until Claude passed away in 1985. In remembrance of his friendship, I named this fly after him." -Robin L. Kaup, Silverton, Oregon

Dry October Caddis

Originator:	Jim Taylor
Tier:	Jim Taylor
Hook:	Mustad 9672, size 8
Thread:	6/0 orange
Body:	Orange Clark's Yarn
Rib:	None
Hackle:	Furnace, palmer and collar
Wing:	Orange Clark's Yarn underwing
Antenna:	8-pound Maxima monofilament (optional)

Fish Catcher Orange (FCO)

Originator:	George Hadley
Tier:	George Hadley
Hook:	Orvis 1510 size 6-8
Thread:	Red 6/0
Tail:	Red hackle tips
Butt:	Peacock herl
Body:	Fluorescent shell pink floss or dubbing
Rib:	Small gold oval tinsel
Hackle:	Red hackle tips as throat. White marabou over hackle
Wing:	White marabou tips

Tier's Note: "The FCO is an excellent pattern for Oregon coastal streams. I fish it on a standard wet-fly swing." -George Hadley, Salem, Oregon

Glow Finn Mickey

Originator:	Jim Brik
Tier:	Jim Brik
Hook:	Daiichi 2052 Alec Jackson, silver
Thread:	Danville fluorescent flame nylon
Body:	None
Wing:	Glow-in-the-dark Mylar or Flashabou. Yellow over pink over yellow, stacked in separate bundles

Tier's Note: "I first had success with this fly on Oyster Creek on Vancouver Island in the summer of 2001. Then I used it with excellent results for silvers on Kodiak Island. I found that our Oregon coastal cutthroat respond to the Glow Finn Mickey as it swings down and across, using a drop-down rather than stripping back toward me." -Jim Brik, Salem, Oregon

Gray Hackle Peacock Variant

Originator:	John Rodriguez
Tier:	John Rodriguez
Hook:	Eagle Claw 1197B, size 6-8
Thread:	6/0 black
Body:	Peacock herl, full, twisted with Krystal Flash
Rib:	Medium copper wire
Hackle:	Grizzly mixed with red or orange
Eyes:	Bead chain or lead dumbbell

Tier's Note: "This is a good pattern for clear, sunny days when brighter colored flies seem to spook cutthroat. I used different eyes to vary the sinking rate and eliminate them for upper-river and low water use." -John Rodriguez, Salem, Oregon

JR Shrimp

Originator:	John Rodriguez
Tier:	John Rodriguez
Hook:	Eagle Claw 1197B, size 6-8
Thread:	6/0 red
Tail:	Orange calf tail, angled 45 degrees down
Body:	Mix of orange, purple, red, olive Antron seal
Rib:	Medium copper wire
Eyes:	Bead chain or lead dumbbell

Tier's Note: "This fly is used in estuarine areas and lower-river stretches. Fish it with a floating line and vary the weight of the eyes for presentation at different depths or over structure. The JR Shrimp is an unstable swimmer due to the eyes and angled tail. I fish it to emphasize its tendency to wobble with short strips and jerks while twitching the rod tip or flipping it from left to right." -John Rodriguez

October Caddis Soft Hackle

Originator:	Keith Burkhart
Tier:	Keith Burkhart
Thread:	6/0 UNI-Thread, fire orange
Hook:	Eagle Claw 1197B, size 6-8
Body:	Hot orange wool yarn
Rib:	Fine silver wire
Hackle:	Partridge flank

Tier's Note: "I developed this pattern to use when October Caddis are present on the coastal rivers of Oregon. When fished sub-surface with a floating line the fly is very effective before and during the emergence when cast to the bank and retrieved back to the boat." - Keith Burkhart

Olive Squirrel

Originator:	Lee Hibler
Tier:	Lee Hibler
Hook:	Daiichi 2051 Alec Jackson, size 7
Thread:	8/0 black or olive
Tail:	Natural gray squirrel
Body:	Front half, peacock herl. Rear half, green copper wire, fine
Wing:	Natural gray squirrel

Tier's Note: "I created this fly for Oregon coastal cutthroat. It has been effective in both salt and fresh water." -Lee Hibler

Peake's Go-Getter

Originator:	Unknown
Tier:	Les Johnson
Hook:	Size 4-8, long shank, down-eye, extra stout
Thread:	6/0 Danville black
Tail:	Red hackle fibers
Butt:	Red chenille
Body:	Yellow chenille
Hackle:	Brown, four turns
Wing:	Natural brown bucktail, length of body and tail

Tier's Note: "This is an old Oregon pattern that may have first been sold by Joe Wharton, purveyor of fine fishing tackle in Grant's Pass, Oregon who ran his shop from 1904 until 1952. I found the fly in a packet of Wharton's sample patterns labeled 'steelhead and cutthroat' given to me by the late Clarence Shoff, owner of Shoff's Sporting Goods in Kent, Washington. The Shoff Tackle Company tied this and other patterns commercially for Wharton's store. I tied a few Go-Getters and used them successfully on cutthroat in the Elk and Sixes rivers on the southern Oregon coast while fishing with Denny Hannah. I have since found the Go-Getter to be equally good in Puget Sound streams, particularly as a change-up pattern.

Pete's March Brown (PMB)

Originator:	Peter Emori
Tier:	Peter Emori
Hook:	Orvis 1877 dry fly, size 10
Thread:	Brown 8/0
Tail:	Brown hackle tips or quail tips
Body:	Brown quill
Hackle:	Brown dry fly hackle, trimmed on bottom
Wing:	Brown hen hackle tips

Tier's Note: "This is an effective coastal river dry fly, particularly in March through May in the Alsea, Siletz and Nestucca rivers. It needs to be fished drag-free or it will sink. It is best in slick water." -Peter Emori, Salem, Oregon

Red Ant

Originator:	Mike Kennedy
Tier:	Les Johnson
Hook:	TUE steelhead, size 6-12
Tail:	Red hackle fibers
Butt:	Peacock herl
Body:	Red floss or wool
Hackle:	Brown, four turns
Wing:	Red fox squirrel tail

Tier's Note: "This version of the Red Ant, developed by Mike Kennedy has been a long-standing favorite pattern for tempting half-pounder steelhead and cutthroat on the Rogue River. The dark, buggy look of the Red Ant with just a touch of red can be exceptionally good for cutthroat when brighter flies are not bringing strikes. Originally the Red Ant was dressed on small double hooks. The contemporary version of the Red Ant shown here is more commonly tied on a single hook."

Sea Runner

Originator:	Randy Sholes
Tier:	Randy Sholes
Hook:	Gamakatsu T10-3H, red, size 4-6
Thread:	Red
Underbody:	Lead wire, optional
Body:	Pearl Petite Estaz
Collar:	Lavender Polar Aire or similar substitute

Tier's Note: "The Sea Runner has been a very effective fly for sea-run cutthroat in Oregon coastal streams from tidewater to the middle and upper reaches. I cast the Sea Runner slightly downstream, mend it, let it swing and then bring it back with varied retrieves. Strikes come both on the swing and the retrieve. I use size 4 and 6 hooks as they don't seem to catch as many small fish or smolts." -Randy Sholes, Tigard, Oregon

Spruce

Originators:	Bert and Milo Godfrey
Tier:	Gene Trump
Hook:	TMC 300 or similar 6X long, heavy wire, down-eye streamer hook, sizes 4-10
Thread:	Black 6/0
Tail:	Three peacock sword tips
Body:	Rear three-quarters, red floss or wool. Front quarter, peacock herl
Wing:	Two matching badger hackles flared
Hackle:	Badger, tied as a collar

Tier's Note: "The Spruce was designed in 1918 or 1919 by Bert and Milo Godfrey, brothers who owned a hardware store in Seaside, Oregon. Bert reportedly tied the first Spruce during a camping trip with Milo on the Lewis and Clark River at the mouth of the Columbia. Bert raised his own chickens to ensure having the proper hackles. The first Spruce was tied on a standard size 8 sproat hook. The original Godfrey dressing has remained unsullied through the years although the Spruce has been tied on a variety of long shank streamer and steelhead hooks as its use expanded. Within a few years the Spruce caught on among trout fishermen throughout the west eventually becoming so popular with customers at Dan Bailey's Fly Shop in Livingston that it was often mistakenly thought to have been originated in Montana." -Gene Trump, Corvallis, Oregon

SRF Cutt-Rat

Originator:	Dwight Klemin
Tier:	Dwight Klemin
Hook:	Orvis 1510 size 6
Thread:	Green 6/0
Tail:	Pink Orvis Super Hair
Body:	Hot green floss (fluorescent)
Rib:	Gold tinsel
Hackle:	Hot pink
Wing:	Olive elk hair over pink Orvis Super Hair

Teeny Nymph

Originator:	Jim Teeny
Tier:	Jim Teeny
Hook:	Eagle Claw
Thread:	Black
Body:	Pheasant rump feather barbules twisted and wrapped forward
Legs:	Ends of rump feather points pulled down and tied off

Tier's Note: "In 1973 I designed the Teeny Nymph to entice cruising rainbow trout along the shoreline of Oregon's East Lake. I first tied it on a size 8 hook with natural pheasant to resemble a bug in its nymph stage. In the beginning years fly tiers requested additional colors of the feathers and we were able to fulfill their needs. We all tried the Teeny Nymph on other species and were successful on steelhead, salmon, bass, bluegill and all trout—including coastal cutthroat in both fresh and salt water." -Jim Teeny, Gresham, Oregon

Umpqua

Originator:	Victor O'Bryne
Tier:	Robert Borden
Hook:	1X long, size 4-6
Thread:	Black
Tail:	White kid goat
Body:	Rear half, yellow wool. Front half medium red chenille
Rib:	Small oval silver tinsel
Hackle:	Brown saddle
Wing:	White kid goat with a few fibers of red on each side

Tier's Note: "The Umpqua was designed by Victor O'Bryne in about 1936 for summer steelhead. However, it soon proved to be a great pattern for Oregon cutthroat." -Robert Borden

Washington - Fresh Water

Adult Damsel

Originator:	Dave Essick
Tier:	Dave Essick
Hook:	Mustad 94831, size 10
Thread:	White 6/0, colored with Pantone #306-T pen. Add black segment markings with a Sharpie
Thorax:	Spirit River "Fine and Dry" dubbing, damsel blue
Abdomen:	30-pound-test braided running line colored with blue and black Pantone marker
Eyes:	Umpqua mono nymph eyes, extra small
Wing:	Dark dun rooster, self posted parachute style

Tier's Note: "Several years ago in the late spring, my friend Preston and I made the short hike into Ebey Lake, a quality lake near the town of Arlington. As we made our way through the down-timber surrounding the shoreline, I

noticed a lot of damsel nymphs crawling out onto the exposed logs and stumps and that the warm morning sun was helping transform some of them into their new adult flight configuration. Some were already trying out their new wings. Never one to pass up an opportunity to fish a surface fly, I tied on one of my adult damsel patterns, cast it next to a stump and immediately had a nice cutthroat slurp it down. Preston and I rose and hooked several beautiful coastal cutthroats that were focusing in on the damselflies and were fooled by my Adult Damsel." -Dave Essick, Seattle, Washington

American Coachman

Originator:	Unknown
Tier:	Les Johnson
Hook:	Any standard wet-fly hook, size 6-10
Thread:	4/0 black Danville
Tail:	Red calf tail or bucktail
Body:	Yellow wool tapered to a heavy shoulder. Dubbing can be substituted for wool
Wing:	White bucktail or polar bear
Hackle:	Brown wrapped in front of wing

Tier's Note: "The American Coachman has been a popular, although perhaps underrated, coastal cutthroat fly for many years, especially in Washington and British Columbia."

Archie's Ghost

Originator:	Archie Herrera
Tier:	Pat Trotter
Hook:	Standard wet-fly hook, size 10-6
Thread:	Black, 6/0
Tail:	Red hackle fibers
Body:	Rear half, yellow chenille. Front half, orange chenille
Rib:	None
Hackle:	Badger, long for hook size.
Wing:	White bucktail or arctic fox tail

Tier's Note: "This is a fly from the 1960s when "harvest trout" still teemed in the waters of southwest Washington during the late summer through fall. I named this fly for an old fishing partner of mine, Archie Herrera, who passed away many years ago. This was Archie's' favorite pattern, although I don't know that it originated with him, and he didn't have a name for it. It is a variation of another old southwest Washington pattern, the Kalama Special, which was tied with an all-yellow body of chenille for sea-run cutthroat fishing.

I fish this fly where the water deepens and slows using a floating, or sometimes a sinking tip line. A 9-foot tapered leader works nicely. I twitch the fly along in sort of an active dead drift. Don't be afraid to cast right up next to obstructions and dense cover." -Pat Trotter, Seattle, Washington

Bead Soft Hackle

Originator:	Unknown
Tier:	George A. LaBlanc
Hook:	Tiemco 2312, size 10-14
Thread:	Black 8/0
Body:	11/0 gunmetal or iris seed beads
Hackle:	Partridge

Tier's Note: "This fly is fished in lakes and beaver ponds in western Washington for coastal cutthroats. In beaver ponds I fish it on a floating line with a 9- to 11-foot leader with a 6x-7x tippet. I allow the fly to sink to the pond bottom, and then retrieve with 1- to 2-foot strips and long, 20-

to 40-second pauses watching the end of my fly line for any movement to indicate a take.

In larger lakes I fish a floating line with a 10- to 14-foot leader with a 5x to 6x tippet. I allow the fly to sink to full leader depth before retrieving using a slow hand roll or figure-eight twist with short 5" to 10-second pauses." -George A. LaBlanc, Seattle, Washington

Black Spook

Originator:	Unknown
Tier:	Les Johnson
Hook:	Standard wet-fly or TUE steelhead hook, size 10-6
Thread:	Danville, black 6/0
Tail:	Black hackle fibers
Body:	Red wool or dubbing, full
Rib:	Flat gold tinsel, four turns
Hackle:	Black, four turns
Wing:	White polar bear or bucktail, body length

Tier's Note: "This is an old pattern that fills the bill for a cutthroat fly with a bright red body and white wing."

Brad's Brat

Originator:	Enos Bradner
Tier:	Les Johnson
Hook:	Any wet-fly or steelhead hook, size 4-8
Thread:	Danville black, 6/0
Tag:	Gold tinsel, three turns
Tail:	Bucktail, white over true orange
Body:	Rear half, true orange wool. Front half, red wool
Rib:	Gold tinsel, four turns
Hackle:	Natural brown
Wing:	Bottom 2/3 polar bear, bucktail or calf tail. Top 1/3 Orange polar bear, bucktail or calf tail

Tier's Note: "The Brad's Brat was originated by well-known Seattle outdoor columnist, fishing writer and angler Enos Bradner. Bradner was one of the eight founding members of the Washington Fly Fishing Club and was elected charter president in May 1939. In his book, *Western Angling* (A.S. Barnes and Company 1950), Bradner recounted using the Brad's Brat during a trip to Alaska for rainbow trout so it has been around a long time. The Brad's Brat is high on my list of attractors for sea-run cutthroat and in larger sizes has a locked in spot as one of my 'go-to' steelhead flies. The Brad's Brat calls for a bucktail wing but I like it with polar bear which adds additional translucence in the water."

Callibaetis Cripple (Quigley Cripple)

Originator:	Bob Quigley
Tier:	Les Johnson
Hook:	Gamakatsu S19, size 14-18
Thread:	Danville tan, 6/0
Shuck:	Tan Z-lon or Antron, sparse
Body:	Nature's Spirit Callibaetis dubbing
Rib:	Single strand of pearl Flashabou
Wing:	Bunch of deer hair out over the hook eye
Thorax:	Butts of deer hair, trimmed
Hackle:	Grizzly, two or three turns

Tier's Note: "The Cripple has gone through several subtle changes, and has in recent years been adopted by many tiers and shamelessly renamed. The origin of this very effective emerging dun belongs only to Bob

Quigley, of Northern California, considered by many to be one of the very best fly fishermen on Fall River. It is a 'must have' companion to the Callibaetis Parachute whenever one is fishing cutthroat in ponds, lakes or river backwaters."

Callibaetis Parachute

Originator:	Unknown
Tier:	Les Johnson
Hook:	Gamakatsu S10, size 14-18
Thread:	Danville tan, 6/0
Tail:	Coastal deer hair, barred, sparse
Body:	Nature's Spirit Callibaetis dubbing
Rib:	Single strand of pearl Flashabou
Wing:	Bunched partridge hackle tied as a post
Hackle:	two or three turns of pale grizzly hackle, parachute style
Thorax:	Nature's Spirit Callibaetis dubbing

Tier's Note: "This Callibaetis parachute pattern is no different in style from the Parachute Adams tied by Del Mazza in the late 1980s for a magazine, the name of which escapes me. There are currently many parachute dressings available that are similar. All will entice coastal cutthroats on western ponds, lakes and river backwaters when a hatch is on."

Charlie

Originator:	Ron Romig
Tier:	Ron Romig
Hook:	TMC 200, size 8-10
Thread:	Orange, 6/0-8/0
Tail:	Golden pheasant tippet
Body:	Red floss
Rib:	Brown hackle
Wing:	White calf tail

Tier's Note: "This pattern can be dressed and floated dry or fished sunk and stripped back under the surface. It works well in western rivers for sea-run cutthroat." -Ron Romig, Fall City, Washington

Chironomid

Originator:	Les Johnson
Tier:	Les Johnson
Hook:	Gamakatsu S10 or equivalent dry-fly hook, size 14-20
Thread:	Danville black, 6/0
Body:	Floss, black, brown, green or red
Rib:	Fine silver wire, optional on size 18-20
Thorax:	Peacock herl
Wing Case:	Quill section or plastic strip to match body
Gills:	White Antron

Tier's Note: "This is a basic, easy-to-tie Chironomid (midge) that does the job for me when coastal cutthroats are feeding on a midge hatch on the surface or in the film."

Conway Special

Originator:	Dan Conway
Tier:	John Olson
Hook:	Any standard wet-fly hook, size 6-10
Thread:	Black 6/0 Danville
Tip:	Small gold rope, four turns
Tail:	Red and white hackle fibers, mixed
Body:	True orange wool or dubbing, fairly thin. A second Conway version used a lighter orange body.
Rib:	Oval gold tinsel, fine, four turns
Hackle:	True orange palmered. Two turns of red hackle in front of final turn of orange.
Wing:	White goose secondary feathers, matched with red and yellow matched strips down either side
Collar:	Peacock herl, turn or five turns

Tier's Note: "The Conway Special was originated the 1930s by Dan Conway, an Irish immigrant who lived in Seattle and was referred to in Enos Bradner's book, *Western Angling*. Conway was respected as one of the all-time great tiers of coastal cutthroat flies among the Pacific Northwest tying fraternity in the 1930s and 1940s despite having only one hand and a hook.

A stickler for tying with painstakingly selected materials, Conway was always faithful to the originator when tying any pattern, never presuming to change or 'improve' anyone's fly. The original Conway Special dressed with matched and married primary wing is a beauty.

A hairwing version of the Conway Special came on the scene some years after the original and was not attributed to Dan Conway. More durable and easier to tie, the Conway Hairwing has a white bucktail wing with wisps of red and yellow bucktail down each side. Both versions remain effective and worthy of a place in anyone's cutthroat box." -Les Johnson and John Olson

Cutthroat Spider

Originator:	Preston Singletary
Tier:	Preston Singletary
Hook:	Tiemco 200RBL, Dai-Riki 270 or equivalent size 6-8
Thread:	Black 6/0
Tail:	Well-marked brown teal or widgeon flank
Body:	Rear 2/3 gold tinsel, front 1/3 hot orange dubbing
Hackle:	Sparse (no more than two turns) of well-marked brown teal or widgeon flank feather

Tier's Note: "This is a style of fly rather than a pattern. The colors may be changed to suit the tier's taste (and that of the fish). The one described here has been a favorite but an alternate version using silver tinsel, kingfisher blue dubbing and any well marked black-and-white waterfowl for hackle and tail has been effective at times. The long, sparse hackle is very mobile in slow moving water.

I fish the Cutthroat Spider quartering downstream on a floating line with a steady, stripping retrieve and concentrate on the slower-moving areas that have an abundance of cover in the form of snags, large rocks and overhanging trees." –Preston Singletary, Seattle, Washington

Dead Chicken

Originator:	Unknown
Tier:	Les Johnson
Hook:	Standard wet-fly hook, sizes 6-10
Thread:	Danville black, 6/0
Tail:	Red hackle fibers
Body:	Yellow chenille, full
Hackle:	Barred grizzly, long and soft
Alternate hackle:	Guinea

Tier's Note: This simple pattern has been effective for all coastal cutthroats in creeks, ponds, lakes and rivers for many years."

Elk Hair Caddis

Originator:	Al Troth
Tier:	Les Johnson
Hook:	Gamakatsu S10, size 12-18
Thread:	Danville, color to match dubbing, 6/0
Body:	Olive, brown, tan, green Nature's Spirit dubbing
Hackle:	Palmered hackle four turns
Wing:	Bunch of elk hair, stacked, length of body. Butts trimmed and left as stubble in front

Tier's Note: "Al Troth's world-famous caddis dry fly needs no introduction. Wherever a caddis is called for this is the one most people tie on. Coastal cutthroat working a caddis hatch take it with little hesitation."

Extended Body Baetis

Originator:	Preston Singletary
Tier:	Preston Singletary
Hook:	Standard dry fly, size 16-22
Thread:	Black or olive dun, 8/0
Tail:	2 or 4 moose body hairs, depending on fly size
Body:	Abdomen, olive tying thread built up on a needle and saturated with Soft Tex
Thorax:	Nature's Spirit Blue Winged Olive dubbing
Hackle:	Dark dun, parachute style
Wingpost:	Blue dun sparkle yarn

Tier's Note: "I was told a long time ago that sea-run cutthroat in the rivers often become quite selective on blue-winged olives in the fall. I had promised myself to act on this tip but allowed many years to pass before doing so. When I finally did I could only kick myself for not having done it much sooner.

Now, whenever I find sea-run cutthroat feeding on the surface, the *Baetis* imitations come out. Catching large cutthroats feeding on tiny mayfly imitations has to be some of the best sport that the Pacific Northwest has to offer.

This pattern is a very good, if somewhat fragile, *Baetis* imitation and the cuts seem to find it very much to their liking." -Preston Singletary

Faulk Special

Originator:	Emil Faulk
Tier:	Emil Faulk
Hook:	Standard wet fly, sizes 6-14
Thread:	Danville white, 6/0
Tail:	Red hackle fibers
Body:	True orange wool
Rib:	Gold rope, medium, four turns
Hackle:	Red, four turns
Head:	White bucktail tied with stubble at the front like an elk hair caddis

Tier's Note: "Tied by Emil Faulk in 1923, the Faulk Special, often called simply 'Faulk,' was a favorite on the Hoh, Humtuplips, Satsop, Wynoochie and other streams of Grays Harbor and the Olympic Peninsula. It was said to be especially effective in clear water conditions in size 14. The version of the Faulk shown here is a sample tied by Faulk and given to Shoff's Sporting Goods, Kent, Washington in the 1940s as a commercial tying pattern. Shoff's tied and distributed the Faulk Special to sporting goods stores throughout southwest and coastal Washington. It was a very popular cutthroat fly at Walt Failor's Sporting Goods Company in Aberdeen, Washington where it was sold from 1946 through the 1950s." - Les Johnson

Fall Muddler

Originator:	Unknown
Tier:	Curt Kraemer
Hook:	Standard TUE Steelhead hook, size 6
Thread:	Black, 6/0
Body:	Rear half; flat mylar tinsel. Front half; orange yarn or dubbing
Hackle:	Brown-dyed mallard flank, spun as a collar
Wing:	Brown-dyed bucktail
Head:	Brown-dyed bucktail clipped

Tier's Note: "This is a favorite cutthroat pattern of mine to use as a bait-fish imitation but it can pass as an October caddis as well, depending upon the color variation used. The light version uses natural mallard flank and bleached deer hair for the wing and head." -Curt Kraemer, Marysville, Washington

Fish Hawk

Originator:	Unknown
Tier:	Les Johnson
Hook:	2-3XL wet fly, size 10-6
Thread:	Danville, black or brown 6/0
Tail:	Brown mottled turkey section
Body:	Flat gold tinsel
Rib:	Gold wire, wrapped opposite direction of tinsel, optional
Hackle:	Brown, tied wet style
Wing:	Brown mottled turkey tail sections, on edge over body

Tier's Note: "The Fish Hawk, an unassuming pattern is a sleeper. The Fish Hawk was in *Pacific Northwest Fly Patterns* by Roy Patrick who established Patrick's Fly Shop in Seattle in 1946. According to Patrick, the Fish Hawk was a favorite cutthroat fly for low, clear water conditions in September and October."

Hoh River

Originator:	Unknown Hoh River guide
Tier:	Bruce M. Ferguson
Hook:	Gamakatsu SS15, size 6
Thread:	Black monocord, 3/0 or 6/0
Tail:	Marabou blood quill, light orange
Body:	Gold Diamond Braid
Rib:	None
Hackle:	Palmered lemon yellow dyed rooster neck
Wing:	Dyed light orange calf tail

Tier's Note: "I was introduced to this fly on the middle to lower reaches of the Hoh River on Washington's Olympic Peninsula a number of years ago while fly-fishing on a guided drift boat in early autumn. Pods of sea-run cutthroat were arriving fresh from the Pacific Ocean and holding in the side channel pools. Other more traditional flies just didn't compare with the "Hoh River". -Bruce M. Ferguson, Gig Harbor, Washington

Muddler Minnow

Originator:	Don Gapen
Tier:	Les Johnson
Hook:	Mustad 9575 down eye, return loop streamer, size 6-10
Thread:	Danville, brown 6/0
Tail:	Mottled turkey section on edge
Body:	Gold Diamond Braid
Wing:	Brown bucktail with turkey section on either side
Head:	Spun deer hair (brown/black/brown) cut to shape of sculpin head

Tier's Note: "Originated in 1949 by Don Gapen, the Muddler Minnow has been one of the best all-around patterns ever designed as a wet or dry fly. The first ones used for sea-run cutthroat were probably brought to the Pacific Coast from Montana. The Muddler can imitate a stonefly or grasshopper on the surface and is deadly when fished deep as a baitfish imitation. My rather scruffy version, something of a cross between a Muddler and a sculpin, has been a consistent producer over the years in both fresh and salt water."

Knudsen's Cutthroat

Originator:	Al Knudsen
Tier:	Les Johnson
Hook:	Standard wet fly, size 6-10
Tip:	Silver tinsel, four turns
Tail:	Red hackle fibers
Body:	Yellow wool, thin to medium
Rib:	Silver tinsel, four turns
Hackle:	Red hackle tied down as beard
Wing:	White over red bucktail, body length

Tier's Note: "This is one of the great Al Knudsen's excellent patterns that is still a good choice combining two popular cutthroat colors, red and yellow."

K Special, Orange

Originator:	Pat Trotter
Tier:	Pat Trotter
Hook:	Standard wet fly, size 8-10
Thread:	Black, 6/0
Tail:	Red hackle fibers
Body:	Hot orange chenille
Hackle:	Badger, long for the hook size
Wing:	White bucktail or arctic fox tail is standard. Orange buck tail or dyed arctic fox tail for the orange-orange variation.

Tier's Note: "This is my personal favorite sea-run cutthroat pattern. I first tied it back in the 1960s when I lived in southwest Washington. It actually derives from the old Kalama Special (hence the name) a sea-run cutthroat fly which is tied the same except with an all yellow chenille body. I fish the K Special Orange the same way as Archie's Ghost. For a changeup I use an orange wing, creating the K Special Orange-Orange." -Pat Trotter

Omak Ogre

Originator:	Mike Hartley
Tier:	Mike Hartley
Hook:	Standard shank wet fly, size 4-8
Thread:	Fine clear monofilament
Tail:	None
Hackle:	None
Body:	White bucktail under red bucktail, under olive bucktail. Red Flashabou sides. Top with sparse bunch of black bucktail
Head:	Build up with monofilament. Add silver Witchcraft stick-on eyes. Cover head with Hard Body or head cement

Tier's Note: "This is my version of the redside shiner, a minnow native to the west and one of the preferred forage fishes of the coastal cutthroat in rivers, ponds and lakes." -Mike Hartley, Seattle, Washington

Polar Shrimp

Originator:	Clarence Shoff
Tier:	Les Johnson
Hook:	TDE heavy wire wet-fly hook, 4-10
Thread:	6/0 black Danville
Tail:	Fluorescent red hackle fibers, length of body
Body:	Hot orange chenille, medium to full
Hackle:	Hot orange, four or five turns
Wing:	White bucktail or polar bear

Tier's Note: "The Polar Shrimp was originated in 1936 by Clarence Shoff, pioneer tackle manufacturer and owner of Shoff's Sporting Goods, a fine tackle emporium in Kent, Washington. The Polar Shrimp first gained fame in Northern California and Southern Oregon where Shoff's company tied flies commercially for shops along the Eel, Smith, Rogue, North Umpqua and Santiam rivers. It continued to gain popularity and today the Polar Shrimp is a standard with anglers from San Francisco to Anchorage not only for coastal cutthroat but salmon and steelhead as well."

Purple Poof

Originator:	Tom Hardy
Tier:	Tom Hardy
Hook:	Tiemco 200R, size 6-8
Thread:	Black Monocord
Tail:	Purple marabou
Body:	Black Crystal Seal
Rib:	None
Hackle:	None
Head:	Silver bead
Wing:	Purple marabou, tied in front of bead

Tier's Note: "I like this fly due to its rather wacky action with the wing tied in front of the bead." –Tom Hardy

Reverse Spider

Originator:	Mike Kinney
Tier:	Mike Kinney
Hook:	TMC 200R, 4-10
Thread:	To match body, 6/0
Tail:	Lady Amherst tippet
Body:	Medium chenille, black, yellow, pink, orange or red
Hackle:	Lady Amherst tippet, mallard or goose flank
Wing:	None

Tier's Note: "I started fishing for sea-run cutthroat as a six-year old boy in a small creek behind my home in Marysville, Washington. In about 1975, a friend, Merle Paddock, took me cutthroat fishing in a boat on the Stillaguamish River. This marked the beginning of my real education on fly-fishing larger streams for sea-run cutthroat.

Merle used a sink-tip fly line and a little black-bodied spider with a white chicken hackle and a bump of chenille behind the hackle to hold it out for more action as it was stripped through the water quickly.

I began experimenting with mallard flank which has longer, stiffer barbules that stand up to more abuse in the water. It worked better than chicken hackle but had a tendency to zip itself back together. Then, at the Monroe State Fair I saw a Lady Amherst pheasant skin and the white hackles glowed. It was just what I was looking for. Tied backwards the Lady Amherst not only held up better but also produced much more attractive action. I also use mallard with white or yellow bodies for low, clear water or over spooky fish. Amherst however remains my favorite for fresh-run fish with black being the best for low light and yellow or pink for bright light. Other tiers have told me that they also use red and orange-bodied Reverse Spiders with success." -Mike Kinney, Arlington, Washington

Royal Trude

Originator:	Carter Harrison
Tier:	Les Johnson
Hook:	Gamakatsu P10-2L1H or equivalent 2X long dry-fly hook
Thread:	Danville black, 6/0
Tail:	Small bunch of deer or elk hair. Black moose optional.
Body:	Butt and shoulder; peacock herl. Center band; Royal Coachman red floss.
Wing:	White deer hair or calf tail, fairly full and evened, length of body and tail
Hackle:	Two Royal Coachman brown hackles wound thick to support the long-shank hook
Head:	Black

Tier's Note: "The Royal Trude was first tied as a joke by New Yorker Carter Harrison and presented to his friend, an Idaho rancher named A.S. Trude. This caddis-style variation of the Royal Coachman proved to be no joke, quickly becoming established as an excellent cutthroat fly from Wyoming to Washington, Alaska to California. At one time or another I've raised coastal, westslope, Yellowstone and Snake River cutthroat to the Royal Trude. I keep a couple stashed in each of my trout boxes."

Royal Wulff

Originator:	Lee Wulff (Series named by Dan Bailey)
Tier:	Carol Ferrera
Hook:	Partridge SEB or Wilson TUE, size 10-14
Thread:	Black 6/0
Tail:	Moose body hair
Body:	Peacock herl with red floss center band
Wing:	White calf tail upright and divided
Hackle:	Royal coachman brown, full

Tier's Note: "I began tying and using the Royal Wulff several years ago on the Coeur d' Alene River in Idaho while fishing with my sister Rose and brother-in-law Tom. It often brought up those westslope cutthroats when nothing else would. When I began fishing for sea-run cutthroat I tried the Royal Wulff in the North Fork Stillaguamish River. I was delighted to discover that it works just as well on the coastal cutts has it does on their westslope cousins." -Carol Ferrera, Redmond, Washington

Salmon Migrant Fry

Originator:	Clifford A. Barker
Tier:	Clifford A. Barker
Hook:	2xl medium wire, size 6-10
Tail:	None
Body:	Mix pearl with either pink or olive gray Angel Hair
Throat:	Red or pink Krystal Flash, sparse
Wing:	Rolled mallard flank feather over sparse pearl Krystal Flash
Head:	Olive deer hair spun and clipped Muddler style. Leave it longer over the back

Tier's Note: "I designed the Salmon Fry Migrant to imitate salmon fry and parr in Western Washington rivers. I fish it down and across and along the edges of current seams and tail outs. The Salmon Fry Migrant is also good around any structure such as rocks, root wads, logs, gravel banks and creek estuaries. Retrieve the fly in 6-inch to 1-foot strips. It works equally well for coastal cutthroat or Dolly Varden." -Clifford A. Barker, Bellevue, Washington

Silver Minnow

Originator:	Unknown
Tier:	Les Johnson
Hook:	Gamakatsu SL11-3H, Mustad 3407, or equivalent, size 4-10
Thread:	Danville, black 6/0
Tail:	None
Body:	Small silver tinsel or rope
Wing:	Mallard flank tied flat over sparse bunch of blue hackle fibers, deer hair or calf tail

Tier's Note: "The Silver Minnow is a nearly forgotten classic with a bit of Canadian influence from Roy Patrick's book, *Pacific Northwest Fly Patterns* that can be very good during low, clear water conditions. Patrick liked this easy-to-tie pattern for coastal cutthroat fishing from July to the end of the season."

Skagit Minnow

Originator:	Ken McLeod
Tier:	Les Johnson
Hook:	Gamakatsu SL11-3H, or equivalent
Thread:	Danville, black 6/0
Tail:	Peacock sword
Body:	Silver tinsel with peacock sword over the top
Head:	Black chenille, small, two turns

Tier's Note: "This Ken McLeod original was probably the earliest effort by a Washington fly tier to imitate chum or pink salmon fry that migrate out of Washington coastal rivers in the spring. The Skagit Minnow is still a good fly worthy of a spot in every coastal cutthroat angler's fly box, not only for use in rivers but estuary fishing as well."

Snoqualmie Spider

Originator:	Tom Hardy
Tier:	Tom Hardy
Hook:	Tiemco 200R, sizes 6-8
Thread:	Black monocord
Tail:	Amherst pheasant overlaid with Pearl Krystal Flash
Body:	Black or yellow Angora goat or other seal substitute
Rib:	None
Hackle:	Guinea, reversed
Wing:	Pearl Krystal Flash, tied like a post, almost straight up
Head:	Silver bead

Tier's Note: "This is another variation on the traditional sea-run cutthroat spider. I like them a little less beefy than those available in tackle stores. The fly is very sketchy and the Krystal Flash seems to be an important addition. I usually fish from a boat and cast to the banks, a traditional cutthroat fly-fishing technique. All sizes of the Snoqualmie Spider listed will work but the size 6 helps to discourage smolt attacks or at least hook-ups.

Like most spider patterns, you cannot fish this one wrong. Cutthroat take it dead drifted or streaking through the water—and every retrieve in between. You just have to see what turns them on during any given day. One-foot strips seem to be the easiest and most consistent method. I rate the yellow and black versions about equally effective." -Tom Hardy, Kirkland, Washington

Split Wing

Originator: Glenn Young
Tier: Glenn Young
Hook: Gamakatsu T10-3H, size 2 and 4
Thread: 6/0, tan waxed nylon
Body: Gray foam cut into stripes and wrapped forward with yellow dubbing at front
Rib: None
Hackle: Grizzly
Wing: Caribou or blonde elk

Tier's Note: "I tie the wing angled back and split. The wings must be divided evenly or the fly will tilt in the water." -Glenn Young, Puyallup, Washington

Stillaguamish Special

Originator: Unknown
Tier: Les Johnson
Hook: Gamakatsu T10-6H, size 4-10, or equivalent wet fly hook
Tip: Silver tinsel or rope, small
Tail: Red and white hackle fibers
Body: Yellow wool, thin, palmered with yellow hackle
Hackle: Red, four turns
Wing: White bucktail or polar bear with a few strands of red mixed in
Head: Peacock collar four turns

Tier's Note: "Once one of the most popular patterns in Washington for coastal cutthroat, the Stillaguamish Special became a standard on streams all along the Pacific Coast. It is still a good choice as a basic yellow coastal cutthroat fly."

Trailing Shuck Midge Emerger

Originator: Preston Singletary
Tier: Preston Singletary
Hook: Any standard dry-fly hook, size 18-20 or to match hatching midge (some may be as large as size 10)
Thread: Color to match hatching midge (commonly black, gray, olive, tan, 8/0 UNI-Thread
Tail: A few fibers of tan or yellowish-tan sparkle yarn
Body: Tying thread, thin with a slight taper toward the thorax
Hackle: Parachute-style, dark dun for darker-colored midges, medium or light dun for lighter-colored ones
Wingpost: Sparkle yarn, to match the shuck; if visibility is a problem use white, it's easier to see and doesn't seem to put the fish off

Tier's Note: "I first tied this pattern for use on a small lake in the foothills of the Cascades that has a self-sustaining population of coastal cutthroat. Although the fish were obviously feeding on emerging midges one morning and, while I was hooking one from time to time on my usual midge emerger (a sort of floating Chironomid pupa imitation), they were ignoring my fly more often than not. I was finally able to observe a couple of fish rising close to my float-tube and to see that they were selectively taking midges which were almost fully emerged, but had not yet completely escaped from their trailing nymphal shucks.

When I got home that afternoon I sat down at the vise to see if I could come with a suitable imitation that would have the slender abdomen and humped thorax of a typical midge. This pattern was the result and has since proven to be very effective when and wherever trout are taking midges; not just cutthroats but rainbows and browns as well." -Preston Singletary

Wingless Bomber

Originator:	Glenn Young
Tier:	Glenn Young
Hook:	Gamakatsu T10-6H, sizes 2 and 4
Thread:	6/0 tan waxed nylon
Tail:	Brown bear
Body:	Deer butt/antelope body/deer head
Rib:	None
Hackle:	Grizzly
Wing:	None

Tier's Note: "I trim the head slightly downward so the fly can be pulled under the surface in rough water." -Glenn Young

Estuary and Salt Water

Bed and Breakfast

Originator:	Mike Croft
Tier:	Mike Croft
Hook:	Mustad 34011, size 4-6
Thread:	Gudebrod clear monofilament, fine
Tail:	None
Body:	None
Rib:	None
Hackle:	None
Wing:	Brown bucktail over white bucktail, one-half each, mixed with a few strands of Flashabou
Eyes:	Witchcraft stick-on, small
Head:	5-minute epoxy

Tier's Note: "This pattern was originally known as the B&B for bucktail on bucktail since bucktail is used for both the white and the dark hair. The dark hair is the part of a white bucktail that we often throw away when the white is used up. The B&B was soon being called by a more common interpretation, Bed and Breakfast. I like this fly because it is inexpensive and easy to tie.

I fish the B&B in shallow water near shore, rarely working over bottoms more than six feet deep. It produces well when young smelt, herring or candlefish are present." -Mike Croft, Tacoma, Washington

Blair's Baiter

Originator:	Blair Alexander
Tier:	Blair Alexander
Hook:	Tiemco 9394, size 4 through 8
Thread:	Olive, 3/0
Tail:	None
Body:	Pearl Diamond Braid
Rib:	None
Hackle:	None
Wing:	Chartreuse over white bucktail
Cheek and Lateral line:	One strand of Flashabou down each side.
Head:	Build up head with thread. Epoxy over thread and stick-on eyes

Tier's Note: "I first tied the Baiter about ten years ago. It is my first choice for saltwater beaches around Puget Sound. The Baiter is an all-around pattern having taken not only cutthroat but also coho and chinook salmon, Dolly Varden and one steelhead at Bush Point." -Blair Alexander, Seattle, Washington

Burgess Braided Baitfish

Originator:	Peter Burgess
Tier:	Peter Burgess
Hook:	Daiichi #2546 (size 4 or 6 for cutthroat)
Thread:	Fine monofilament
Body:	Clear wire looming with silver Flashabou inside
Wing:	Sparse bucktail or synthetic hair topped with flash. I like Wing 'n Flash topping.
Eyes:	Adhesive mylar
Head:	Three coats of epoxy

Tier's Note: "I originated this pattern to imitate the Pacific sand lance, an important forage fish for the coastal cutthroat trout. The black wing with emerald green topping has been my favorite color combination although the lavender and light olive seems to be equally effective. The Braided Baitfish is light for its size, very durable and of medium buoyancy. Fished with long strips and it has an enticing, jig-like action. It can also be dead drifted in moving water and holds itself naturally as it swings through the current at the end of a drift. Colors shown are; black/emerald green flash, light olive/olive flash, lavender/purple flash." –Peter Burgess, Tonasket, Washington

Cam's Mini Tube Candlefish

Originator:	Bill Knox
Tier:	Cam Sigler
Tube:	1/2" of 1/8" I.D. hard tubing with 1/2" of 1/8" I.D. PCV tubing for hook holder
Tube Body:	Braided silver mylar
Thread:	Danville clear monofilament, fine
Wing, Top:	Olive FisHair and pearl Flashabou. Middle: Yellow FisHair
Bottom:	White FisHair
Eyes:	2mm Witchcraft stick-on
Head:	Braided pearl mylar tubing covered with 5-minute epoxy

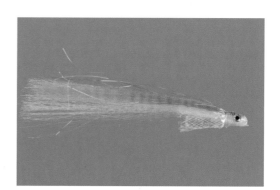

Tier's Note: "I cannot take credit as the originator of this fly. I learned about tube flies when I first moved to Washington in the late 1960s from Bill Knox of Vashon Island. At the time he used them to troll for salmon. I tie this particular pattern to imitate baitfish that cutthroat trout and coho salmon feed upon when they are cruising the beaches around Vashon Island. I usually fish this fly on a sink-tip line. It is a great generic baitfish pattern that takes fish all year around. If I need a smaller bait I simply snip off a bit of the FisHair to match smaller baitfish.

The most productive retrieve is a series of four or five short strips, pause and then strip again. I've had cutthroat take this fly within a foot or two of the beach. Other colors I use are (with colors listed top to bottom); black/yellow white; blue/green/white; red/yellow/white; purple/yellow; and purple/yellow/pink." -Cam Sigler, Vashon Island, Washington

Clouser Minnow

Originator:	Bob Clouser
Tier:	Les Johnson
Hook:	Gamakatsu SL11-3H, size 4 and 6
Thread:	Monofilament or Danville flat waxed nylon to match fly color.
Eyes:	Spirit River Real Eyes Plus or Hot Real Eyes. 3/16" for size 4; 5/32" for size 6.
Wing:	Underwing, white bucktail or FisHair. Topwing, chartreuse or fluorescent green bucktail or FisHair.
Flash Tail:	Silver Flashabou under top wing

Tier's Note: "An East Coast striper guide, Capt. Tony Biski told me one

day while we were fishing off of Cape Cod that the chartreuse and white Clouser Minnow 'is the most popular fly in America' and he is probably right. The Clouser Minnow can be tied large or small, bulky or sparse for freshwater or salt, with bucktail or synthetic fibers – and it nearly always produces. During the past several seasons the Clouser Minnow has become increasingly popular with Washington and British Columbia anglers. It is tied in a variety of color combinations including some of the West Coast classics like the Lambuth Candlefish and Coronation. Other combinations that work well include blue over white; blue over green over white; red over yellow; or olive over white. Tie your favorite streamer or bucktail Clouser style and you are likely to be delightfully surprised how cutthroats will land on it." -Les Johnson

Cutthroat Candy

Originator:	Steve Raymond
Tier:	Steve Raymond
Hook:	Size 8, 2X fine
Body:	Brown nylon or polypropylene wool
Hackle:	Chocolate brown, palmered under the overlay
Overlay and wing:	Dark brown deer hair tied in with the tips pointing aft then pulled forward over the back forming the overlay. The tips are then tied back forming the wing.

Tier's Note: "The inspiration for this pattern came from Lloyd Frese's Salmon Candy series developed for Hosmer Lake. Lloyd used a deer-hair overlay to improve the floatation and I learned to tie the Salmon Candy series under his tutelage. Using his design as a starting point I first tied the Cutthroat Candy as an adult caddis imitation and fished it with great success at Hosmer and in a number of BC lakes, although I never bothered to give it a name. But when I began using it in estuaries it became even more successful than it had been in fresh water, quickly becoming my standard pattern for sea-runs. That is when I began calling it the Cutthroat Candy.

I think the Cutthroat Candy is the first dry fly used for cutthroat in salt water. I started using it in the winter of 1974. By then I'd been fishing sea-runs for about five years, using the tactics I had learned from others, primarily Ed Foss. Essentially these were to search for rising fish and then cover the rises with a sinking pattern. With those tactics you could go a long time between rises and when you finally saw one and covered it, the chances of getting a strike were not very good. I decided there had to be a more efficient way to catch sea-runs and it suddenly occurred to me if I were fishing them in fresh water I would cover the rises with a dry fly. That is what led me to start experimenting with dry flies in the estuaries.

I found that using a dry fly as a searching pattern is far more effective than using wet flies. Even when no rises are visible, a skated Cutthroat Candy often brings up fish whose presence otherwise would go undetected. I've also risen steelhead, coho and chinook salmon and sea-run Dolly Varden to this fly. I've seldom used a wet fly since that day in 1974 when I first used the Cutthroat Candy." -Steve Raymond, Whidbey Island, Washington

Disco Sand Lance

Originator:	Les Johnson
Tier:	Les Johnson
Hook:	Gamkatsu SS15, size 6-8
Thread:	Clear, fine monofilament
Body:	Silver Flashabou reinforced with monofilament criss-crossed.
Wing:	Pearl green Flashabou topped with bright green Flashabou. Wing should be sparse
Eyes:	Spirit River mini bead chain, anodized black
Head:	Built up with bright green flat waxed nylon covered with two coats of Softex.

Tier's Note: "This is a late-season fly that appeals to cutthroat and coho salmon that are marshalling around the mouths of creeks before moving back into fresh water."

Euphausid

Originator:	Don Simonson
Tier:	Don Simonson
Hook:	Mustad 3408 or Mustad 3407, size 4-8
Thread:	Red, 6/0
Tail:	Strands of pearl Flashabou
Body:	Medium white chenille
Beard:	Strands of pearl Flashabou
Head:	Red, 6/0

Tier's Note: "Euphausids, amphipods and cocapods, generally known as krill, are residents of our Puget Sound estuaries. Sea-run cutthroat delight in feeding on these tasty morsels. I have found krill to be evident in the estuaries throughout the year. This pattern has become my go-to fly, which usually is the one I start out with when fishing a shoreline or estuary. I like to fish it using either a floating line or an intermediate sinking line. Wading and casting out into small tide rips and retrieving with short, 4" to 8-inch strips is an effective method. I personally enjoy fishing from my pram and casting into the shoreline, normally starting my retrieve with the fly in a foot of water or less.

A variation of this pattern that is also effective is a pink chenille body, black head and the same pearl Flashabou." -Don Simonson, Seattle, Washington

Ferguson's Green & Silver

Originator:	Bruce M. Ferguson
Tier:	Bruce M. Ferguson
Hook:	Single; Mustad 34011, size 6. Tandem (front) Mustad 34007, size 6 (trailer) Daiichi 2556, #6
Thread:	Black monocord, 3/0, waxed
Body:	Rear half, silver Diamond Braid. Front half, four turns of medium chartreuse chenille
Tail:	Short bunch of white polar bear
Wing:	White polar bear, calf tail or bucktail, 1 1/4 to 1 1/2 inches long
Sides:	Four or five strands of pearl Krystal Flash
Eyes:	None or optional stick-on black on silver

Tier's Note: "This fly was originated in the early 1970s for Washington's Puget Sound resident coho salmon. However, when fished close along the beach, it has proven to be a steady, year-around producer on sea-run cutthroat. In fact, you never know that it is not a coho you've hooked until you see the brownish, spotted back and square tail of the cutthroat.

The tandem hook tie (not shown) is great for coho salmon since they habitually strike short, plucking at the trailing wing. The rear hook greatly increases hookups. When you know cutthroat are present though, it is best to go with the single hook version since cutthroat generally don't hesitate to smack the fly full bore, often swallowing it or gilling themselves on the trailer hook. This is nearly always a fatal situation for the cutthroat."
-Bruce M. Ferguson

FJ Pink

Originators:	Bruce Ferguson and Les Johnson
Tier:	Les Johnson
Hook:	Gamakatsu SP11-3L3H, size 6-10
Thread:	Fine monofilament, clear
Tail:	A few strands of pale pink Krystal Flash
Abdomen:	Pale pink Nature's Spirit or Wapsi dubbing.
Back:	Clear Scud Back or Thin Skin strip
Rib:	Micro Stretch tubing to match body
Thorax:	Pale pink Spirit River dubbing topped with Clear Scudback or Wapsi Thin Skin
Eyes:	Spirit River mini bead chain, anodized black
Legs:	A few strands of Krystal Flash. Pick out the dubbing with a bodkin to simulate legs

Tier's Note: "This is an accurate representation of a euphausid since I tied it from University of Washington School of Fisheries identification photos blown up and supplied by my detail-oriented friend, Bruce Ferguson. The FJ Pink (FJ for Ferguson/Johnson) has, since its conception several years ago as a salmon fly, also proven to be an outstanding cutthroat pattern throughout Puget Sound and into the lower reaches of rivers. For often-effective variations, tie the FJ Pink with the same materials in cerise, pale orange or off-white." -Les Johnson

Frank's MVP

Originator:	Frank Vangelder
Tier:	Frank Vangelder
Hook:	Sproat, standard shank, size 6
Thread:	Brown
Tail:	Brown grizzly saddle hackle
Body:	Medium brown floss
Rib:	Salmon colored thread
Hackle:	Brown grizzly saddle hackle

Tier's Note: "This fly is effective from spring through fall. I've fished it over rocky shores and smooth, sandy areas as well and had good luck on both types of beaches. The fly is allowed to sink as far down as safely possible without snagging and then hopped along the bottom in quick, 4- to 6-inch strips with a few short pauses. Sometimes cutthroat will follow it fly in quite a ways before they hit, so don't give up on it. The MVP gets aggressive strikes from cutthroat and salmon—and has accounted for quite a few flounder as well. The name stands for Frank's Marine View Park, but the connotation of MVP is well deserved for this fly." -Frank Vangelder, Tacoma, Washington

Gripper

Originator:	Steve Damm
Tier:	Steve Damm
Thread:	Clear fine monofilament
Tubing:	3/4" of 1/8" ID hard tube with short soft tube hook holder. Add a turn of Twist On lead for weight
Body:	Sparkle Flash, pearl, or green pearl.
Wing:	FisHair, olive green
Overwing:	Two strands of black Flashabou
Sides:	Slender grizzly hackle
Eyes:	Stick-on, small, black on silver
Head:	5-minute epoxy or Sally Hansen's Hard-As-Nails

Tier's Note: "I have fished this fly for several years in the early part of the season when cutthroat and Dolly Varden are waiting in estuaries or along beaches near river mouths to ambush outbound salmon smolts. When cutthroat or Dollies hit the fly there is no doubt about it, which is why I call it the Gripper." -Steve Damm, Seattle, Washington

Guinea and Gold Sea-Run Spider

Originator:	Gary Oberbillig
Tier:	Gary Oberbillig
Hook:	Tiemco 206, Mustad 37160, Gamakatsu C12U, size 10.
Thread:	Orange, 6/0
Tail:	Golden pheasant crest
Body:	Transparent stretch tubing (medium) over base of tying thread
Hackle:	Golden pheasant crest, 3-4 turns. Orange dyed guinea, 1-2 turns
Wing:	Root beer Krystal Flash, 4-6 strands
Eyes (Optional):	Hourglass, mini or micro size wrapped and secured with Super Glue

Tier's Note: "Fish this fly as though it might be a shrimp and chances are the cutthroat will agree. Let it sink deep in the water column and retrieve it in short, deliberate strips. It is best when fished during the two hours before and the two hours after high tide. The orange version has generally been most dependable but the pink dressing has been surprisingly effective for large fish. The design of the Guinea and Gold Sea-Run Spider is simply my recombination of good ideas from several sources. The use of golden pheasant crest as hackle has been popularized by Mike Croft with his Croft Bead Head Spider, a highly regarded pattern for waiting period coho salmon in South Puget Sound. The segmented body is a bit like a fat Bowstring Spider. The Krystal Flash along with trusted cutthroat colors and guinea hackle surely can't do any harm." -Gary Oberbillig, Olympia, Washington

James Peach

Originator:	James Schmidt
Tier:	James Schmidt
Hook:	Mustad 34011, size 6
Thread:	Chartreuse
Body:	Fluorescent orange chenille, medium
Rib:	Silver wire wrapped counter to chenille
Head:	Chartreuse chenille, medium
Wing:	Polar bear with four strands of silver Flashabou topping

Tier's Note: "This is my most productive sea-run cutthroat pattern. The body of orange and chartreuse is, in my opinion, the best color combination for sea-run cutthroat. I usually fish this fly right on the beach with an intermediate line using short, quick strips." -James Schmidt, Seattle, Washington

Johnson's Beach Fly

Originator:	Les Johnson
Tier:	Les Johnson
Hook:	Gamakatsu SP11-3L3H or SS15, size 6-12
Thread:	Danville fluorescent orange, 6/0
Tail:	Sparse bunch of fluorescent orange calf tail
Rib:	Flat gold tinsel
Body:	Spirit River seal dubbing, or Danville wool, light fluorescent orange, brushed out.
Hackle:	Brown neck hackle, four turns
Wing:	White polar bear, Arctic fox or calf tail, length of body and tail, sparse

Tier's Note: "The conception of this fly is simple. I wanted a pattern just a bit lighter orange than the Polar Shrimp or Thor. The Beach Fly has taken cutthroat trout, coho and chum salmon from Puget Sound beaches and pink salmon all the way north to the Queen Charlotte Islands. I believe that the success of this fly is attributable to the pale fluorescent orange color of the body that shows through the white wing when the fly is wet. It is highly visible in the water yet not too garish. I consider a basic orange fly with a white wing a necessity in anyone's cutthroat fly box."

Knudsen Spider

Originator:	Al Knudsen
Tier:	Bob Young
Hook:	Mustad 34011, or equivalent long-shank hook, size 6
Thread:	Danville 6/0
Tail:	Mallard flank fibers
Body:	Medium black chenille
Rib:	Flat silver tinsel, optional
Hackle:	Mallard flank

Tier's Note: "Al Knudsen, first tied this fly, originally called the Wet Spider, in the 1930s. It became very popular for cutthroat trout on the Stillaguamish River. Any originality to the pattern I have contributed is the dressing down or simplification associated with the way I tie it. I have used this fly through many seasons and at all times of the year and find that it works to some extent almost all of the time. A novice tier can knock this pattern out quickly and easily. The materials are simple, readily available and a snap to apply.

Fishing mostly from beaches of Puget Sound, decorating driftwood and rocks (the result of low back casts) is not very expensive with the Knudsen Spider. It is compact enough to cast with a 5- or 6-weight and takes cutthroat just as well as it takes Puget Sound resident coho salmon. The Knudsen Spider also has a substantial enough silhouette to tempt mature salmon in the fall. Black always seems to work best for me but yellow or orange versions make a nice change-up." -Bob Young, Seattle, Washington

Lambuth Candlefish

Originator:	Letcher Lambuth
Tier:	Les Johnson
Hook:	Gamakatsu SS15 or SP11-3L3H, size 4-8
Thread:	Danville black and clear monofilament
Body:	Flat silver Mylar tinsel strengthened with a criss-cross pattern of clear monofilament
Wing:	Bucktail or FisHair. Underwing; mixed light blue and green. Median; small amount of red. Overwing: French blue and olive mixed

Tier's Note: "One of our early Washington saltwater tiers, Letcher Lambuth went to great lengths to imitate the colors of Puget Sound baitfish by dying

his own polar bear and comparing his flies with the actual fish in a fish tank. Lambuth's attention to detail resulted in a very effective pattern that has stood the test of time in Washington and British Columbia. Originally tied on large hooks with dyed polar bear for coho salmon, it is now more often tied with bucktail or FisHair. Dressed on smaller hooks the Candlefish is a great cutthroat fly from spring through fall."

Marabou Candlefish

Originator:	Mike Croft
Tier:	Mike Croft
Hook:	Mustad 34011, Size 4-6
Thread:	Gudebrod clear monofilament, fine
Tail:	None
Body:	None
Rib:	None
Hackle:	None
Wing:	Marabou, Olive over tan over white, one-third each
Gills:	Red thread
Eyes:	Witchcraft stick-on, small, covered with epoxy

Tier's Note: "I originated this fly in 1993 in an attempt to make a better swimming candlefish (sand lance) pattern. This fly has worked very well for both cutthroat and coho salmon. I dress it on a long shank hook for cutthroat and a short shank hook for coho. It works best very close to the shoreline where young candlefish dwell. This fly looks funny until it gets thoroughly wet. For variations use dark olive/chartreuse, brown, black or pink marabou." -Mike Croft

Marabou Clouser Minnow

Originator:	Bob Clouser
Tier:	Mike Croft
Hook:	Mustad 34011, Size 4-6
Thread:	Black, 6/0
Tail:	None
Body:	None
Rib:	None
Hackle:	None
Wing:	One-half white marabou, one-half brown marabou with a few strands of Flashabou mixed in

Tier's Note: "Tom Wolf took my original Marabou Candlefish pattern and tied it Clouser style. This has turned into our most consistent South Puget Sound cutthroat fly. Fished in six to twelve feet of water and letting it settle a for a few seconds before retrieving works best. The fly is more durable and lasts longer than one would expect. When tying the Marabou Clouser, keep it less than two inches in length." -Mike Croft

Miyawaki Beach Popper

Originator:	Leland Miyawaki
Tier:	Leland Miyawaki
Hook:	Gamakatsu Octopus size 2 and 4. Front hook shank only is used. Barb is cut off upon completion of tying. Rear hook is secured with double loop of 25-pound-test Maxima leader
Head:	Edgewater Dink Component, size 4 and 6. Colors can be varied
Thread:	3/0, match popper color
Wing:	Matched grizzly hackles, chartreuse or yellow, tied to cove together. Add six uneven lengths of Krystal Flash down each side of the feathers. Add a strip of holographic mylar down each side topped with a sparse bunch of polar bear or equivalent

Tier's Note: "Richard Kamrar of Gig Harbor showed me his surface popper some nine years ago. I really liked his idea and began experimenting with — and modifying — Kamrar's original concept until I arrived at the popper I use exclusively on the beaches today.

I use a 6-weight rod, floating line and a 15' leader tapered to 3x. I fish along our local Puget Sound beaches where I can utilize the movement of the tide to pull my popper. Think of the popper as a wounded baitfish and that you are appealing to the natural predatory instincts of fish that are cruising the beaches looking for something good to eat.

Retrieve the popper with short pulls or jerks, making sure that you leave a v-wake. It is not necessary to make it spray or hop. If you get a follow retrieve twice as fast to taking the fly. If you get a hit, let the popper play dead then twitch, or change direction with your rod tip. Cutthroat should hit the fly before it reaches your rod tip. If the fish turns away at the beach, pick up and direct it immediately back out into the water in the direction the fish was last seen. Oftentimes the fish will literally fly out of the water to pounce on the popper. Always retrieve the popper all the way in. Just before you pick up, stop and make a quick change of direction with your rod tip. If you see a fish boil, drag the fly across the water parallel to the beach with the rod tip. This will usually do the trick. I'm sure you'll find that fishing with a popper is the most fun you can have on a beach—with your clothes on." -Leland Miyawaki, Kent, Washington

Nothing - With An Attitude

Originator:	Jim Koolick
Tier:	Jim Koolick
Hook:	Tiemco, salt water, size 4 to 8
Thread:	Black, 8/0
Tail:	Polar Flash
Body:	Spirit River New Age Volcano, hot pink, 1-1/2 turns
Hackle:	Polar Flash
Head:	Thread base covers front 1/3 of hook shank. Extend Polar Flash 1/3 longer than hook shank. After tying in the hackle, finish off the head bullet style

Tier's Note: "I fish this fly off the Puget Sound beaches using a rapid, short-stroke retrieve. The Nothing-With an Attitude is particularly effective in low light. In addition to sea-run cutthroat, the Nothing- With an Attitude entices coho salmon and has accounted for a variety of flounder and rockfish. My favorite size is a sparsely dressed number 8."
-Jim Koolick, Seattle, Washington

Omnibus

Originator: Wes McGaffey
Tier: Curtis E. Jacobs
Hook: Mustad 3906B, size 6 or 8
Thread: Black, 6/0
Tail: Plume from base of red, yellow and white hackle quill, mixed
Body: Peacock herl, 4 or 5 strands
Rib: Fine oval silver tinsel
Hackle: Red, yellow and white, two turns of each
Wing: Fine polar bear or calf tail

Tier's Note: "Wes McGaffey was using this pattern well before he joined the Washington Fly Fishing Club in the early 1960s. He used the Omnibus regularly in the South Puget Sound area as well as in Hood Canal near Mission Creek around Belfair. Wes regularly fished for sea-runs wading out in hip boots. He fished it both with floating and sinking tip lines."
-Curtis E. Jacobs, Bothell, Washington

Polar Bear Baitfish

Originator: Capt. Tom Wolff
Tier: Capt. Tom Wolff
Hook: 1/8 " I.D. hard tube with soft tube hook holder
Rib: Wrap tubing with silver mylar tinsel or sleeve with braided mylar piping
Wing: Green over white polar bear hair or substitute
Eyes: Silver Witchcraft eyes with black pupils

Tier's Note: "This is my go-to fly when cutthroat are keying in on Northern anchovy. It also works as a sand lance along the beaches. I now tie all my baitfish patterns on tubes." -Capt. Tom Wolff, Sumner, Washington

Pregnant Guppy

Originator: Preston Singletary
Tier: Preston Singletary
Hook: Gamakatsu SP11-3L3H, size 8
Thread: Fine monofilament tying thread
Body: Silver Diamond Braid and a strip of white, 2mm closed-cell foam, approximately 3/16" wide
Wing: chartreuse or olive Seahair, chartreuse Krystal Flash and dark brown Krystal Flash, layered, sparse
Eyes: Chartreuse Spirit River 2.5 mm stick-on eyes

Tier's Note: "I've been interested in floating patterns for coastal cutthroat in salt water ever since being introduced to Steve Raymond's and Leland Miyawaki's waking flies. I had hoped that a pattern that looked a little more like a wounded baitfish would result in a better strike-to-hookup ratio, unfortunately this has not proven to be the case. Although I don't hook and land as many fish on the surface patterns, they do engender a lot more activity, and the variety and violence of the surface rises make it a very exciting way to fish.

I fish this fly on a floating line, casting at about a 45-degree angle along the beach, and varying the retrieve to find something that will interest the cutthroat (or coho). The pattern will sometimes float on its side and creates a variety of disturbances in the surface film, ranging from a smooth v-wake to a sputter and pop, depending on how fast it is retrieved."
-Preston Singletary

Puget Power

Originator:	Jimmy LeMert
Tier:	Jimmy LeMert
Hook:	34011 Mustad, size 6
Thread:	Clear monofilament, fine
Body:	None
Wing:	White hair topped with a few strands of olive hair. Pearl Flashabou down sides, sparse.
Eyes:	Witchcraft eyes covered with Softex

Tier's Note: "I rarely have much time to tie flies which was the reason for developing the Puget Power. It is a very simple sand lance pattern that I can knock out quickly. I've landed cutthroat throughout Puget Sound with this little fly all year long. It is at is best though in late spring through early summer when the young-of-the-year sand lance are emerging along Puget Sound beaches." -Jimmy LeMert, Seattle, Washington

Ray's Fly (Reduced)

Originator:	Ray Bondorew
Tier:	Seth Taylor
Hook:	Gamakatsu SC15, size 6-2
Thread:	Olive, 6/0
Body:	Pearl Flashabou
Wing:	Light olive bucktail over yellow bucktail, sparse
Topping:	Strands of peacock herl
Cheek:	Jungle cock neck feathers, matched

Tier's Note: "This is a reduced version of Ray Bonderew's Striper Fly, a pattern well known with New England anglers as a killer for striped bass. I have reduced the basic Bonderew dressing to better imitate a Pacific sand lance, essential forage for sea-run cutthroat in salt water. I use it as an alternate to my Marabou Sand Eel." -Seth Taylor, Seattle, Washington

Seth's Marabou Sand Eel

Originator:	Seth Taylor
Tier:	Seth Taylor
Hook:	Gamakatsu SC-15, size 4-6. TMC 800, size 8
Thread:	White Danville, 6/0
Body:	Marabou fibers, olive over maroon over yellow over white. Single strands of pearl or olive Flashabou are layered between each color of marabou. Short mono loop can be placed on shank of hook under marabou for anit-fouling.

Tier's Note: "This is a sparse, reduced version of a sand eel that I used for fishing stripers in my native state of Maine. When I relocated to Washington I simply pared down my favorite striper patterns and started incorporating northwest color schemes into their dressings. An important color that began showing up in my streamers was the red lateral line first used by Pacific Northwest fly tying innovator and legend, Letcher Lambuth. Capt. Tom Wolf and Mike Croft have tied similar patterns for use in Washington's South Puget Sound. Several tiers along the way have actually arrived at some form of a marabou fly for cutthroat and coho in salt water." -Seth Taylor

Silicone Candlefish

Originator:	Cam Sigler Jr.
Tier:	Cam Sigler Jr.
Hook:	Owner Spinnerbait, size to match fly
Bottom Wing:	White FisHair over silver Flashabou
Top Wing:	Blue FisHair, blue Flashabou
Eyes:	Witchcraft black on silver
Special Instructions:	When the fly is completed, coat the wing completely with silicone or Softex, forming it into a tapered, bullet shape. A rattle may be pushed up into the fly and covered with silicone after the initial coating. Let the fly dry and it is ready to use.

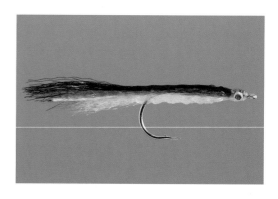

Tier's Note: "This pattern is a basic streamer. The difference from most streamers or baitfish imitations is that I add silicone or Softex to the wing, which stiffens it and maintains a larger silhouette when bigger baits are needed. The silicon application also keeps the wing from wrapping around the hook when casting during windy conditions. I fish the Silicon Candlefish in several quick strips, a pause and then quickly strip again." -Cam Sigler, Jr., Vashon Island, Washington

Silver Bullet

Originator:	John Olson
Tier:	John Olson
Hook:	Mustad 34011, Size 6
Thread:	Black, 6/0
Tail:	None
Body:	Silver Cactus chenille
Wing:	Pearl Krystal Flash. Alternate: silver Krystal Flash

Tier's Note: "The Silver Bullet is my go-to fly in salt water for cutthroat and coho salmon. It is a very simple but effective pattern. My first choice is the pearl wing but the silver-wing version is a good change-up. I fish the Silver Bullet with a clear camo intermediate line just below the surface, stripping it erratically to imitate a frightened or wounded baitfish." -John Olson, Seattle, Washington

S. S. Candlefish

Originator:	Roger Stephens
Tier:	Roger Stephens
Hook:	Tiemco 9394, size 6
Thread:	Fine clear monofilament
Sequin:	8mm pearl (found at most craft stores)
Body:	Pearl Sparkleflash over shaped, closed-cell foam form
Tail:	Pearl Krystal Flash or white bucktail
Topping:	Peacock herl over entire fly
Eyes:	Stick-on, black on silver
Gills:	Red permanent marker
Finish:	5-minute epoxy.

Tier's Note: "Cutthroat and coho tend to strike this fly aggressively. However, you have to be quick on the trigger when setting the hook or you will miss the grab, particularly if you have a lot of line on the water. The SS Candlefish is a good searching pattern. If there are any sea-run cutthroat present they will generally hit it within a couple of casts. Move down current if there are no takers. Cover a lot of water with this fly as it does bring them up.

If the SS Candlefish is not skating or popping continually on the surface the tail material may be wrapped around the hook. Cutts won't hit it when this happens. Stiffer material helps to reduce tail-wrapping the fly.

I cast the fly at 45 to 90 degrees down current and skate it with the current when the line bellies, or pop it and pause, then let it swing. I repeat this action until it is straight down current. The up-current retrieve can be skated and popped continuously, or with a 1- to 2-second pause between strips. Both retrieves take fish." -Roger Stephens, Olympia, Washington

Williams Point Sand Lance

Originator:	Les Johnson
Tier:	Les Johnson
Tube:	HMH
Hook:	Gamakatsu SC-15, size 2-8
Thread:	Fine, clear monofilament
Tail:	None
Wing:	Olive over gray over white bucktail, sparse
Topping:	A few strands of olive pearl Flashabou
Median line:	A few strands of silver Krystal Flash
Eyes:	Spirit River mini bead chain, anodized black.
Head:	Softex over the entire head, two coats.
Black Phase:	Substitute black hair for overbody and black Flashabou for topping.

Tier's Note: "This pattern is named after its inauguration on Williams Point at Lincoln Park in Seattle, a great late-season cutthroat beach. Sand lance often swarm the shallows at Lincoln Park, where they are preyed upon by cutthroat trout and resident coho salmon. The sand lance range in size from little more than an inch, up to four inches. I carry the Williams Point Sand Lance in a variety of sizes to "match the hatch."

The olive phase is good on overcast days with the black phase best on sunny days. It has a very realistic baitfish shape and the hair rarely wraps around the hook during casting. The bead-chain eyes provide just enough weight so that when I stop the retrieve the fly dives for the sand — just like a real sand lance attempting to avoid becoming an entrée for a feeding sea-run cutthroat."

Woolhead Sculpin

Tier:	Mike Croft
Originator:	Unknown
Hook:	Mustad 34011, size 4-6
Thread:	Tan 6/0
Body:	Tan chenille
Back:	Tan Indian hen, Matuka style
Rib:	Small oval tinsel
Hackle:	None
Pectoral Fins:	Partridge
Gills:	Red floss
Wing:	Tan wool
Head:	Tan wool

Tier's Note: "The Woolhead Sculpin is not a year-around fly. It works best for me when small sculpins show up in less than a foot of water along beaches and around boat ramps, usually from June through December. The fly fishes best when cast and retrieved. I don't know who invented the first Woolhead-style sculpin since there are many variations of the pattern around. All I did was match the color to the shallow-water sculpins found in South Puget Sound. I tie the pattern in tan through dark brown." -Mike Croft

Cuddler

Originator:	Cecillia "Pudge" Kleinkauf
Tier:	Cecillia "Pudge" Kleinkauf
Hook:	Mustad 9672 size 8-10
Thread:	UNI-Thread, 6/0 tan
Tail:	Deer hair, half the length of the hook shank
Body:	Dubbed hare's ear with Antron, tan
Rib:	Gold
Hackle:	None
Wing:	Deer hair extending just past tail
Head:	Elk hair clipped caddis-style

Tier's Note: "I fish the Cuddler (part caddis, part Muddler) in the spring when cutthroats are chasing salmon smolt that are outmigrating to the ocean. It works best with short, erratic strips." -Pudge Kleinkauf, Anchorage, Alaska

Linda's Lovely Unit (LLU)

Originator:	Loyal J. Johnson
Tier:	Loyal J. Johnson
Hook:	Mustad 3665A, size 8-12
Thread:	Danville flat waxed, black
Body:	White wool yarn
Rib:	Silver mylar or oval tinsel
Wing:	20 strands of peacock Krystal Flash with grizzly hackles tied along each side, streamer style
Eyes:	Chrome dumbbells in front of black thread built up as a thorax

Tier's Note: "I developed this fly for coastal cutthroat trout in Sitkoh Creek, Chickagof Island, Alaska. It is named for a pleasant young lady named Linda. The LLU works well in spring when fish are migrating from streams for the sea. I cast out into deep pools, let it settle and bring it back in 6 to 10-inch strips. The LLU works not only on cutthroat but all other salmonids; coho and chum salmon, Dolly Varden, grayling and rainbow trout. -Loyal J. Johnson, Sitka, Alaska

Thorne River Emerger

Originators:	Dan Lemaich and Les Johnson
Tier:	Les Johnson
Hook:	Gamakatsu SS15 or SP11-3L3H, size 6 through 12
Thread:	Danville black 6/0
Tail:	None
Body:	Silver Mylar tinsel reinforced with fine monofilament criss-crossed.
Wing:	Underwing, white Super Hair, sparse. Midwing, pink Super Hair, a few strands. Topwing, olive Super hair, sparse.
Topping:	Peacock herl, sparse
Median Line:	One strand of Krystal Flash down each side.
Eyes:	Mini, black Spirit River bead chain

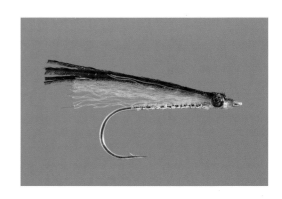

Tier's Note: "Dan Lemaich and I developed the Thorne River Emerger one evening over a couple of glasses of Bushmills in 1994 during a fishing trip to Prince of Wales Island, Alaska. It was tied to imitate tiny pink and chum salmon fry emerging from the gravel to head downstream for Clarence Straight and the Pacific Ocean. That day we had been fishing the Thorne River and each time a surge of salmon fry would emerge from the gravel to head downstream, schools of hungry cutthroat would waylay them in a frenzy that whipped the surface of the Thorne River to a near froth. Not knowing that tiny pinks and chums were triggering the orgy, we had been attempting to catch the cutthroat with what we had in our boxes, finally hooking one suicidal cutthroat on a Hair's Ear nymph. The cutthroat was killed for the next day's breakfast, cleaned and found to be jammed with little salmon fry. That evening we tied a few reasonable imitations from materials available at the lodge tying bench. The following morning when Dan and I cast our new creations into a melee of feeding cutthroat we hooked up almost simultaneously and the Thorne River Emerger was born. In larger sizes it has proven to be a better than average imitation of emerging sand lance and when tied on size 10 and 12 hooks it continues to gain favor on streams where pink and chum fry emerge from the gravel each spring to run a gauntlet of hungry cutthroat in their effort to reach the Pacific. The black bead chain eyes give the Thorne River Emerger just enough nose weight to give it an erratic up and down swimming action but not enough to make it difficult to cast or turn it upside down." - Les Johnson

Tony's Pretty Good Fly

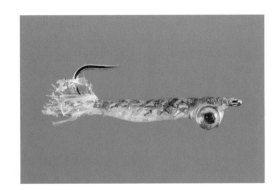

Originator:	Tony Soltys
Tier:	Tony Soltys
Hook:	Tiemco 9394, silver, size 6-10
Thread:	Clear, fine monofilament
Body:	Pearl Body Braid unraveled at hook bend as tail. Top tinted with olive permanent marker (Prismacolor PM-27 or PM-28.
Eyes:	Nickel-plated barbells with Witchcraft stick-on eyes.

Tier's Note: "Tony's Pretty Good Fly works well in still or running water, fresh or salt in the Juneau area. It often works well in size 10 when fish ignore larger sizes or other patterns. The best retrieve for the fly is short strips and pauses" -Tony Soltys, Juneau, Alaska

British Columbia, Canada - Fresh Water

Blue Ninja

Originator:	Dr. Hiro Imai
Tier:	Rory E. Glennie
Hook:	Mustad 9672, size 8
Thread:	Black 6/0 UNI-Thread
Tail:	Black hackle barbules
Body:	Pale blue yarn or chenille
Rib:	None
Hackle:	Black, palmered sparsely
Wing:	None

Tier's Note: "My good friend and oftentimes fishing companion, Dr. Hiro Imai from Tokyo, Japan, is an astute observer of the fish's world. He has a home along the banks of his beloved Oyster River where he stays while on visits to Canada. Hiro loves to fly fish for cutts in the river. He saw that there are some big stonefly nymphs in the river which the cutthroats seem to relish. These particular nymphs appeared to exhibit a bluish cast about their exoskeleton. In about 1986 Hiro came up with a simple and very effective rendition of the black nymphs. He started with a pale blue body and wrapped it sparsely with a poor-grade hackle feather. He wanted to give the fish the bare impression of one of the stonefly nymphs. As well, he wanted and easy-to-tie, cheap pattern that could be lost to a snag on the bottom without too much grief. The Blue Ninja has gained local acceptance as a must-have pattern for many of the sea-run waters of Vancouver Island.

Hiro likes to fish during the low-light hours particularly in the evening when sca-runs probc boldly into shallow waters searching for these nymphs.

Hence, he named his creation in deference to those mythical martial arts warriors of his homeland that operate best under the cover of darkness - the Ninja." -Rory E. Glennie, Gold River, British Columbia, Canada

Bulkley Mouse

Originator:	Andre LaPorte
Tier:	Les Johnson
Hook:	Wilson dry fly, size 6-8
Thread:	flat waxed nylon to match deer hair
Tail:	A few strands of pearl or blue Krystal Flash extending just beyond deer hair tips.
Body:	None
Wing:	Thick build-up of black-dyed or natural deer hair on top of the hook shank and not much longer than the hook shank
Head:	Deer hair clipped full to push a lot of water.

Tier's Note: "I first used the Bulkley Mouse on the Bulkley River near Telkwa, British Columbia while fishing with guide Andre LaPorte several years ago. This high floating skater proved to be outstanding at bringing dour steelhead to the surface. When I returned home I began using it on occasion for steelhead on Puget Sound rivers. When skated it has proven to bring explosive strikes from cutthroat as well as steelhead. Like other surface offerings, cutthroat seem to miss the Mouse as often as they connect with it. When they nail it squarely though, the grab is heart-stopping. The black Bulkley Mouse has a blue Flashabou tail and the natural has a pearl Flashabou tail."

General Fry

Originator:	Roderick Haig-Brown
Tier:	Arthur Lingren
Hook:	Low water salmon, size 4-6
Thread:	Black
Tail:	Small orange or red feather tip or section
Body:	Flat silver tinsel
Rib:	None
Wing:	Yellow, orange, blue and green dyed polar bear mixed with white polar bear.

Tier's Note: "The Campbell River is home to most Pacific salmon and rather than dress imitations of coho, chinook, chum or pink fry, Haig Brown turned his fly tying talent towards producing an all-purpose imitation. In Fisherman's Spring (1951), for his all-purpose fry imitation, Haig-Brown recommends a pale red or orange tail which both the Silver Lady and Silver Brown sport. All of his other flies had silver bodies and that important feature was also retained. A hairwing rather than the conventional feather-strip wing, because hairwings had more movement; polar bear rather than bucktail because it was more translucent and flexible; and a variety of colors; orange, yellow, blue, green and white perhaps to cover the many different light conditions encountered in a day's fishing." -Arthur Lingren, Vancouver, British Columbia

Gold Rolled Muddler

Originator:	Tom Murray
Tier:	Barry Stokes
Hook:	4xl, size 6 to 12
Thread:	Fluorescent red
Tail:	Mallard flank, dyed gold.
Body:	Medium flat gold mylar tinsel.
Rib:	Fine gold wire
Hackle:	None
Wing:	Mallard flank, dyed gold, over 4 strands of gold crystal Flashabou.
Head:	Gold-dyed deer hair clipped top and bottom with a few hairs left down each side as a lateral line. Leave red thread exposed at rear of body and under head.

Tier's Note: "The Gold Rolled Muddler is most effective when fished close to the bottom with short, quick erratic strips. It can also double as a fry pattern if fished higher in the water column. Colors can be varied to imitate different specific fry. Try rusty orange for coho and olive/orange for chum." -Barry Stokes

Humpback

Originator:	Roderick Haig-Brown
Tier:	Arthur Lingren
Hook:	Low water salmon, size 8
Thread:	Black
Tail:	Yellow hackle fibers or golden pheasant crest
Body:	Flat silver tinsel
Rib:	None
Hackle:	Yellow
Wing:	Mixed green and blue polar bear hair with a few strands of peacock sword overall as topping

Tier's Note: "While runs of coho, chinooks and chums number in the thousands, the pink salmon returned to many British Columbia streams in the tens of hundreds of thousands and to some in the millions. They are late summer and fall spawners with the eggs incubating over winter and hatching in the spring, when they immediately begin their seaward migration. The small fry are a feast of spring when in the millions they emerge from the gravel into the jaws of opportunistic cutthroat trout.

"Haig-Brown thought that the fly dresser should strive to reproduce the characteristic silver-blue-green of the humpback fry. His Humpback fly was his attempt and about this pattern, in Fisherman's Spring (1951), he asserts that it "is an effective fly when the humpback fry are going down in good numbers' and that 'it has also caught fish, including steelhead and coho salmon....much later in the season.' (p.33)." –Arthur Lingren

Invicta

Originator:	James Odgen (Circa 1880)
Tier:	Stuart McIntosh
Hook:	Tiemco 5262 or Mustad 94840, 2xL, size 8-12
Thread:	Brown
Tail:	Yellow from golden pheasant topping
Body:	Dubbed seal (ginger and yellow mixed).
Palmered Hackle:	Ginger, clipped short
Rib:	Oval gold tinsel
Hackle:	Blue jay, throat only
Wing:	Hen pheasant tail

Tier's Note: "I have no idea what the Invicta, an old pattern from the

United Kingdom, imitates from the trout's pantry but it has worked for me on browns in Britain and cutthroats near Comax. I first purchased this pattern in the 1960s. I usually fish it on a 13-foot leader from a floating line with very little movement. A strike indicator 5-feet up from the fly is sometimes useful." -Stuart McIntosh, Comax, British Columbia

Orange Knudsen

Originator:	Al Knudsen
Tier:	Conall Connelly
Hook:	Mustad 3906, size 8-12
Thread:	Red, orange or black, size 4/0 or 6/0
Tail:	None
Body:	Orange seal fur blended one-half red, one-half yellow
Rib:	Flat or oval, silver or gold tinsel
Hackle:	Gray mallard flank feather

Tier's Note: "This pattern is a variation of the Knudsen Spider. I have found it most effective in rivers during low, clear water. I fish it across and down, mending as required either with a natural drift or occasional short twitches or pulses. I have also taken jack coho on both variations of the Knudsen Spider and once, a steelhead on the number 8 orange. I also tie a Red-Yellow Knudsen variation with the rear 1/2 of the body yellow and the front 1/2 orange." -Conall Connelly, Campbell River, British Columbia

Oyster Grub

Originator:	Stuart McIntosh
Tier:	Stuart McIntosh
Hook:	Tiemco 200R or 5263, sizes 10-14.
Thread:	Black
Tail:	None
Body:	Ginger seal dubbing, teased out to form legs
Back:	Black wool, five strands pulled over dubbing
Rib:	4 to 6-pound test monofilament leader material
Tail:	None
Wing:	None
Head:	Black wool or thread

Tier's Notes: "Roy Dash and I had been fishing the lower reaches of the Oyster River all of a July day. We new the cutthroat were in; 10-inch to 15-inch fish had shown themselves by rising consistently but not to anything we tossed their way. Then Roy caught one just at quitting time. It being a keeper, he took it home. Next morning Roy called me to say that upon cleaning the cutthroat he had found three or four "caterpillar-like" grubs in it, about 1/2 to 3/4-inches long. They had black heads and underbodies about the same color as the weedy, muddy coating on the riverbed rocks. To the tying benches! I tied up four imitations of the grubs from Roy's description and we met back at the Oyster River later that day. Understand that this was before I added the nylon rib to give the fly some resistance to sharp cutthroat teeth. By the time I had caught five fish from 10 to 17-inches, the first grub had "had it."

The duration of effectiveness for the Oyster Grub seems to be from early July to early September, perhaps coinciding with availability of the natural.

We fish the Oyster Grub on a 13-foot leader and either a floating line in slow moving water or a medium sink tip in moving water, retrieving with 4-inch pulls. I've seen both caterpillars and caddis larvae/pupa that look like the Oyster Grub. A taxonomic identification of the natural would be interesting." Stuart McIntosh - Puntledge River

Puntledge

Originator:	Rory E. Glennie
Tier:	Rory E. Glennie
Hook:	Mustad 9671, size 6
Thread:	Uni-Thread, black 6/0
Tail:	Mallard flank or bronze shoulder feather
Body:	South American Kid fur, dubbed rough and spikey.
Rib:	fine oval gold tinsel
Hackle:	Barred rock or natural brown rooster feather
Wing:	Wild goose secondary flight feather strips.

Tier's Note: "Back in the 1920s young Jack Hames sneaked a well-chewed trout fly from his father's fly wallet. Jack was a bright, inquisitive youngster who loved to fish the local waters near his home in Courtenay on Vancouver Island. He pursued the sea-run cutthroat with a passion. Jack found that this dull, unimpressive looking "borrowed" wet fly — without a name at the time — was a killer. He opined that the dubbed fur body was the main active ingredient. The fur did not mat together when wet but stood out in relief while under water. After that sole fly was snapped off on a bad cast he went searching for the right fur to make copies. Years passed without a suitable material being discovered until one day while pawing through his mother-in-law's sewing basket he came upon a spikey gray patch of fur that served as dubbing for many of his killer flies–and then the small piece of fur was used up.

His long-time friend Bob Taylor from Vancouver took the last small bit of fur from Jack for a sample and proceeded to track down the mystery fur. It turned out to be South American Kid at a local furrier. Now they both had a source for the right dubbing. Only then did Jack name the fly after his home stream, the Puntledge River.

The Puntledge has also been my home river since the 1970s. In the late 1980s the same Bob Taylor passed along a swatch of South American Kid fur to me, telling me about its history. I still use the Puntledge River pattern just as Jack Hames showed it to me. It is a good bet to use well upstream when the sea-runs are searching for caddis and provides me with a link to a bit of true sea-run fly-fishing history." -Rory Glennie

Silver Brown

Originator:	Roderick Haig-Brown
Tier:	Arthur Lingren
Hook:	Low water salmon, size 6-8
Thread:	Black
Tail:	Small whole Indian crow feather
Body:	Flat silver tinsel
Throat:	Natural red-brown hackle
Wing:	Slender strips of golden pheasant center tail feather enclosing a few strands of orange polar bear hair.

Tier's Note: "Developed in the 1930s as an imitation of a cutthroat trout or coho salmon fry, Haig-Brown claims that the Silver Brown is an effective cutthroat pattern for "maturing fish in August and September" (The Western Angler, vol., p.174). Tommy Brayshaw was with Haig-Brown on September 4, 1936 at the Campbell's Canyon Pool and later recorded in his diary that Haig-Brown "got three of 3-3/4, 1-3/4 and 1-1/4 on a slim, silver-bodied fly: #6 low water hook, brown hackle and golden pheasant tail wing."

Haig-Brown's original dressing didn't include the orange polar bear hair; that came later and the full dressing is given on page 32 of Fisherman's Spring (1951). In that book Haig Brown recommends that it be fished just under the surface and worked slowly and that it is just as likely to move a steelhead to the surface as it will a two or three-pound cutthroat." -Arthur Lingren

Silver Lady

Originator:	Roderick Haig-Brown
Tier:	Arthur Lingren
Hook:	Low water salmon, size 6 or larger
Thread:	Black
Tail:	A small, whole golden pheasant tippet feather
Body:	Flat silver tinsel
Throat:	Badger hackle
Wing:	Two badger hackles side-by-side, slender strips of teal, four strands of peacock herl with a golden pheasant tippet topping overall.

Tier's Note: "The Silver Lady stirs fond memories of steelhead, Dolly Varden and cutthroat trout that I have taken on this eye-catching pattern. Haig-Brown designed this fly to imitate salmon fry and found that it was especially good as "an early season fly, effective for feeding trout when spring and dog salmon fry are abundant." (*Fisherman's Spring*, p.32)." -Arthur Lingren

Tryityou'lllikeit

Originator:	Peter Caverhill
Tier:	Peter Caverhill
Hook:	Tiemco 9394, nickel-plated size 8
Thread:	Fine clear monofilament
Tail:	Yellow hackle fibers
Body:	Bright olive green Antron, wool or floss
Wing:	Yellow hackle fibers, sparse
Eyes:	Plastic bead chain (translucent bright green)

Tier's Note: "The green version of the Tryityou'lllikeit described here has been the most effective for me. I have tied this fly with different colored plastic bead-chain eyes and different wing, tail and body combinations. However, I haven't had a chance to fish the other colors although I feel that they should work well. The hook size is worth fooling with but my preference is to use fairly small flies with a size 8 being standard and a size 10 being a good option in really shallow water or slow current situations.

This fly has accounted for coho, char and chum salmon in addition to cutthroat. I have given the pattern to other anglers and they have also taken fish with it. Most often I fish the Tryityou'lllikeit on a clear, intermediate sinking line such as the Scientific Anglers Stillwater or Cortland Camouflage intermediate. I fire out the longest possible cast (to cover the maximum area) and retrieve the cast in fairly rapid foot and-a-half long pulls. It rides with an every-so-slight upward bias on the front. The eyes do not really add weight; in fact there may almost be some buoyancy affect from them." -Peter Caverhill, Port Moody, British Columbia

Arrowhead Sculpin

Originator:	Loucas Raptis
Tier:	Loucas Raptis
Hook:	Tiemco 9394, size 6
Thread:	Grey, 3/0 pre-waxed
Tail:	Mallard flank feather
Rib:	Small oval silver tinsel
Body:	Olive dun dubbing tied 2/3 up the hook shank
Wing:	Rabbit strip, chinchilla color
Over-wing:	A mallard flank feather cut into a V and folded over the wing. Two strands of pearl Flashabou on either side.
Throat:	A piece of grizzly hackle fluff cut into a V and tied by the stem so that the stem functions as a weed guard.
Head:	Natural color deer hair, spun and clipped into the shape of an arrowhead.
Olive Variation:	All materials are the same in the olive phase of the Arrowhead Sculpin except that they are dyed olive rather than natural.

Tier's Note: "In the spring of 1993, when I went to the beach for the first time looking for sea-run coastal cutthroat, I was directed to the mouth of a little creek flowing into Bazan Bay just north of Victoria. As I was crossing it, I couldn't fail to notice the dozens of sculpins darting in all directions. These were all Tidepool Sculpins (Oligocottus maculosus), speckled gray in general appearance and between 2 and 4 inches in length.

After observing them for a while, I went home and tied the Arrowhead Sculpin as an imitation. On my first trip back, fishing with this pattern, I hooked two beautiful sea-runs in quick succession. Since then, the Arrowhead Sculpin has been a very consistent pattern in the mouths of little creeks, in tidal pools of larger rivers and near eelgrass beds, where my olive variation works best. Fishing it with a sink-tip line in the main body of rivers, I have caught sea-runs on a dead drift as well as on the retrieve. Along the beach I fish it with a clear intermediate fly line and cast it almost parallel to the shoreline. I let it sink close to the bottom and retrieve it with quick, short strips but with many pauses in between. The natural week guard in the form of pectoral fins makes it a particularly practical pattern when fishing over eelgrass or when there is troublesome flotsam in the water." -Loucas Raptis, Victoria, British Columbia

Asellus

Originator:	Roderick Haig-Brown
Tier:	Arthur Lingren
Hook:	Size 8
Thread:	Black
Body:	Olive-dyed seal fur
Rib:	Fine gold wire
Back:	Peacock herl
Hackle:	Badger

Tier's Note: "Haig-Brown's Asellus imitation had a bulky olive seal's fur body with a back tied in at the hook bend and again at the eye. And, to give that ever-so-critical-to-success life and movement, Haig-Brown wound on, just behind the hook eye, a large, soft badger hackle. With the enthusiasm that fly tiers who fly fish often have for their creations, this pattern showed great initial promise but then "tapered off from the dramatic to the normal." (Fisherman's Fall, p.119). -Arthur Lingren

Barry's Ultimate Deceiver

Originator:	Lefty Kreh
Tier:	Barry Stokes
Hook:	Mustad 34007, size 6 or 8
Thread:	Fine monofilament
Tail:	White saddle hackles, 4 to 6
Body:	Pearl Diamond Braid
Rib:	None
Hackle:	None
Throat:	White polar bear past hook bend
Wing:	Peacock herl over blue-died polar bear. Pearl Flashabou down each side of wing.
Head:	Dark blue glitter nail polish over chartreuse glitter nail polish. 1.5 mm stick-on eyes. Epoxy overall.

Tier's Note: "The Barry's Ultimate Deceiver is a basically a Lefty's Deceiver, the standard saltwater streamer in the fly-fishing industry. What I've done is tie it in a small version for our western cutthroat and cohoes, and then added some contemporary materials to make it more effective in our British Columbia waters.

I use the Deceiver either casting to actively feeding fish or as a searching pattern. I cast out and vary countdown times before beginning my retrieve. I alternate the retrieve speed and method until a productive result is achieved." -Barry Stokes, Victoria, British Columbia

Crystal Mickey

Originator:	Unknown
Tier:	Rory E. Glennie
Hook:	Eagle Claw 1197B, size 6
Thread:	Danville black, 6/0
Tail:	None
Body:	Silver Poly Braid
Rib:	None
Wing:	Layered; 3/4 yellow polar bear hair, 1/4 red polar bear hair (over yellow)
Topping:	12 strands, Pearle scent Crystal Hair over wing

Tier's Note: "This fly was originally tied as an eastern brook trout fly by Toronto anglers and proved to be so effective that it was named the Assassin. It was renamed the Mickey Finn by renowned author, Gregory Clark and introduced to the fly-fishing world in 1936 by another noted author, John Alden Knight. It is a venerable fly, which I had used for sea-runs for many years. A simple fly which works well most of the time but most of the time is not good enough. I wanted to fiddle with the pattern to improve its allure. Topped with pearl Flashabou it was an ace pattern for coho salmon but a dud on sea-run cutthroat. Then I turned to playing with Crystal Hair as a topping of the basic color scheme and that was it. It was, I figured, bound to be noticed by the fish at a greater distance than was the plain original.

The sea-runs have approved of my tinkering. I find that the Crystal Mickey attracts the interest of cutthroat throughout the season and becomes a bona fide first choice searching pattern for both salt water beaches and larger upstream pools of the sea-run's home rivers." -Rory Glennie

Golden Needle

Originator:	Rory E. Glennie
Tier:	Rory E. Glennie
Hook:	Eagle Claw 1197G, Size 8
Thread:	Black, 6/0 Uni-Thread
Tail:	None
Body:	None
Rib:	None
Hackle:	None
Wing:	Mixed dyed polar bear hair (white, blue, green, yellow, red, and black). Mixed wing should be sparse and about 1-1/2 inches long.

Tier's Note: "Juvenile needlefish (sand lance), share the same near-shore coastal beaches with sea-run cutthroat. At times these small (1-1-1/2 inch long) baitfish are a prime food source for cutthroats. As they mature, needlefish move into deeper water further from the beach becoming less available as a food source for the shore-hugging cutthroat. Exploring needlefish nurseries provides good opportunity for exploiting the sea-run's penchant for eating baby needlefish.

The north shore of Tsapee Narrows in Clayoquot Sound on the west coast of Vancouver Island is a good place to witness this piscatorial interaction. Tsapee Narrows separates Meare's Island from Esowista Peninsula at Tofino. The tidal current rages through the center of the Narrows at about 7 knots. Ramparts of rock jutting from the northern shoreline create a long, near shore, slow water back eddy; the nursery. My years of guiding cutthroat seeking fly fishers highlighted the importance of intimately knowing such areas.

When sea-runs key in on a baby needlefish "hatch" they can becoming stubbornly single-minded in their preference for a suitable imitation The melding of various hues of dyed hair in each of these patterns impart a spectral, luminous impression of a tiny baitfish. For the most part I find that impressionism stands head and shoulders above precise imitation when it comes to duping sea-run cutthroat trout. This fly is best when tied on a gold-plated hook." -Rory Glennie

Holder's Sea-Through

Originator:	Dan Holder
Tier:	Dan Holder
Hook:	Mustad 34007, Size 4-8
Thread:	Green Monocord
Tail:	Red calf, trimmed
Rib:	Oval silver tinsel
Body:	Light olive/brown yarn or dubbing
Wing:	Polar bear or bucktail, long and sparse
Hackle:	Full natural brown
Head:	Green Monocord with painted eyes (optional).

Tier's Note: "This pattern was originally tied by mistake as a wrong version of the American Coachman, but with its shortened olive-colored body, large green head and long, sparse wing, it instantly proved itself a lot more effective than any comparable coachman-like pattern. In its first try on sea-runs along Bazan Bay in Sidney, the Sea-Through hooked three fish on three successive casts (at the amazement of competent companions who had been fishing the same water without success). Along the beaches of Fulford Harbor and on Saltspring Island it is the sure fly and just recently it turned out to be deadly on difficult coho salmon in the tidal waters of the Sooke River. It is most effective in my experience when stripped very slowly.

My speculation behind its effectiveness is that it imitates small baitfish, which often appear translucent in the water with their abdominal area and head being the clearly visible target. A sea-through baitfish for sea-run cutthroat — hence the name, Holder's Sea-Through." -Dan Holder, Sidney, British Columbia

MLF Epoxy Fry

Originator:	Lisa Peters
Tier:	Lisa Peters
Hook:	Mustad 34011, size 6
Thread:	Pink or burgundy thread wrapped along hook shank.
Underbody:	Core material from mylar piping.
Back and belly:	Two strands of blue Flashabou on top and bottom, stacked.
Body:	Pearl mylar tubing over entire body sticking out past end of hook.
Eyes:	Stick-on Witchcraft eyes, 1.5mm.
Epoxy:	Cover entire body with epoxy to bring out the colors from under the piping.

Tier's Note: "This is a great cutthroat fly when fished from the beach in quick, short strips." -Lisa Peters, Tofino, British Columbia

Mysid

Originator:	Roderick Haig-Brown
Tier:	Arthur Lingren
Hook:	Size 10-14
Thread:	Orange
Tail:	Five strands of golden pheasant tippet
Body:	Flat silver tinsel
Wing:	Woodduck flank

Tier's Note: "During his visits to Mohum estuary fishing for cutthroat Haig-Brown encountered many of his frustrations such as taking short, following and swirling with taking the fly, just as other anglers experienced when fishing sea-runs. Convinced that the solution to his sea-run cutthroat problems rested with the development of good asellus and mysid imitations, he set to work.

The mysid is a small shrimp that abounds in great numbers and is a readily available trout food. Haig-Brown pondered why they are not under constant attack. However, he learned when he captured some for his aquarium that the small coho were enthusiastic but totally ineffective in catching the tiny shrimp. The Mysid worked but he turned is thought to another estuary insect, the asellus, a close aquatic relative of the wood louse." –Arthur Lingren

Pink Worm

Originator:	Bernie Marchildon (Original procedure by Dave Lornie).
Tier:	Barry Stokes
Hook:	3 or 4xl streamer, size 4-10.
Thread:	Florescent hot pink, 6/0.
Tail:	Fluorescent hot pink chenille tied in at hook bend, doubled about 1-1/2" from tie-in point and twist using a dubbing twister until it doubles back on itself (about 20 turns). Secure with tying thread near original tie-in point and remover dubbing twister.
Body:	Fluorescent hot pink chenille, medium.
Rib:	Medium silver flat mylar tinsel.
Wing:	None

Tier's Note: "Bernie Marchildon of Victoria, British Columbia designed this pattern in late 1993 for use in estuaries and along saltwater beaches.

He had run out of marabou for a tail and used the twisted chenille as a substitute. He took the fly out for a test and the rest, as they say, is history. Cast out the Pink Worm and either retrieve is slowly or let it swing in the current. It needs virtually no movement but do not underestimate its effectiveness." –Barry Stokes

Prairie Oyster

Originator:	Rory E. Glennie
Tier:	Rory E. Glennie
Hook:	Mustad 94842, size 12
Thread:	Black, 6/0 UNI-Thread
Tail:	Natural brown deer body hair
Body:	Bright orange nylon floss or thread
Rib:	None
Hackle:	Natural red (brown) neck hackle
Wing:	Prairie Dog hair tied Trude style

Tier's Note: "The Prairie Oyster, named in reference to materials used in its wing construction and the place it was first fished, is a dry fly which is primarily fishing attached to a slow sinking, sink-tip fly line

Situated on the East Coast of Vancouver Island, the Oyster River boasts a growing population of sea-run cutthroat. Some of the finest fishing occurs during a rising tide. Cutthroats are quite showy fish when the tide is rising in the channel. They often break the surface in what appears to be a top water feedings spree. The sea-runs seem to be keying in on sunken fodder delivered via the overhead freshwater conveyor belt. Few aquatic nymphs are found that far down in the estuary. There are however a good number of drowned adult insects being carried off to sea, i.e., Caddisflies, bees, houseflies, ants, beetles, etc. The Prairie Oyster is designed to be generic in silhouette with an eye-catching spot of color. It hollow deer body hair tail assures a modicum of buoyancy.

The idea is to present the fly as near to the salt/fresh water interface as possible. Hence the slow sinking, sink-tip fly line is employed to hold the buoyant fly below the surface. The technique of fishing a buoyant fly on a sinking line is old hat to many stillwater trout fishers where keeping the fly above the weed tops is necessary to be effective, but the crossover into the estuarial arena is fairly recent." -Rory Glennie

Pussywillow

Originator:	Unknown
Tier:	Cliff Olson
Hook:	Mustad 94840, size 6
Thread:	Black 6/0
Tail:	Black marabou topped with black Flashabou
Body:	Black chenille
Rib:	Silver chenille
Hackle:	Black, palmered (prior to rib).
Wing:	None

Tier's Note: "The Pussywillow has been good in both salt and fresh water (rivers and lakes) for coastal cutthroat. It is also effective on coho in fresh water and rainbows in lakes." -Cliff Olson, New Westminster, British Columbia

Red-Tailed Hawk

Originator:	Jack Grundle
Tier:	Conall Connelly
Hook:	Mustad 9672, size 6-8
Thread:	Black 3/0 or 4/0
Tail:	Red dyed polar bear hair
Body:	Flat silver tinsel
Rib:	Oval silver tinsel (optional)
Hackle:	None
Wing:	Yellow over white polar bear or synthetic

Tier's Note: "Jack Grundle, editor of *Western Fish & Game* magazine (which also went by other names over the years, from 1965 until the late 1970s) first described the Red-Tail Hawk in the March/April 1972 issue of that magazine. It was one of several variations on the American Coachman with which he had experimented around that time. I believe that Jack used the fly mainly off of various beaches along the Sechell Peninsula between Howe Sound and Gervis Inlet northwest of Vancouver. I have never fished or visited the area but hear that its fishing has fallen victim to development during the last two decades.

I fish the Red-Tail Hawk along beaches and estuaries between Kelsey Bay and Deep Bay on the east coast of Vancouver Island. For years this has been my favorite pattern for beach and estuary fishing, generally retrieved with a fast strip. I have recently also found it to be very effective fished in the same manner along beaches off of creek mouths in coastal lakes." –Conall Connelly

Salt Pill

Originator:	Dave Lock
Tier:	Dave Lock
Hook:	Varivas 990S, size 8
Thread:	Bennechi number 12, white
Tail:	Gliss 'N Glo, mop olive or mop green
Body:	Arizona Scud dubbing, olive to match seaweed
Rib:	None or optional fine wire or monofilament
Hackle:	Gliss 'N Glo, mop olive or green, tied as beard

Tier's Note: "This pattern is like a Baggy Shrimp using the mother-of-pearl Gliss 'N Glo for the back. It has been effective when fishing tides that are flooding over shorelines that have had seaweed exposed during the ebb. Cutthroat will be browsing on pill bugs in very shallow water, sometimes like bonefish with their tails sticking above the surface. Steve Raymond deserves credit for making me aware of this cutthroat appetizer in his fine book, *The Estuary Flyfisher*. -Dave Locke, Victoria, British Columbia

Sea Spider Dawn

Originator:	Dave Lock
Tier:	Dave Lock
Hook:	Varivas model 990, size 8
Thread:	Bennechi #12, white
Tail:	Same as hackle
Body:	Gliss 'n Glo Mop, natural
Hackle:	Pink-dyed mallard flank

Tier's Note: "This fly is derived from Knudsen's Spider using Mike Kinney's tying method. My thinking is that when you have strongly colored low angle light it illuminates translucent euphausids near the surface so the fish will find them easily. This pattern has worked well during these times and will be taken even when cutthroats or coho are feeding on bait.

The Sea Spider Dusk version is the same except that the body is deep gold Glis 'N Glo with a dusk orange mallard flank tail and hackle.
-Dave Locke

Something Else (Swan Fly)

Originator:	Ken Ruddick
Tier:	Barry Stokes
Hook:	4xl, sizes 2-10
Thread:	White 6/0 or fine monofilament
Tail:	Fine, short pearl piping, picked out.
Body:	Clear "v" rib over pearl tinsel piping.
Rib:	None
Hackle:	None
Wing:	Mallard flank, dyed Kool-Aid Green over a few strands of white polar bear hair and two strands of pearl Krystal Flash.
Head:	Clear monofilament with collar of red thread. Eyes can be added on larger sizes.

Tier's Note: "Ken Ruddick of Vancouver, British Columbia showed this fly to me in 1988. The original pattern had a wing of dark brown mallard flank over a few strands of white polar bear. The head was tan thread with a slim bank of red for a collar. After experimenting with many colors of mallard flank for the wing, including two-color wings, I have found that Kool Aid green and yellow to be most effective. This fly is most effective when fished sunken in estuaries and retrieved in quick strips. The name "Swan" came as a result of using clear Swannundaze for a body before we started using the more supple v-rib." -Barry Stokes

Chapter 10 - Tackle and Accessories

"Always it was to be called a rod. If someone called it a pole, my father looked at him as a sergeant in the United States Marines would look at a recruit who had just called a rifle a gun."

—Norman Maclean
A River Runs Through It

Tackle for fishing coastal cutthroat has not really changed much since the days of Roderick Haig-Brown, Enos Bradner and other pioneer west coast fly fishers who were early champions of this unique trout. Since those days some seventy-odd years ago, the cane rod gave way to fiberglass which in turn has been largely replaced by graphite but this addresses technology rather than function. Even in light of today's elevated prices an angler can have a dependable, if not fancy, coastal cutthroat outfit put together for a reasonable outlay of cash. Most anglers who presently fish for trout already own the basic outfit needed; a standard trout rod and reel in 5 or 6-weight matched up with a modern floating line.

Since there has never been a requirement for anything more than a well balanced basic outfit, tackle manufacturers have not found a red-hot market when it comes to extracting great sums of the coastal cutthroat angler's disposable cash for a specialized rod and reel, waders, or anything else out of the ordinary which only seems fitting when pursuing a trout that carries its blue collar reputation with pride.

Rods

I began fly-fishing with a three-section cane rod that had been repaired in two places by my Grandfather Ed. It carried a Shakespeare Russell reel (which I still own-and which still works) with an on/off click check and a full spool of E diameter enameled level line. The outfit was probably heavy but I don't recall thinking much about rod weight in those days. It was my fishing rod and it caught fish. That first rod was eventually replaced with a used but beautifully maintained 8-1/2 foot Granger cane rod and 3-5/8" Hardy Perfect reel that was spooled with a good silk

Reels machined of aircraft aluminum and anodized like these Islanders are lightweight and serve the author for both fresh and saltwater fishing. The top IR-3 has an adjustable click drag. The LX-3.4, a mini big game reel has a full disk drag. The rods are by Lamiglass.

double-taper line. I purchased the outfit at Reiner's Pawn Shop in Aberdeen, Washington. It served me well through most of the 1950s (It spent a few years in storage during the Korean Conflict when I served a hitch in the Marine Corps) until its spine was unceremoniously snapped one day by the strike of a big, cock coho salmon on the Toutle River just downstream from the North Fork confluence.

My replacement rod was an off-the-rack Fenwick fiberglass, 8-1/2 feet long for a 6-weight line. This was a very popular rod of the day that would handle a bit larger flies and even endured the strain of large coho salmon. It was later joined by a 7-foot Philipson for a 5-weight line. Eventually I acquired a Scientific Anglers 6-weight, which was one of the best fiberglass rods I ever owned. My first graphite rod was made at Shoff's Sporting Goods Kent, Washington custom shop on a Fenwick blank. All of these rods have long since passed on into fly rod Valhalla. Today most of my rods are graphite. I also own a few 7- to 8-foot, 4-weight fiberglass rods for fishing little jump-across creeks or during extremely low water conditions.

I consider a 4-weight the lightest practical rod for coastal cutthroat fishing, with a 5-weight probably being the best all-around rod to use in fresh water. A 6- or 7-weight does a nice job for fishing larger rivers and the salt. This is not to infer that one cannot catch a sizable cutthroat even on

The Hardy Lightweight (top) has been used regularly by the author for more than thirty years and is still going strong. A high-quality reel purchased today, like the G. Loomis Adventure 5 shown here, will provide the same long years of service given reasonable care.

a tiny 3-weight outfit. However, rods lighter than 4-wieght will not always beat a cutthroat quickly because larger specimens often fight so hard that a lighter rod simply allows the battle to wage on too long. A case in point occurred when I was fishing with Preston Singletary a few seasons back on the Stillaguamish River.

Preston was at the oars of his raft and set me up nicely on a heavily covered undercut bank. I made a cast with a 7-1/2-foot, 4-weight fiberglass rod and was immediately fast to a large cutthroat. The fish fought with astonishing strength and tenacity, at times rattling the rod so hard that I thought the guides would shake loose. Upon finally landing a handsome, deep-bodied 19-incher I spent considerable time reviving the spent warrior and watched it swim slowly away apparently no worse for wear. Preston rowed back up to the top of the pool to cover some water we had missed.

As we drifted once again down into the heart of the pool we saw a trout thrashing around in the shallows. Rowing over we found the cutthroat I'd just released in an obvious state of suffering. Another even longer effort to revive the cutthroat failed so I killed it and placed it in the ice chest. It may be that if I had played the cutthroat out more quickly on a stronger rod that it would not have fought to complete exhaustion and subsequently died, although this is strictly speculation on my part. Having a cutthroat fight to the death is, I admit, the exception. For today's cutthroat angler a fast action, 4- to 7-weight graphite rod 8 to 9 feet long is ideal and there is a fine selection of good ones on the market. I purchase fly rods made in the United States by manufacturers who have been building rods for a long time. It has been my experience that if I should break a rod that it will be repaired and returned in a timelier manner from an established local or regional manufacturer than from a company that imports rods manufactured offshore. Also, as I get longer in the tooth I feel ever more strongly about spreading my limited disposable shekels completely within the borders of the United States, or Canada, whenever possible.

The fittings on a fly rod are important, particularly if you plan to use it for both fresh and saltwater fishing. Many expensive trout-weight rods have beautiful nickel silver reel seats with fancy wood inserts. These are highly vulnerable to the ravages of salt water and should be thoroughly cleaned upon returning home.

Fly rod guides should be made of corrosion resistant materials and have every niche and cranny around the guide feet sealed with rod varnish or epoxy. Water can crawl into some very tiny places and will soon begin corroding guides under the wraps where you may not detect it until the damage has reached a point that the guides will have to be replaced.

If you plan to use your fly rod in both fresh and salt water consider one that has an all metal reel seat of anodized aluminum or a combination of graphite and stainless steel. Both are highly corrosion resistant. Metal or graphite reel seats lack the aesthetics desired by some anglers but they certainly are functional, especially for the angler who needs a rod to do double duty in fresh and salt water.

The saltwater angler will eventually identify the need for a 7-weight. This rod will be a shade on the heavy side for use on coastal cutthroat but is the right tool for the late saltwater season when some very large northern coho salmon are cruising along the beaches with the cutthroat I am after. It will also come in handy when fall steelhead are shouldering into the rivers along with the cutthroat. The rod I use for this fishing is a fast action, 9 1/2 -foot, 7-weight graphite rod. Some anglers who are also steelheaders find that their 8-weight steelhead rod doubles quite handily for late season fishing on cutthroat and coho. I consider the 8-weight overkill for combination cutthroat and coho fishing.

I have had the opportunity to cast nearly every American manufactured rod during the past forty or more years and nearly all of them have proven to be excellent tools. Most of my rods are made by Lamiglas, Inc., a Woodland, Washington company that has been in business for years. Other fine rods that I have used, or owned are manufactured by Fenwick, Orvis, Sage, Scott and St. Croix. My list is only a modest sampler of all the good fly rods available.

Never purchase a rod unless you are given the opportunity to first try it out. Most fly shop staff members will encourage you to try the rods they carry. You may have to cast several before finding one that suits you. Finally, always purchase the best rod you can afford and take good care of it. Even an entry level fly rod from a reputable manufacturer will be fairly expensive and it should last a lifetime provided you don't smash it in a car door or leave it balanced

A landing net is a necessary tool for landing a cutthroat safely. A long-handled net like this one used by Preston Singletary is best when fishing from a boat or raft.

precariously on the roof of your vehicle as you drive away from a parking area. So, save your money and don't plunk it down on the fly shop counter until you can get the fly rod you really want.

Reels

There are enough snazzy reels on the market today to boggle the mind. To say that we have come a long, long way since the utilitarian Shakespeare Russell reel of my boyhood years would be the epitome of understatement. Most reels costing more than $150 (and many of them do cost more than $150) are made of aluminum and are anodized to resist saltwater corrosion. Reels with a price tag upwards of $300 are usually machined of aluminum bar stock, also anodized and will ward off corrosion for a lifetime with a bit of reasonable routine maintenance.

For cutthroat I prefer a reel that holds at least 100 yards of 18-pound test backing under the fly line. Although cutthroats are better known for their dogged fighting qualities rather than long runs, I have had extraordinary fish get into the backing on numerous occasions. The more pertinent reason to have adequate backing is to handle a summer steelhead or coho salmon that will occasionally take a fancy to a cutthroat fly.

A reel for cutthroat should have a substantial spring and pawl drag which is more than adequate for even for cutthroat up to 4 pounds or more. I have a couple of old Hardys, a Princess and a Lightweight with very modest drag adjustments that have accounted for a great many cutthroats and are still going strong. More recently manufacturers have designed click and pawl drags which are, admittedly better. A disk drag is rarely needed but is a welcome feature when the odd steelhead or coho salmon grabs my cutthroat fly.

My guideline for buying a reel is the same as with a fly rod; purchase the best one you can afford. I laid out $65.00 for a Fin Nor reel forty years ago, a whopping deduction from my bank account at the time. I still own and use the reel which has never required repairs and it works like a Swiss watch. The old Fin Nor has taken steelhead, coho salmon, chinook salmon, striped bass and a host of other finny critters and has done it all for the paltry sum of about $1.63 per year.

I purchased my Fenwick World Class IV reel in 1985 and it has provided the same good service even taking on such bad actors as big bull dorado and black skipjacks. My two original Ross model 3.5 reels (from the old Etna, California plant) have seen steady work through the years for steelhead and salmon in freshwater and salt and are still going strong.

The Cortland Ltd Graphite Large Arbor reel in size LA70 or LA90 is inexpensive and solidly built. It is highly resistant to saltwater corrosion and a good looking reel especially considering its economy price tag. For the angler on a strict budget, the Ltd Large Arbor Cortland is a good investment that should endure decades of hard fishing with reasonable care. I have a brace of Cortland large arbor reels that have served me well and have withstood the rigors of inexperienced guests who have fished with me on Washington waters.

Reels that I have acquired during the past several seasons are Islander large arbor models that I really like. I find that the amount of backing capacity sacrificed by the large arbor design is more than made up for in my ability to rapidly recover line. Islander reels are made of aircraft aluminum that is heavily anodized so that I can use them interchangeably in either fresh or saltwater. Islanders are lightweight, handsome and about as bulletproof as a reel can be. My compact Islander LX 3.4 is a mini-saltwater model but doubles nicely for freshwater use since it is very lightweight while incorporating the durability of the larger big game models. The click and pawl drags on the IR3 and IR4 Islanders are excellent for freshwater use but have served equally well in the salt.

Other reels that have served me well and will probably still be serviceable long after I have gone to that great pea gravel drift in the sky include; Orvis, Scientific Anglers and G.Loomis. The reels I own represent a noticeable disparity in price. The best reel one can afford does not always mean the most expensive reel in the shopkeeper's case. The reels I have listed here including the ones I've owned for years and still have years of use left in them. There are a great many more available that you can examine before whipping out your Visa. Whenever I have attempted to get by too cheaply over the years I have wound up sending many reels that were not up to the intended task into early retirement. In each case the bargain reels were attractively priced. These are reels that in retrospect I consider overpriced.

Fly Lines

Fly-fishers still count on the tried and true floating line for most coastal cutthroat fishing but new high-tech fly lines are not being ignored. Intermediate sinking fly lines are becoming increasingly popular for certain conditions in saltwater. Lines that sink very fast in deep, swift runs or multi-tip lines are also counted in the cutthroat flyfishers line arsenal. So, although the basic floating line remains the backbone of coastal cutthroat fishing, today's angler is able to fish a wider range of conditions more efficiently thanks to the many specialty lines we now have available.

Floating Fly Lines

For fishing in rivers or lakes a floating line either in weight-forward or double taper is the answer most of the time. Cutthroats hang out in fairly shallow areas and don't miss very much that moves through their territory. A floating line will put your fly into a cutthroat's view in water up to ten feet deep. A floating line is also a popular choice for salt water use on calm days and for working a surface popper or gurgling bug.

When considering a floating fly line for use on large rivers or in the salt, it is prudent to consider the wind which can range from a nuisance to a curse-provoking frustration. On days when the wind hits in powerful gusts coming in from the side or straight into one's teeth I strongly recommend one of the new lines designed specifically for use in windy conditions. Floating lines made for use in windy conditions are

sold under a variety of names and designed with short front tapers that carry most of the casting weight. They load the rod quickly and will punch a fair-sized streamer into the wind much more efficiently than lines with a longer front taper designed for presentation.

Clear Intermediate Lines

Beach and lake anglers are also devotees of clear or camouflage intermediate sinking lines mentioned earlier, which are nearly invisible in the water, a distinct advantage when casting over a trout that can be very spooky at times regardless of its aggressive reputation. In addition, an intermediate sinking line settles very slowly just under surface chop and will not get pushed around by the wind like a floating line. An intermediate sinking line riding just below the surface chop pulls straight even during a fairly stiff breeze.

Fast-Sinking Heads

There are times when cutthroat in salt water will feed just over the lip of a steeply incline. When this phenomenon occurs it can be very difficult to reach them with either a floating or intermediate sinking line. This is when a very fast sinking 25-foot head is the answer. Once only made in heavier line weights these heads are now available from Cortland, Scientific Anglers, Teeny Nymph Company and others in weights as light as 175, 200 and 225 grains which makes them

Bob Young with a nice sea-run cutthroat taken near Olalla, Washington. His stripping basket, to keep coiled line from settling into the water, is an inexpensive Rubbermaid dishpan with a few drainage holes drilled in the bottom and slots for a belt.

suitable for 5- through 7-weight rods and perfect for reaching down after cutthroat that are holding off of deeper beaches.

Multi-Tip Fly lines

The multi-tip fly lines that have been introduced over the past few years by Cortland, Scientific Anglers and others complete with a series of tips that float, sink slowly, fast and extra-fast have been all the rage, and for good cause. Being able to carry a wallet full of tips that can be quickly changed to meet a variety of river flows and depths is very handy and a lot less bulky than having a pocketful of extra spools clanking around in ones' vest.

Truth be told, those of us who cast flies along the Pacific Coast have been building these hybrid fly lines for some forty years but having them available, at long last, tailor-made right off the fly shop shelf is much more convenient.

When Presentation Counts

There are times late in the autumn season when the preponderance of sea-run cutthroat have made it into their natal waters prior to spawning that they become very attracted to small dry flies. When tempting cutthroat at this period — sea-run or river dwellers — with tiny Blue Wing Olives, presentation becomes critical. This is the time to use a weight forward or double taper line with a long front taper that will lay one's miniscule offering down light as a feather. Even with all of the hip-and-trendy lines we have at our disposal a floating line is the answer for the thistledown presentation that is needed when cutthroats are sipping mayflies.

Leaders

At one time I tied up all of my leaders from lengths of level monofilament. With the superb ready-made tapered leaders now offered by nearly every tackle manufacturer I no longer spend hours trying to tie seemingly endless numbers of perfect blood knots. Commercial leaders taken straight off the shop pegs cast very nicely, turn over well and save me valuable time that can be devoted to fly tying.

Corrosion-proof plastic fly boxes are the way to go for fishing in salt water and work fine in fresh water as well. One box will carry all the flies an angler needs for fishing in fresh water or salt.

I employ 7 1/2-to 9-foot, 2X or 3X leaders for saltwater and 9- to 12-foot 3X to 5X leaders for fresh water. When fishing gin clear water I add a 24- to 30-inch length of lighter tippet section to the end of my leaders. When fishing dry flies size 16 and smaller on very clear water I will add a couple of sections to taper down to 6X tippet. Although I do not usually find cutthroat to be particularly leader shy, the smaller diameter tippet is needed to accommodate the small eye of tiny fly hooks. I have used this uncomplicated system almost exclusively for several years to handle cutthroats upwards of 18 inches and have never experienced a break off that I could honestly attribute to failure of the leader.

Poly Leaders

Poly leaders in floating and several sinking rates are actually mini-sinking tips rather than actual leaders. These tips, available in 6- to 10-foot lengths, depending on the manufacturer, are very useful as they can be quickly looped to the end of one's floating fly line, turning it into a short sink tip. I find that the poly leaders are particularly effective when combined with one of the short front taper wind lines previously addressed in this chapter. Whenever I fish a wind taper I always have a selection of poly leaders stashed in a vest pocket.

Accessories

There are a few important accessories that all fly fishers need. Good polarized glasses are very important for cutting glare. A couple of good fly boxes will carry all the flies one will ever need. A leader cutting tool should be pinned on one's vest or hung around the neck on a thong so it won't be misplaced. A small package of adhesive bandages doesn't take up much room and will eventually come in handy. A tube of floatant is needed for dry flies. A hemostat or small pair of long nose pliers is invaluable for removing hooks from cutthroat and mashing down barbs on flies.

For packing all of one's accessories a good vest or shoulder bag is a must. With so many on the market I am hesitant to make recommendations. The best way to make a selection is to take all of your peripheral gear along with you and head for your favorite tackle shop. Before you buy a vest, chest pack or shoulder bag, make sure that all of your gear will fit into it comfortably with a bit of room left over for expansion.

When I was a much younger man I would plow into the heavy current of a river without a second thought. I did float my hat a few times while fording streams that were a bit too deep or swift and finally, as the years added up inexorably on my bones, I purchased a wading staff. Now, as a senior citizen who has become considerably less adroit than in my younger days, I consider a good wading staff standard equipment.

Waders or hip boots are a necessity for the serious cutthroat angler. Whatever brand or style you choose should have felt soles for negotiating slick river rocks. For very low water conditions when rocks become exceedingly slimy, felt soles with metal studs provide an additional measure of sure-footedness. For fishing saltwater beaches, a lug sole boot foot will hold up better than felt.

You will need chest-high waders for most river or beach fishing. I use breathable waders for all my fishing nowadays, having discovered that by layering fleece under them they are warm enough for west coast winters and far more comfortable than neoprene waders. During spring through fall I use stocking foot waders with a sturdy wading shoe. Through the winter I like an insulated boot foot breathable wader which is much warmer and easier to get on and off.

If there is a single element that can be counted upon throughout the coastal cutthroats' range from California to Alaska it is rain. Fish in the fall and early winter and you can count on being dumped on by some very serious storm fronts. Fortunately we now have rain gear available that turns the most drenching of cloudbursts nicely and the once intimidating price tags for good rain parkas have been dropping steadily downward to a point where we don't have to offer up outlandish sums of cash along with our first born child in order to obtain one. Look for a breathable jacket that will fit over your waders and a sweater, with a sturdy hood big enough to pull over a stocking cap and that will shield your eyeglasses. Make sure the sleeve cuffs can be tightly secured to keep determined rivulets of rain from finding a way up your arm during casting. And check to see that the outside pockets are cavernous enough to engulf a large fly box or two, leader spools, line cleaner pads and other necessary items for a day of fishing if you are a person who doesn't like to use a vest or shoulder bag.

You will, of course, need warm underwear. I like polypropylene in lightweight, expedition weight and 200 weight. With these three weights of synthetic underwear I can adjust layers to handle everything from a relatively balmy October afternoon on the Rogue River. to a morning of wind-driven sleet on the Sol Duc.

Just about everything you employ for cutthroat fishing will fit handily into a large, inexpensive duffle bag that is easily toted around in your vehicle. You may want to add a folding chair for ease of putting on shoes and waders or for simply sitting in upon returning from fishing while enjoying a good sandwich washed down with a nice bottle of amber.

Once you have acquired all of your tackle and related accessories you won't have to replace anything expensive for a good many years. Cutthroat trout don't tend to be very tough on tackle.

Boats and Rafts

Although many of us like walking the streams and beaches there is no arguing that the convenience and mobility that one gains with a car-top pram or a raft with a rowing frame. Most of the fishing the sea-run cutthroat angler enjoys is near shore and on protected water. For this fishing a 12-foot aluminum pram fills the bill. For low, clear autumn rivers a raft is probably preferred to a drift boat. I've fished for several years with Preston Singletary in his raft and it has taken us to places we would not have been able to fish on shank's mare.

Polarized sunglasses are important during sunny days. Carol Ferrera spotted this cutthroat through the glare in a shallow run and took it on a size 14 Royal Wulff.

A good rain parka is vital to fishing on rainy days in comfort. Jimmy LeMert was well prepared when he landed this nice cutthroat while fishing from a Washington beach during a day of steady rain.

Bob Young

Chapter 11 - Fly-Fishing in Fresh Water

"The cutthroat is at his best in a river that is open to the sea; he should then be a short, thick fish of two pounds or more, not too long in fresh water, with a clean white belly and a heavily spotted, green—or olive-brown back."

—Roderick Haig-Brown
A River Never Sleeps

For many Pacific Coast fly anglers the coastal cutthroat is a freshwater trout to be sought in creeks, rivers, ponds, and lakes. These same fly fishers prefer to fish for the coastal cutthroat in its sea-run form during the late summer and autumn when it returns to its river environment.

Self-sustaining populations of coastal cutthroat that live in small, brassy-bottomed beaver ponds or western lakes grow to good size and if they are not caught and killed, can become surprisingly spooky, shy feeders that sip mayflies and midges with all the delicacy of any selectively feeding brown or rainbow trout.

In small creeks above impassable barriers or draining back country ravines, coastal cutthroat are easily taken on almost any dry fly. Since they often mature at a length of little more than eight inches, it generally takes a legal limit to make up a meal for just one hungry backpacker.

Coastal cutthroat that live in large rivers such as Oregon's Willamette, the Cowlitz in Washington or the Fraser in British Columbia are similar but not all are sea-runs. Willamette cutthroats migrate only within the mainstem and its tributaries. Most Cowlitz River cutthroats travel all the way down the Columbia River to push out into the Pacific Ocean. Fraser River cutthroats are a mix of river-dwelling

An angler works his fly under a canopy of cover near the bank. This is one type of cover that should never be overlooked when fishing sea-run cutthroat in parent rivers.

and sea-run fish. Regardless of migratory differences, cutthroats in all of these rivers have the potential to grow to the same good size and provide a similar sport fishery.

It is in smaller, low gradient coastal rivers open to salt water that the cutthroat really seems to be in its element. These are rivers that glide slowly through gentle slopes, stands of Douglas fir, spruce, and cedar; into deep, dark undercut banks that are tangled with woody debris and overhead canopies of willow, alder and brambles. This is intimate habitat that has always seemed to me to be the right size of river for the coastal cutthroat. Perhaps it is just because it is the size of river that I most enjoy fishing, especially for sea-run cutthroats.

It is the sea-run cutthroat whose natal streams allow them direct access to salt water bays or into the Pacific Ocean where they spend a good period of their lives are the western river angler's trout of autumn. They are sometimes still called bluebacks for their saltwater coloration, or harvest trout since they ascend parent rivers at harvest time. Anglers, who enjoy fishing coastal rivers for cutthroat either on foot or floating via raft or drift boat, anxiously await the arrival of sea-run cutthroat into coastal rivers. Vanguard cutthroats are often in the lower reaches of their rivers as early as mid-June and they will continue to arrive until mid-November with stragglers clearing the estuaries well into the winter. This wide time span of freshwater entry is one of the many facets of the cutthroat's mystique and just one of the scores of reasons that it remains an enigma among all the western trout.

Woody debris and overhead canopy of streamside vegetation

Deep center river slot with cooler water.

Boulders to break the current

Feeder Creek

Ron Jenkins Illustration

Freshwater habitat utilization of the coastal cutthroat

Fishing in Beaver Ponds

Busting brush on my way upstream to the beaver ponds at the head of a small Hood Canal river, really just a creek was once one of my favorite spring outings. There were two ponds, one on the main stem of the stream and another smaller, narrow, deeper one at the top of a little tributary. I first made my way to the ponds after being told about them by a neighbor who lived down the beach from our family summer place on Collins Lake. It was not an easy hike. The trail, little used, was heavily grown over each spring and nearly disappeared in places.

The first time I made it to the larger of the two ponds it looked so heavily strewn with timber felled and limbed by beavers that there seemed to be no place to drop in a fly. At the far side though there was a fairly substantial area that was free of down-timber. Standing at the edge of the dam, a rise between two logs caught my eye. I carefully skirted the dam and its jagged rim of sharp pointed, beaver-chewed branches that can shred the toughest waders. Removing a small Coachman from the keeper of my 7-foot fiberglass fly rod, I checked behind me for a crease in the surrounding trees where I could direct an abbreviated back cast.

It took a few attempts to drop the fly in between the logs where it was immediately taken down in a splashy rise. Just as quickly my little rod bowed tightly as the leader was yanked back under the maze of logs by an obviously heavy trout that set my little reel buzzing for a few brief seconds before easily snapping the tippet.

When my second Coachman fell on its sword just as quickly I decided to cut back the leader a foot. With both of my Coachman patterns gone, I tied on a Blue Upright, a precursor to the contemporary Blue Winged Olive. It was taken without hesitation and I stripped line quickly bringing a fat cutthroat flopping onto a shoreside log where I managed to keep it balanced until I could pin it down. The cutthroat was a golden yellow/olive with vivid orange slashes on its gills; a heavy-shouldered 13-incher, glaring up at me from its position of disadvantage. I backed the hook out and returned the handsome, densely spotted trout to the dark depths of its sanctuary. With the heavier leader point, which did not impede the takes one bit, I brought four more cutthroat to hand that morning keeping a brace that nicely complimented a mid-morning family breakfast of eggs, bacon and fried potatoes.

I have generally found cutthroats in relatively remote and lightly fished beaver ponds to be easily tempted with sparsely dressed flies that have a nice buggy look, tied on size 14-18 hooks. A good adult midge or callibaetis dun will score well at times as will the old Royal Wulff which has always been a reliable change-up dry fly perhaps due to its bright red midriff.

I have nearly always been more successful fishing dry flies on snag-filled ponds than wets or nymphs since cutthroats seem to spend considerable time looking up. Nymphs and wet flies have always garnered strikes for me but in my experience are best reserved for ponds that have a reasonable amount of open water where a fish can be kept clear of snags. Any good size cutthroat given the opportunity to grab a fly that has sunk a couple of feet down into its digs delights in systematically wrapping a leader around a submerged snag to break off with irritating regularity. By using a floating fly to bring the cutthroat to the surface for the grab I can occasionally at least gain an advantage by quickly spiriting it up onto the logs or shore before it can dart back into the maze of cover; which still happens more often than not.

My little Philipson was a great rod for beaver pond fishing although a 4-foot rod, which was not available to my knowledge, would have been even better. My first leader, which I had cut back evolved into a straight 5-foot section of 6-pound test. This proved to be perfectly functional for short casts and using it I managed to work most of the cutthroat I hooked through the labyrinth of logs and branches that are characteristic of all the good beaver ponds I have fished over the years.

The largest beaver pond cutthroat I have ever landed was taken from the smaller of my two favorite ponds. It was a muscular 18-incher that chose to slug it out directly under an opening at the edge of the pond where I had a good spot to land it. I dispatched the cutthroat, a monstrous beaver pond fish that tipped the scales at 2-1/2 pounds and slipped it into my backpack.

I discovered several more ponds and small lakes throughout the Mason County peninsula that held native coastal cutthroat during the ensuing years. Many of those ponds probably still hold populations of native cutthroat although I have not checked them out for several years.

Cutthroat in Western Lakes

There were once almost endless lakes along the western slope of the Cascade Mountains and throughout the lowlands bordering the Pacific Coast that held strong populations of coastal cutthroat. These were self-sustaining populations that utilized small feeder streams for spawning. Cutthroat in these lakes always grew to good size if given the chance. The occasional bruiser to 20-inches is still landed every season and 13 to 16-inchers show up regularly in angles' bag limits. Some large lakes with a good forage fish populations hold cutthroats upwards of 10-pounds or more.

The native coastal cutthroat stocks in most of these lakes suffered during the days when state and provincial fish and wildlife agencies stocked them heavily with hatchery rainbow trout to provide additional sport for anglers who bought a license for which they expected limits of trout. Hatchery rainbows that supplemented native cutthroat worked just fine for filling legal limits; except that the addition of the highly competitive hatchery mongrels soon put some of the most vulnerable native cutthroat populations on the ropes. Many of these lakes now hold only vestige populations of cutthroat.

In recent years however there has been a cutback in hatchery stocking of rainbow trout into coastal cutthroat lakes with the intention of rebuilding native populations.

Where rainbow stocking programs still exist in cutthroat waters they are carefully monitored by fish and wildlife agencies.

Coastal cutthroat in larger ponds and lakes become very selective feeders at times. The western slope lakes they inhabit are rich with midges, callibaetis mayflies, damsel and dragonflies — and with the opportunity to scrutinize every offering very carefully — these cutthroat are not always easily hooked. Unlike fishing in beaver ponds where thick leaders are actually an advantage, a long, fine tippet combined with a clean presentation is vital if you have any hope of hooking suspicious and selective lake-dwelling coastal cutthroat.

Most fly-fishing in lakes throughout the Cascade foothills can be enjoyed from a float tube or pontoon boat and with nothing more sophisticated than a 4 to 6-weight rod and a floating or intermediate sinking line. Some anglers like the added security of a strike indicator. I prefer to fish without an indicator as I look upon the pesky things as bobbers which I associate with bait fishing.

Fishing Midges (Chironomids)

Coastal cutthroat are no different than any other lake-dwelling trout when it comes to carefully checking out an insect before deciding whether or not to eat it. They can be very fussy. Midges in western waters range from tiny critters not more than 1/4 of an inch long with some larger specimens growing to nearly an inch in length. A selection of colors to carry should include; black, brown, green and red. Matching the hatch when fishing midges is very important, just as it is with mayflies.

A floating line works most of the time for fishing just under the surface. The introduction of clear or camouflage intermediate sinking fly lines however has been a boon to the midge (chironomid) aficionado. A nearly invisible intermediate sinking line settles under the surface very slowly. Unlike a floating line that gets pushed around when even a slight wind scuffs the surface, the intermediate, riding just under the surface always pull straight and true. Being able to maintain a tight line from one's rod tip to the fly results in a higher percentage of hookups even if the take is light.

For fishing midges nearer to the bottom in ten to fifteen feet of water, a full sinking line in type III to VI sinking rate is the most efficient delivery system. Some anglers carry spare spools with a full sinking line but the more dedicated lake angler will usually have two rods strung, one with a floating or intermediate sinking line and the other with a full sinker that will get down deep and quickly.

Midges in the larva and pupa stage are not red-hot swimmers, exiting their tubes in the bottom detritus to slowly ascend to the surface. Anglers who fish midges successfully learn to work their offerings from the bottom up, either with very short, erratic strips of line or by employing a hand-twist retrieve. The cutthroat's take of a chironomid is often light but in my experience, is almost always firm enough to send me a signal that it is time to set the hook. At other times I've nearly lost my rod to a violent strike that took the tip into the water right up to the ferrule.

Presenting the Dry Midge

When midges begin to hatch, fishing on top becomes a very viable option as cutthroats rarely miss the opportunity to feed on this important food form, particularly early in the spring. A good emerger is the Raccoon with the Lady McConnell a very effective adult. Both of these patterns are most effectively fished on a long, fine leader. The Raccoon should be dressed and buzzed along the surface like an actual midge hatching out. The adult can be fished either with movement but is sometimes effective sitting dead still on a tight line right in the middle of a feeding lane until a cutthroat decides to pick it off.

Fishing Mayflies

Callibaetis mayflies are high on the list of the coastal cutthroat's menu in lakes. Veteran lake anglers will tell you that working a callibaetis hatch on a western lake can be just about the most challenging and rewarding fly fishing one can experience. It is however a game of patience because coastal cutthroat never seem to be in a rush to gulp their mayflies down.

Presenting the Dry Mayfly

A mayfly hatch building along the shallows of a lake rarely escapes the notice of a hungry cutthroat, usually within a very short time. When a callibaetis hatch is on, the angler needs to match not only the insect but display infinite patience for the fly to be taken.

A cutthroat that is sighted feeding along the shore should be approached quietly and set up on so that the fly can be turned over cleanly with an easy cast. For this work I like a high-floating, double taper and a leader of 9 feet with about 30 inches of tippet added.

If I make a good cast my fly will land gently, right in the middle of the hatching mayflies. I carefully pull any slack out of my fly line and wait with my rod pointed right at the fly. It then becomes a game of waiting for a cutthroat to work through the naturals to take a look at my ersatz offering.

If my fly is eventually sucked from the surface the trick is to simply tighten up on the line although it is a technique that I have yet to perfect even after a good many years of practice. When I see a good cutthroat feeding around my fly the excitement invariably builds to a peak and I am still guilty of really laying back into the grab now and then, which always results in a straightened hook or broken tippet. When I get it right though, the throbbing surge of a hooked cutthroat is the exhilarating result.

Fishing Baitfish Imitations

Most coastal cutthroat that live in lakes in Washington and British Columbia and attain sizes larger than 12 inches feed on minnows as an important part of their diet. Some of the very largest cutthroat that live in lakes in fact become exclusively minnow-eaters, cruising the depths and shallows, under and around logs and docks, and through patches of reeds in quest of a mouthful that provides a more substantial meal than all but the largest dragonfly nymphs. There is no place for light tippets here.

Cutthroat looking for baitfish are on the hunt and hit minnows hard. Any fly that looks or moves like a minnow is going to receive a savage strike from a foraging cutthroat and a leader point of less than 3X will be popped more often than not. I find a 7 1/2-foot leader works just fine for fishing minnow-imitating streamers. Either a floating, sinking tip or full sinking line may be required to present minnow imitations, depending upon the depth I am fishing.

I don't carry a large or sophisticated selection of minnow-imitating streamers and bucktails for fishing cutthroat in lakes. My rather disheveled version of the tried-and-true Muddler Minnow still works well for me. I also like olive and black Woolly Buggers and a couple of streamers like the Mickey Finn, a classic attractor, and more recently I've begun using a redside shiner bucktail, a common minnow that occurs in western lakes and streams. Minnow patterns dressed on size 4 through 8 3XL hooks cover the bases for me.

Casting around woody down-timber or stickups along the shallows I simply allow my baitfish imitation to settle to the bottom and then retrieve it in a series of short, erratic pulls. If cutthroat are around and in the mood for a minnow lunch the take will be quick in coming and all business.

If, on the other hand cutthroat begin playing the maddening game of following my streamer and then refuse it at the last moment—and I've had them follow almost to the rod tip before turning away—I know that they are either not really interested in minnows at the moment, or that I am not offering the one they want. A change or two of flies will usually determine what the cutthroat prefers

In late summer and fall, when rivers drop very low, clear and warm, cutthroat may be found in good numbers in the outflow of a feeder creek's cool waters.

Carol Ferrera

as its minnow entrée of the day, or if it is simply checking out my fly box.

Monster Coastal Cutthroat

In large lakes that have a good population of minnows, coastal cutthroat trout reach their most impressive size. Lake Washington cutthroat approaching 15 pounds are caught on occasion. Such a cutthroat is often 5 to 7 years old, about the same age as a 16-inch sea-run. In Lake Crescent on Washington's Olympic Peninsula the Crescenti, a coastal cutthroat subspecies, which was anadromous at one time eons ago before it became land-locked by massive earth slides, has been taken to 12 pounds. True to the adaptive nature of the coastal cutthroat, the Crescenti upon becoming landlocked in Lake Crescent, began spawning in Barnes Creek and has survived. Crescenti cutthroat are meat eaters most efficiently caught by trolling deep with plugs or spoons. They are rarely within range of the average fly fisher.

Small-Stream and Headwater Creek Cutthroat

There are streams scattered from Northern California through British Columbia and into the Misty Fjords of Alaska that hold resident populations of coastal cutthroat. Oftentimes these fish are separated from other cutthroat and anadromous salmonids by impassable barriers. Headwater creeks and other small mountain streams are not rich with feed thus the cutthroats mature at a small size. With competition for food very spirited, these small headwater cutthroats will come charging boldly to the surface to smack almost any dry fly. The high creek angler needs only a light rod and a small box with leader tippet and a mixed dozen flies in sizes 12 through 18 to partake of these spunky little trout.

Since they are always hungry, high country coastal cutthroats are easy pickings for backpackers who regularly catch a mess of them on the way to the evening campsite. Cleaned and rolled in a bit of flour and fried until the

Downtimber, overhead canopies of branches and deep, dark slots are prime cutthroat stations.

skin is crisp, or sprinkled with salt and pepper and wrapped tightly in foil to be cooked right on the coals, they are delicious.

Sea-Run Cutthroat

It is when the wandering sea-run cutthroats return to ascend home rivers that flow into protected salt water bays or directly into the Pacific Ocean that freshwater anglers get serious about stringing up their fly rods. For the most dedicated among those who traditionally begin fishing during the first chill of autumn, there is no other time for challenging the sea-run cutthroat than when they show up in fresh water pools above tidewater and continue upstream to lurk under the dark cut banks and around the down-timber fortresses typical of coastal rivers. Cutthroats returning from their sojourn in the salt are fully up to the challenge; sleek, silvery, strapping and primed to slam into a well placed fly with lightning speed and intensity not unlike that of an NFL strong safety.

In western Washington where I live we enjoy a long season for fishing coastal cutthroat. With South Puget Sound cutthroat spending most of their lives in salt water and those that inhabit North Puget Sound rivers spending spring through fall in natal rivers there is just a short few months in mid-winter when fishing drops off. My fishing companions and I usually make our first earnest move to fresh water in September or early October, although we still make regular forays to late-season saltwater spots through the winter months.

Fishing Techniques

I use a 5- to 6-weight rod and matching reel for my freshwater cutthroat fishing as I do in the salt and during low, clear water when fishing dry flies, I use a soft-action 4-weight. In small to medium-size streams I have never found that I require anything other than a floating line for all the situations I encounter.

If there is one element necessary to consistently hook coastal cutthroat in fresh water it is to keep the slack out of one's line. I cast only the amount of line needed to reach the cutthroat's lie with the leader nicely turned over and then quickly take up any slack. After a cast that hits close to a good cutthroat lie I aim my rod tip straight at the fly then begin a series of rod tip lifts and drops. After lifting the rod smartly to move the fly, I use my line hand to take up all the slack when I drop the tip back down. This lift and drop retrieve gives the fly excellent continuous, undulating movement while never allowing any slack line to be left on the water. A cutthroat comes out from under its cover to attack a fly with blinding speed. If there is any slack line the cutthroat will grab the fly and reject it in the blink of an eye.

While fishing the Stillaguamish River several years ago with guide Mike Kinney, sea-run cutthroat expert and developer of the Reverse Spider fly, I had missed a couple of very good fish in a row by not dealing efficiently with my slack fly line.

Finally, after I missed yet another cutthroat, Mike said softly. "You were about three minutes too late setting the hook on that one." He then rowed his raft onto a gravel bar and patiently went through the lift and drop retrieve with me. Once back on the water my hookup percentage improved considerably

For all its intensity and speed when slamming into a fly, a coastal cutthroat will be most quickly aroused when the fly is cast directly into its territory. It cannot be too strongly stated that to get a cutthroat's attention on a regular basis your fly should be dropped right on its nose. This requires accurate casts tight to the bank or right into woody cover where cutthroats like to hold.

Fishing the Lower Reaches

From the upper push of tidal influence through the first few lower river pools I look for at least a vanguard run of cutthroat to be holding as early as June although I am still concentrating on the action available in salt water. A fair number of these early cutthroats are quite often large specimens that have spawned at least one time previously. The largest among them tend to be cliquish, usually sharing cover only with others of similar size. Although cutthroats are aggressive and highly territorial in freshwater they are not stupid. If I miss a grab I will give the cutthroat a couple of more looks at the fly and if there is no further interest, I move on to the next likely spot.

In the lower, tidal reaches of rivers I find cutthroat especially susceptible to patterns that imitate small salmonids. This may be due to the fact that they are fresh in from the salt where sand lance and other baitfish have made up a large portion of their diet. For the past several years my number one minnow-imitating pattern in the lower pools of rivers has been the Silver Brown in sizes 4 through 8. The Spruce is another feather wing streamer pattern that has a good reputation with cutthroat anglers. My selection of bucktail

This unusual log is in the mainstem Stillaguamish River. It is a prime holding spot for big cutthroat and almost never fails to produce a good-sized fish.

attractors changes from time. to time, always includes three standbys: the Polar Shrimp, Alaska Mary Ann and Mickey Finn.

Fishing the Middle to Upper River

When cutthroats move into the pools above tidal influence I go to the Reverse Spider on a regular basis. Strange as it looks, the Reverse Spider is as reliable as any fly I have ever used for autumn cutthroat fishing. It is a unique pattern that looks more like a tiny swimming octopus or a caddis on steroids than anything else when used with the lift and drop retrieve. The lifelike movement of the Reverse Spider apparently gives it the appearance of something to eat, even when dressed with a bright red or yellow chenille body. The sight of a cutthroat barreling out from under cover after a Reverse Spider, utterly intent on a kill-shot, is a sight to behold.

As the season pushes into October urging sea-run cutthroats to migrate further upstream they may begin seeking out spawning salmon or steelhead. Holding downstream of spawning salmon cutthroat feed on drifting eggs that wash out of the redds. This is not an infallible rule however as I've seen a lot of spawning salmon paired up in Puget Sound rivers through the years with little or no evidence of cutthroat hanging around to eat drifting eggs. Conversely, when my wife Carol and I fished the Rogue River for fall steelhead our guide, Del Steyaert made a point of working salmon and steelhead spawning water with single egg patterns and we took several nice cutthroats along with a few steelhead.

In the upper stretches of a cutthroat river, as the season wears on and the cutthroats grow choosy, I often switch to attractor patterns more often than I would further downstream. when fishing over fish that have just moved in from the salt. I have at times coaxed some very nice cutthroat out from cover to hit a bright attractor pattern after they have turned away even from the reliable Reverse Spider. I tie most of my attractors on size 6 and 8 hooks but find when fishing very low, clear water conditions the Polar Shrimp, Brad's Brat or Stillaguamish Special dressed sparsely on hooks as small as size 14 will trigger strikes when larger flies are refused. If small brightly colored flies don't get dour cutthroat excited I will throw them a changeup like the Black Spook or Fish Hawk. A lot of experienced cutthroat anglers are so confident in the Reverse Spider though that they fish it to the exclusion of all other dressings throughout the season.

Fishing Dry Flies and Skaters

There has always been a small but dedicated corps of cutthroat fly fishers with a passion for fishing the dry fly. There are skeptics who eschew floating offerings feeling that they are not as effective as a well presented wet fly, a contention that has mounted vigorous discussions especially during the past few seasons.

The sea-run cutthroat has received a bad rap from those who denounce its propensity to take a floating fly. Some of the more savvy cutthroat anglers in our ranks use dry flies regularly. Steve Raymond, a long-time cutthroat angler relies on his Cutthroat Candy almost exclusively in fresh and salt water.

Coastal cutthroats return to their parent rivers in the late summer through fall which coincides with the late-season hatches of blue winged olives and caddis, the same insects they feed upon as fry soon after emerging from the gravel. Adult cutthroat quickly recognize a hatch of mayflies, caddis or crane flies as a snack, if not a meal, and will readily rise to pick these morsels from the surface. I figure that if a cutthroat decides to sip a few mayfly duns in my presence the very least I can do is have a small selection of size 16 to 22 parachute-style dry flies on hand to offer. Since a cutthroat dry fly selection takes up very little room, I can easily fit a few mayfly cripples and parachute style duns along with the consistent Elk Hair Caddis and a skater to imitate a crane fly into a corner of my fly box. I keep a big, orange October Caddis or two on hand although I am convinced that the best time to fish this big, gaudy western sedge is well after dark which is usually when I have completed my fishing day.

Nearing the end of a late-season float on the Stillaguamish River, Preston anchored up at the bottom of the canyon, picked up his rod and as he stepped into the river, said, "I took several cutthroats on dry flies here last week. Let's see if they're still in the mood." With that he cast out a small BWO and hooked up. Carol and I shouted encouragement as he hooked a second rising cutthroat. When he hooked a third straight cutthroat however, Carol who likes nothing better than dry fly fishing, grabbed her rod and said, "I can't stand this. Move over Preston." She stepped in above him and was hooked up to a nice cutthroat in no time. I stayed in the raft to get a few photos of the action.

Waking patterns can be effective for bringing apathetic cutthroats to the surface. Flies like the Waller Waker, Bomber or old Steelhead Bee are good examples of effective waking patterns. None of them however in my experience seems to have quite the confrontational effect on cutthroat as the Bulkley Mouse, a nondescript deer hair fly designed by Andre LaPorte, a steelhead fly-fishing guide from Quesnell, British Columbia.

Stan Reeve and I were fishing the Bulkley River in British Columbia with Andre when he introduced me to his Mouse which he said would, "bring up the most reluctant steelhead in low, clear water." He was correct. After showing me how to skate and control his Mouse to make it plow a big bow wake across the surface I hooked a couple of steelhead that had refused all other offerings.

More recently on a summer morning when I was fishing with my friend Chris Bentsen on the Snoqualmie River for summer steelhead I discovered that the Mouse also rouses the interest of coastal cutthroat. We were fishing an exceedingly low, clear Snoqualmie River for summer steelhead so the prospects were not great. Chris had gone upstream to cover a wide pool with his two-handed rod. I chose to work a stretch of water downstream from Chris where a thin seam of current formed below a lone

midstream boulder. After a few changes of wet flies I tied on a Mouse. I set a cast out just below the boulder. A downstream mend got the Mouse waking when a swirl from a heavy fish bounced it from the surface but missed. I thought it was a steelhead. A second cast to the same spot brought another grab and this time the barb took a hold. To my surprise I was hooked to a large cutthroat rather than a steelhead. Upon releasing a prime 18-incher, I managed to hook two more cutthroats from the same run with the Mouse.

The Mouse is fished like any waking fly using a series of upstream and downstream mends to get it plowing along the surface and it does kick up a commotion. If the water is moving at a good flow I make an upstream mend to slow the speed of the Mouse. In slow water a downstream mend will get it moving. LaPorte often riffle hitches the Mouse behind the head, which is almost dead center on the fly to make it really go nuts.

The Mouse has earned a regular spot in my fly box and has provoked strikes from cutthroat with warming regularity. The Mouse is not available in every fly shop and tying such a large wad of deer hair onto the top of a hook is hard work—but the results I have realized with the Mouse make the effort worthwhile.

Low-Water Tactics

Water tables are usually at the lowest point early in October on most Pacific Coast rivers. This also means the water is warm – and that the rocks are very, very slick. This is the time when coastal cutthroat may abandon their cozy lairs in an effort to find a bit of respite from the tepid flow.

On another of our October floats, Carol, Preston and I had beached his raft and were sitting on a sun-washed gravel bar during an unseasonably warm day finishing up a lunch of pasta salad, hummus-filled tortillas and good cold beer when a guide came gliding around the bend with two anglers in his drift boat and three others tagging along in small pontoon boats. He was teaching an on-the-river sea-run cutthroat class. Anchoring up perhaps twenty-five feet out from a long undercut bank he set his charges to casting and retrieving flies, giving encouragement and advice as they did so. After about twenty minutes with no action he ordered them to weigh anchor and follow him down the river. A short distance downstream from where they had been casting, a small creek tumbled down a steep little ravine into the river. The guide's little fleet drifted right past it and out of sight around the next bend.

"OK." Preston said. "Let's spread out along that little run below the creek and see what transpires." We grabbed our rods and within minutes were all into nice cutthroat. The low water had prompted the cutthroat to move from the slack, dark, uncomfortably warm undercuts into the run fed by the gentle, cooler flow of the creek. We followed well behind the guide and his students for the remainder of our float, concentrating our efforts on the runs downstream of a few small feeder creeks and enjoyed a banner afternoon of cutthroat fishing.

The Late Season

As October passes into November the weather turns colder as storm fronts bring the first series of rain squalls from the southwest. Those of us hoping to hit a few prime late-arriving cutthroats watch nervously as the first heavy rains that the approach of winter begin raising and coloring coastal rivers. It is our hope that the increased flow will be just enough to bring the late-returning cutthroat up from the estuaries. Several days of hard rain in succession will invariably push coastal rivers too high, oftentimes finishing the cutthroat fishing for the season.

Although I never count on great numbers of cutthroat fishing during the wet, windy tag end of the season I still manage to catch a few of the better fish I will hook all year.

The cutthroat I find during the late season are holding low in the river apparently awaiting another burst of rain before moving upstream. They come in quietly, usually swimming alone or with two or three others and tend to take on freshwater coloration more quickly than earlier arriving sea-runs and the males often have pronounced kypes that indicate spawning readiness.

Late-arriving cutthroat can be difficult to engage, at times ignoring just about every pattern I send their way. When the cutthroats get tough, I dig out a fairly large attractor like a number 6 or 4 Brad's Brat, Mickey Finn or similar gaudy dressing in an effort to get a cutthroat's attention. If an attractor fails I switch to a big Muddler Minnow or brightly colored Reverse Spider. Several casts close enough to a late-run cutthroat's lair will sometimes trigger its territorial nature and bring a smashing strike.

Even with icy rain hitting my face like shrapnel and finding a route under the cuffs and hood of my parka the last days of the cutthroat season hold a special thrill. It always seems like the strikes are the most savage of the entire season with every battle in doubt until the last second.

Once the rivers rise to near spate and we are pushing into the winter steelhead season, cutthroats will begin exploring small feeder streams in preparation for spawning. When spawning is completed, spent cutthroats will stay in natal creeks for the remainder of the winter, or drop down into sheltered eddies in the main rivers to rest and recover until spring. This is when the angler who prefers to fish for cutthroat only in coastal rivers begins checking out other rivers for rainbows or browns—until the following autumn.

Deep pools should never be overlooked as they hold cutthroat that will move significant distances to smack a fly.

Chapter 12 - Fly-Fishing in Salt Water

"The sea-run cutthroat bears scant resemblance to its land-locked cousins of the interior basins. After a summer of feeding in the estuaries its sides are typically as bright as a switchblade and its back is a cold blue-green."

—Steve Raymond
The Year of the Trout

There is a long history of fly-fishing in the northern expanses of saltwater along the Pacific Coast from the southern reaches of Puget Sound in Washington northward through the nearly endless bays, fjords and beaches of the mainland and island coastlines of British Columbia and into southeast Alaska. In fact Washington and British Columbia fly fishers were testing the brackish mix of estuarine waters and probing out into saltwater bays with fancy feathered patterns in the 1930s, years before plying flies in the salt ever became popular along the Atlantic Seaboard of the United States.

Anglers who have pursued coastal cutthroat in ponds, lakes and rivers, may feel upon venturing out to the expansive beaches of Puget Sound and Hood Canal in Washington, mainland British Columbia, Vancouver Island or the Queen Charlotte Islands that they are gazing upon a rather intimidating sight. Staring at an expanse of salt water that stretches beyond the far horizon does not create a comfort zone for an angler accustomed to fishing within the clearly defined boundaries of most lakes or streams. It is important to remember however that the coastal cutthroat spends most of its saltwater period each season cruising within an easy cast of the shoreline because that is where most of its favorite forage; pill bugs, krill, sand lance, and

Cam Sigler brings a big cutthroat over the net for Cam Sigler, Jr. Anglers who like to cover a lot of water often opt for a seaworthy 15- to 18-foot boat that can move fast.

sculpins are found. So, by either wading or working from a small boat, fly fishers will almost always be casting their flies close to shore.

I genuinely enjoy fishing for coastal cutthroat trout in ponds, lakes and rivers. I have found that over the years it is every bit as challenging as salt water fishing given the weather swings of fall which can serve up bluebird days and low, clear flows that quickly roil into spate by a front of hard rain. Even within the confines of a small river locating cutthroat can be difficult. If fishing success were based simply on locating the best shoreline cover or subsurface structure where cutthroat find protection from predators, or lie in wait as predators, it fishing in creeks and rivers would be always be easy.

Fishing for coastal cutthroat in saltwater is, in my opinion a somewhat more dynamic quest than fishing a lake or stream simply because cutthroat have so much room to roam in the salt and are not nearly as attached to the heavy cover they seek out in natal rivers. Whether fishing in freshwater or saltwater the angler who succeeds is the angler who becomes

Steve Raymond in his "office" working on a cutthroat. Action took place near Hoodsport on Hood Canal, Washington.

Leland Miyawaki

a student of the cutthroat's environment and learns to adapt the entire spectrum of fly fishing methods to the situation. Fishing in either fresh or saltwater is not more or less difficult than the other in my view. They are simply different, with each having its own variables that must be addressed.

Fishing in salt water is tied directly to the rise and fall of the tides rather than the clock. Long run outs, called minus tides, can scatter weak swimming baitfish and krill. When baitfish or krill are being swept away, a bay or estuary that had been productive at mid-tide will quickly become barren of cutthroat. Conversely, a tide with a gentle or soft low turn that doesn't scatter the feed, will allow cutthroat to forage heavily the entire day along the same stretch of beach.

Wind, which can often be avoided along a river by moving around the next bend, can blow straight into the face of the saltwater angler who enjoys little opportunity to find respite. Pounding one cast after another into the teeth of a blustery onshore wind can make for a difficult day along the beach. Wind often brings with it acres of flotsam and jetsam that drapes tenaciously along fly lines and fouls flies on every cast, turning what was intended to be a pleasant day of fishing into a true test of one's character.

All the many caveats that challenge the saltwater cutthroat angler are overridden by a sense of adventure that is framed in the awesome beauty of our Pacific coastal shoreline. From steep evergreen covered hills reaching down to narrow beaches of steep incline; to shallow cobbled flats and oyster-strewn beaches; to estuarine mud flats and vast deltas where feeder streams wind and braid like slender ribbons to reach the low tide line only to return and surge well up into their estuaries, the saltwater angler's surroundings are in every respect majestic. Even fishing along a developed beach though, lined with houses is just fine with me if there are cutthroats around. Throughout this varied foreshore water, within reach of an easy cast there can be sea-run cutthroat foraging and more than ready to chase your fly.

Time and Tide

Most of us have chalked up a lot of years dragging ourselves out of bed to the dirge of a pre-dawn alarm so that we may stake out the best spot on a steelhead drift or to get a place in line at a popular boat launch during trout season. Often as not, no matter how early we manage to reach our fishing destination in an effort to be ahead of the crowd, we find that there are always a few who have arrived even earlier, downed a thermos of coffee and are killing time with a few hands of pinochle.

A race to secure a place in the boat launch line or on the bank is seldom critical to the fly fisher who seeks cutthroat in the salt. Time is important but only as it relates to the rise and fall of the tide rather than the grim knell of a pre-dawn alarm clock. However, tides throughout a given region can fluctuate by an hour or more from one arm, bay or estuary to the next so the clock cannot be treated with total disregard. So, while it is not possible to toss one's alarm clock aside, it is important to supplement it with a good tide table.

Tide tables are available on the Internet where they can be printed out at no cost. A better solution is to purchase one of the pocket tide tables that not only show the daily tides but have a graph of the high and low turns which is a very helpful feature.

Make Friends and Keep Records

When embarking on the adventure of fishing in the salt for coastal cutthroat trout, having an experienced partner to fish with is a huge advantage. It is also extremely helpful to become a regular customer at a reputable local fly fishing store staffed by people who are experienced saltwater fly fishers. It is further worth consideration to join an active local fly-fishing club to meet others who share your enthusiasm for coastal cutthroat. Lastly, take notes after each outing to a new beach or bay in search of cutthroat. Through experience, either yours, or through the courtesy of a fishing pal, you are going to find that different places fish well on certain turns of the tide. While some beaches will fish best after the low turn, others may fish best at the middle of an incoming tide or on a high turn. Some areas will fish better during certain weeks of the year. Your notes will grow into a priceless personal guide to the best cutthroat beaches in June or July and the estuaries that become productive in October and November.

Once you have learned the nuances of the tides and how they affect the fishing in your favorite areas, employment of productive fishing techniques come into play. Although cutthroat fishing in saltwater is a straightforward game, a variety of techniques are necessary to work one's fly to advan-

tage around the diverse cobble, hidden structure and wash rocks that may hold cutthroat during a day of fishing.

Sandy and Cobble-Bottom Beaches

Gently sloping beaches with bottoms of small rocks interspersed with sandy openings and a scattering of large boulders are usually bordered at the high tide line by drift logs and willows. Such spots generally rich with krill, sand lance, sculpins and other forage. On Puget Sound beaches where I do most of my fishing these are the places where I find cutthroat that are already moving out of parent streams, feeding ravenously by mid-March and in good numbers by mid-April. I also find cutthroats along these same beaches during this same time frame that have not yet entered freshwater to spawn. There is usually a stream close to my favorite late winter/early spring fishing spots and outmigrating cutthroats – or those that have not yet returned to spawning creeks — stay close this freshwater source for a time. Later in the spring and in the summer they can be found several miles from freshwater.

I travel light when fishing along the beaches, carrying a small shoulder bag that holds a box of flies, a spare leader, leader spools, and extra spool for my reel and nippers. My stripping basket is strapped around my waist and I most often carry a 9-foot, 6-weight rod. The line that gets the call most often during my beach fishing is a clear or camouflage intermediate full sinker. I keep an eye peeled for diving birds surfacing with beaksful of baitfish or Bonaparte gulls busily gossiping while they peck amphipods and euphausids from the surface. Rarely do feeding birds fail to signal a good opportunity to

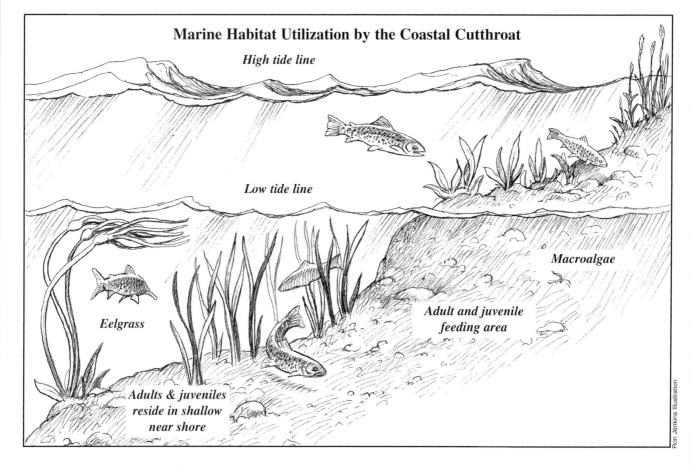

Marine Habitat Utilization by the Coastal Cutthroat

High tide line

Low tide line

Macroalgae

Eelgrass

Adult and juvenile feeding area

Adults & juveniles reside in shallow near shore

Ron Jenkins Illustration

hang into a cutthroat. Fishing beaches, whether from a small car-topper or on foot, is a game of observation as one walks along, for many times cruising cutthroat are clearly visible swimming a scant distance from shore in water barely three feet deep. Wading nonchalantly into the water before looking things over carefully can send any cutthroat in the area scurrying off down the beach out of casting range.

Swinging the Fly

I begin casting while standing back several feet from the water to set out my first exploratory casts, especially on a clear morning when the surface is flat calm. I lengthen subsequent casts and use various retrieves until I'm sure that I have shown my fly to any cutthroat that may be feeding within range of my cast. I then begin working down the beach.

At times tidal action will swing the fly in one direction or the other. I always work the in direction the fly swings as I retrieve and allow it to almost reach the beach before stripping it back for a pickup to send it straight out again. I have come to expect a strike just about anywhere on the swing and retrieve.

The Parallel Presentation

Another technique is to wade out only a few feet and then slowly work parallel to the shoreline walking slowly and casting and stripping the fly through the very shallow water close to shore. This is a technique favored by my friend Leland Miyawaki whom I've watched catch a lot of nice cutthroat by wading parallel to the beach, casting his ever-present surface popper in water barely knee-deep. Regardless of the fly employed, a cutthroat that has not been spooked by other anglers will often chase bait into water a scant few feet from shore.

Fishing Baitfish Patterns

When fishing a sand lance, sculpin or any general baitfish imitation I try to closely mimic the swimming action of

small baitfish by combining short pulls, pauses and an occasional foot-long strip of the line. If I see a cutthroat tracking my baitfish pattern but not moving to it I will stop the retrieve allowing the fly to dive toward the sand to imitate the escape method utilized by sand lance. At times this stratagem will prod the cutthroat into a savage strike, sometimes actually grabbing the fly off the bottom in the belief that it is going to burrow into the sand and escape.

Fishing Krill

Fishing amphipod, cocapod and euphausid imitations under the same conditions requires a bit diffcrent technique since these little shrimp-like creatures offer very little resistance to even moderate tidal movement. Again I prefer a camouflage intermediate sinking line but go to a floater on calm, windless days. For fishing krill patterns I lengthen my leader to about twelve feet with the addition of a section of light fluorocarbon tippet. Working out my longest comfortable I allow the tiny krill pattern to swing along with just the slightest retrieve consisting of strips barely more than two or three inches of line at a time. This gives my fly the longest possible time in the strike zone. When the fly has swung parallel to the beach I retrieve it a bit faster until the leader knot is almost to the rod tip because cutthroat will slam a fly when the leader butt is practically into the tip guide.

Working Deep

Although I find fishing for cutthroat near the surface and over shallow bottoms most enjoyable, there are where beaches deepen off rather quickly in four to five fathom curves and cutthroat do work along these bottoms, particularly on very bright, sunny days. When I know that I am going to work one of these curves I always carry a fast sinking line with a 25-foot sinking head and intermediate running line. This line casts very easily and drops quickly down over the curve to put my fly into sight of any cutthroat that may be probing the depths for a meal.

A word of caution when fishing a sinking line over a drop-off or curve is to cut back a bit on your leader. It is not out of the realm of possibility for a local immature chinook salmon to be foraging in the same area as the cutthroat you seek and with a bit of luck, plus a heavier leader point, you just may bring one of these special fly rod prizes to hand.

Fishing on the Surface

More years ago than he probably cares to remember noted angler and author, Steve Raymond began experimenting with surface flies for cutthroat in the waters of Puget Sound and Hood Canal. Through trial and error he came up with a pattern called the Cutthroat Candy, a small deer hair bug which has become the go-to fly for all of his saltwater cutthroat trout fishing. Since Raymond's early experimentation and subsequent success with floating flies for saltwater cutthroat, others have followed suit, adding dimension to Raymond's pioneering effort. Leland Miawaki, Preston Singletary, Roger Stephens and othcrs have developed poppers and floating baitfish patterns that have proven effective

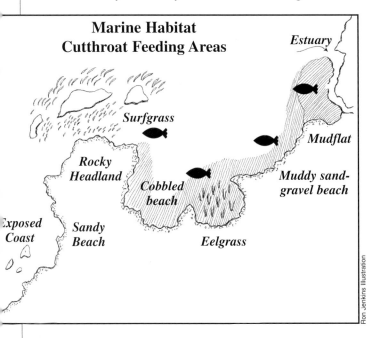

Marine Habitat Cutthroat Feeding Areas

Estuary

Surfgrass

Mudflat

Rocky Headland

Cobbled beach

Muddy sand-gravel beach

Exposed Coast

Sandy Beach

Eelgrass

Ron Jenkins Illustration

for taking beach-cruising cutthroats. They regularly work their floating poppers and baitfish imitations along the surface to entice cutthroat into explosive surface strikes.

Miyawaki has spent the past several years developing his saltwater popper which has been effective on cutthroat trout and salmon. Miyawaki's popper, a bait fish imitation built with a small trailing hook has successfully risen scores of cutthroat. Leland has become so confident in the fish-attracting properties of his popper that he rarely uses any other pattern for his saltwater fishing.

If there is a downside to fishing top water flies for cutthroat in saltwater it is that although they grab eagerly at a fly sputtering and gurgling along the surface, they are almost universally inept at actually getting a hold on the pesky thing. At times an excited cutthroat will take three, four or five vicious cracks at a fly moving noisily along the surface before either taking it down or, after too many misses, simply turning away in frustration.

To maximize success in fishing a surface fly it is critical to maintain a tight line and a low rod tip aimed straight at the fly. This usually dictates fishing over fairly flat water with minimal wind action. Cast out and take up any slack quickly then dropping your rod tip begin popping and gurgling your fly in an erratic retrieve. When a cutthroat shows, allow it to take the fly solidly and turn away before

Judith O'Keefe shows a big sea-run coastal cutthroat before releasing it back into Puget Sound. Action took place near Port Townsend ferry dock.

tightening up on your line. This does not guarantee a hookup but it does, according to those who practice this sort of fly-fishing alchemy, improve the odds considerably.

Experimentation is destined to continue in an effort to perfect surface patterns and techniques that will consistently take cutthroat due to the visual rewards involved when a strike is coaxed up. The grabs are often spectacular knocking the fly well clear of the surface, even when the cutthroat has missed the mark completely. At times when cutthroat have been completely indifferent to subsurface patterns I have seen big cutthroat explode through the surface to hit Leland's popper.

In addition to fishing on top for cutthroat, I've had some experience using poppers on East Coast striped bass and on our Pacific coho salmon and have found that they too have trouble consistently finding the range on a surface chugging fly or popper.

Points of Land and Current Seams

Points and outcroppings along any beach or bay deserve special attention by the saltwater cutthroat angler. Even a small protrusion along any beach can become a Venus Fly Trap for baitfish and krill during certain phases of the tide and when this phenomenon occurs some very fast fishing can result. This event takes shape when the tide pushes a seam of current moves in close to a point of land. The current seam, running parallel to the beach develops an eddy in the lee between the current line and the beach behind the point. Rather than get swept along in the seam of current, forage fish and krill will slide into the calm water of the eddy and there they sit feeling secure but are actually trapped and at the mercy of foraging cutthroat. It can make for some very fast and furious fishing. As the tide shifts, the same phenomenon usually occurs on the opposite side of the land point and the angler is afforded another go at the cutthroat which usually lasts until the tide has dropped and the eddy is lost until the next tide turn.

At times cutthroat can be seen feeding along the outside edge of a current seam. This is when you utilize a fly-swinging techniques not unlike tracking your fly through a river pool when steelhead fishing. A cast is made angling in the direction of and slightly outside of the current seam. Then you simply throw a big mend and allow the fly to swing along the seam. Use a slow, deliberate retrieve as the fly swings. If a strike doesn't come on the first part of the swing, always allow the fly to drift into the calm water all the while continuing an erratic retrieve. Remember that it does not require a large protrusion of land to create a current seam and even a moderate eddy between the seam and shoreline filled with trapped baitfish and krill can provide some very productive cutthroat fishing.

Estuaries and Tide Flats

The nearly endless estuaries that form deltas along the Pacific Coast range from mighty flows of the Columbia or Frazer, which are not the most conducive to fly fishing; to smaller rivers like the Puntledge in British Columbia;

Washington's Nemah; the Sixes in Oregon or the Matole in northern California on down to tiny jump-across creeks that flow almost anonymously into often overlooked bays and inlets.

Some rivers terminate in estuaries of long incline that run out upwards of a mile at low tide, winding through oyster beds and mud flats before consummating their union with the salt. Large rivers that flow into expansive grassy deltas braid and twist forming oxbows and cut banks that are prime cover for cutthroat from the low turn to high ebb. Others tumble rather quickly into the salt and are of comparatively miniscule flow, often being mere trickles during the summer, easily jumped across. Each is important to the coastal cutthroat angler – and each provides a uniquely different type of home base for the coastal cutthroat. Learning the distinctive differences of each type of estuary or tide flat can extend the knowledgeable saltwater angler's season from spring through fall to nearly a year-around sport.

Long Incline Tide Flats

Mud bottomed tide flats where there is a long daily run out through grassy meadows and over oyster beds are common throughout the protected waters of Washington and British Columbia. If these estuaries have not been hopelessly sullied by extensive logging, water diversions or other forms of human development they provide prime habitat for coastal cutthroat trout. The mix of fresh and salt water that runs daily through tide flats and estuaries forms a food-rich blend that makes them absolute smorgasbords of succulent sculpins, pill bugs, salmon smolts, small crabs and shellfish. Such a culinary spread never escapes the attention of the sea-run cutthroat.

Estuaries and tide flats, and I include in these all of the tiny feeder creek outlets that run onto the gently sloping mud shoulders of coastal bays, are wonderful places to be; alive and vital, and very attractive to coastal cutthroat.

Dan Lemaich checks out a prime cutthroat beach near his Camano Island home.

Such places are very special for me in the fall when maple and alder leaves are turning yellow; the first chill of winter's bite rides in on the breeze and rafts of early migrating mallards and pintails are forming out in the bays. Having fished estuaries for a lot of my life, I have always felt that fall is the best time to be tramping along a salt marsh trail in quest of the cutthroats that I know will be surging up into the river's flow on each inward turn of the tide then dropping back slowly as the tide runs out, feeding at will on an energy-packed variety of fish, krill and other small crustaceans.

My bond to tide flats and estuaries began on the Johns and Elk rivers in Grays Harbor County along with several nameless creeks a short hike or bicycle ride from my home in Bay City, Washington. These two rivers and nearby creeks made up just about my entire fishing environment until I entered high school. At low tide the rivers wound out through vast black mud flats and were not fishable without caking my clothes completely with the thick gumbo which was looked upon with precious little pleasure by my mother on wash day. On the incoming tide however it was a very different story when the water flooded back into the tidal reaches of the rivers and the brackish lower pools came alive with big cutthroat trout. I would then fish from just after the low tide turn until the high ebb quitting only after it had run out again for at least two hours when the shoreline mud once again displayed its slick, black barrier.

To this day, more than fifty years later, many of the same tide flat streams of Washington's Grays Harbor and Pacific counties that I fished as a boy continue to host fishable runs of coastal cutthroat that move easily in and out of the lower tidal pools throughout the summer before moving into the river for spawning in late autumn. On the incoming tide they are quite easily fished by simply walking the grassy banks and casting a baitfish imitation or attractor pattern to any cover that will provide a hiding spot for a foraging cutthroat. On small, shallow estuaries I employ a floating line for most of this fishing. On broader and deeper tidal areas I may employ a sinking tip or sinking head line that will carry my fly down into deep, dark holes and undercuts.

Through the years, particularly during the spring and early summer, I have found a high percentage of exceptionally large cutthroats in tide flat estuaries although not in great numbers. It may be that big cutthroats stake a claim to these places due to the abundance of food. Later in the season, as the numbers of cutthroat build in the tidal pools prior to the spawning run, there is a broader mix of large and small cutthroat. Since I find cutthroat fairly consistently through the summer and into early autumn in and around long incline estuaries I have determined that they do not venture very far out into the adjacent bays or inlets. Although they have migrated out of the upper river, they seem to remain almost resident from the brackish area between upper tidal pools out to the complete mix of fresh and salt water.

While baitfish, krill and pill bug imitations are effective in tidal pools, bright patterns should not be overlooked. Attractors like the Mickey Finn, Brad's Brat or Omnibus will very often trigger a strike from a cutthroat that has inexplicably turned away from a more realistic offering. Having often plied attractor patterns to entice a strike from cutthroats that have shown cool indifference to more imitative offerings accounts for the selection of bright, hair wing flies stashed in a corner of my saltwater fly box.

Small Rivers with Broad and Braided Flats

Small rivers that either braid extensively or have developed a wandering shoreline as they flow through deltas and salt marsh flats offer superb angling for coastal cutthroat. They provide so much cover that can be easily reached with a cast fly as they flow through grassy fields before joining the salt that it is rare not to locate at least a few cutthroats on any given day.

When the tide floods, the broad flats and channels attract a cornucopia of forage which in turn brings cutthroats onto the hunt. Many such rivers of easily fished size, like the Nemah and its forks, feed into Willapa Bay. The Dosewallups, Duckabush and Hamma Hamma rivers are a few examples of streams that flow into Hood Canal through many channels in the salt marsh grass to provide one hiding place after another for feeding cutthroat trout. Edged with trails beaten down by a variety of wildlife, waterfowl hunters or anglers and laced with muskrat dens along the intertidal line, these estuaries hold a lifetime of mysteries for the cutthroat angler to solve. Each cut bank, deep hole and root wad is a potential hideout for cutthroats that have moved in with the incoming tide to forage on krill and bait fish. Every spring young, outmigrating salmonids that sweep down from the stream add additional substance to the rich estuarine broth to keep the cutthroats around.

Fishing these shanks, bends and woody cover can be rewarding but approaching a likely looking spot with too heavy a foot fall is not the way to go about it. I have found that just like when I fish the beaches, making my first couple of casts while standing back from the bank will avoid spooking a cutthroat and sometimes trigger a strike. If a strike is not forthcoming, I crouch down, before inching closer to the edge of the bank, a technique advised more than once in the articles of one of my favorite fishing writers of years past, Tom McNally. From my low-to-the-ground position I cast several more times through the likely water and to all sides of any cover while offering the lowest possible profile. This stratagem has worked for me too many times in such situations to be discounted.

Small-Stream Estuaries

Small creeks, particularly those that drain narrow ravines along evergreen shrouded banks of the Olympic Peninsula coastline, Hood Canal or lesser populated areas of Puget Sound in Washington and similar small brooks in British Columbia support an important facet of the fishery that can extend the season considerably for the dedicated salt water angler. Small streams usually do not receive a large enough head of water to allow cutthroat up into the spawning gravel until late autumn or early winter. Since these small stream cutthroats spend a much longer period each season in saltwater, they offer the beach angler a longer period of time to tempt them than do fish born to larger rivers.

These little creeks are almost always heavily bordered with brush and so narrow as to be nearly impossible to fish much further than the upper reach of high tide. My angling pals and I know several little creeks that provide good late-season fishing when cutthroat homing in on larger rivers have long since moved well upstream. I'm sure that most saltwater cutthroat anglers have similar favorite spots that produce good beach fishing into late fall.

Fishing the salt water within a hundred yards or so on either side of these little creek mouths during an incoming tide and through the high turn is most productive. However, baitfish and krill imitations that usually bring strikes become less effective on cutthroat that are near spawning readiness. This is when I switch to sparsely dressed attractor patterns like the Allard Yellow, Allard Orange, or my own Beach Fly.

Small-Stream Flats

In Washington we have a great many fairly expansive, shallow, hard-bottomed flats that are fed by small streams. Similar flats can be found throughout coastal Washington, British Columbia and Alaska. These are easily waded as the footing is firm and it is possible to walk out for a long distance without ever being in much past one's knees. Streams feeding these flats are usually associated with fall runs of chum salmon in Washington. From early summer until October when the vanguard chum salmon show up, these shallow estuaries, rich with eel grass, oyster shells and clutches of mussels attract krill followed by small baitfish which in turn bring in foraging cutthroat trout.

Late in the season, school after school of chum salmon arrive at these little flats, roiling the water and jamming the mouth of the feeder creeks at each high tide and running the cutthroat off in the process. Experienced anglers use the antics of the love-struck dog salmon to their advantage. Casting along the outside edges of these estuaries anglers often find cutthroat slashing into scattered baitfish that have been driven away from the creek mouth by the ruckus of the rampaging chums.

Timing for Fishing Estuaries and Tide Flats

I have found through the years that small estuaries and tide flats usually fish best before and after the high turn. Conversely, large, expansive tide flats produce better after the low turn and until the tide is about halfway in. I attribute this to the fact that I am able to cast over most of the productive water on a small tide flat all the way through the flood. On very large, wide flats there is almost always too much water at high tide to negotiate easily on foot and far too much room for cutthroat to ramble around putting them out of casting range — unless some of the edges have easily reached side channels.

When a very low tide occurs, called a minus tide, I rarely enjoy what I would call good fishing. It seems that a nearly dewatered estuary brought about by a minus tide becomes devoid of bait, thus does not hold the attention of feeding cutthroat.

My personal observations on the best times to fish estuaries and tide flats should not be construed as absolutely infallible. Every estuary has its own rhythm and each fishes a bit differently. Furthermore fishing success can vary greatly depending on the height of the flood or length of run out before the low turn. Even with all the scientific knowledge we now have on the tides I doubt if we will ever completely figure out the mysteries of fishing estuaries. Perhaps this is as it should be. The coastal cutthroat is a mysterious trout. Why shouldn't one of its favorite haunts also be shrouded in a cloak of mystery?

Looking Ahead

With our long history of seeking cutthroat trout in salt water one might think that every beach and bay has been discovered and that anglers are casting shoulder-to-shoulder from Puget Sound in Washington to Southeast Alaska. Although some urban beaches do get crowded at times, for the most part there are still miles of easily accessed beaches that are practically barren of anglers. Since the earliest days of coastal cutthroat fishing in the salt more than seventy years

ago the sport has indeed experienced significant growth, especially during the past twenty years. It has been slow growth though when compared to other trout fishing throughout western North America. At no time has the growth been so dynamic that that salt water angling for coastal cutthroat can be considered crowded. There is still room to fish comfortably on mile after mile of shoreline yet to be explored in Washington. In British Columbia there are estuaries and bays draining wilderness areas that are crying out to be discovered. In Southeast Alaska the cutthroat is very lightly fished on the lower mainland and Prince of Wales Island.

Some of the angling growth that has occurred on coastal cutthroat in Washington and British Columbia can be explained by the burgeoning fishery along the beaches for coho salmon. Cutthroats are taken incidentally by anglers seeking coho, in part at least since both species cruise the same water and feed on the same forage.

Another reason for the growing interest in coastal cutthroat can be attributed to the increasingly tough fishing for steelhead through the 1990s. With so many restrictions and closures placed on steelhead, anglers looking for a diversion have turned to the cutthroat trout. This has happened before. If and when some of the problems surrounding steelhead are resolved, fishing impact on the coastal cutthroat will very likely decrease again. At the merest inclination of improved steelhead fishing the swains of Oncorhynchus mykiss, two-handed rods at the ready, will abandon the coastal cutthroat like a used Saturday night doxy and return with breathless ardor to the courtship of their first love.

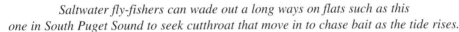

Saltwater fly-fishers can wade out a long ways on flats such as this one in South Puget Sound to seek cutthroat that move in to chase bait as the tide rises.

Fishing from a boat or skiff

I have always preferred to fish on my feet, walking my favorite beaches and casting without worrying about the movement of my boat in the current, or being driven too near, or swept too far from a likely spot. I readily admit, however that a boat surely does allow the angler mobility that far exceeds shank's mare and can be the difference between success and the skunk on any given day.

One day during the shooting of our television series, "Fly-Fishing Northwest", Pete Van Gytenbeek and I grew restless floating around on Captain Keith Robbins' camera boat while Steve Raymond and Cam Sigler were being featured fishing from an open skiff for the saltwater segment of a coastal cutthroat program. Pete finally grabbed one of Robbins' fly rods and cast out a squid pattern on a sinking line. Within seconds of hitting bottom in about thirty-five feet of water and beginning a retrieve, Pete was hooked up to a fish that we first thought was a coho. It turned out to be a 20-inch coastal cutthroat that was cruising a good 200-feet offshore over a relatively deep sandy bottom. I grabbed a second rod from the rack and was soon into another cutthroat only slightly smaller than Van's. We'd have never reached these fish from shore or without the fast-sinking lines on Robbins' light salmon fly rods.

I fish often with Bruce Ferguson who has a custom-outfitted 15-foot Tiderunner that is seaworthy and fast. It is a smooth, solid ride that quickly covers the best spots around Bruce's South Puget Sound bailiwick. Moving from place to place in his boat we've certainly enjoyed good days that would not have been nearly so productive if we had been fishing on foot.

For several years I fished South Puget Sound from a 12-foot aluminum Jon boat powered by a 4-horsepower Evanrude outboard. This was a great little craft that I could easily load and unload from the top of my truck. It held all my gear and would scoot around the protected bays of South Sound safely and was a perfect casting station. When I moved from Gig Harbor to Seattle I sold the boat and have yet to decide whether or not to purchase another.

Throughout the realm of the coastal cutthroat there are areas that can certainly be fished more productively or explored more thoroughly by boat. From South Puget Sound northward through British Columbia waters and into Southeast Alaska, there is cutthroat water that will only ever be cast over by an angler in a boat.

The Quiet Boat

Although coastal cutthroat will sometimes follow a fly right up to the gunwale of a boat, or hit a lure trolled practically in the engine wake, at times they can be surprisingly easy to frighten off by excessive noise from the motor or from walking around carelessly in the boat.

Muffling undue boat noise is easily accomplished by laying down indoor/outdoor carpeting on the deck. This not only reduces the sound of unduly heavy footfalls but keeps the deck from getting slippery when it is raining.

More important in regard to actually fishing is engine noise. The trick here is to be observant and when you spot rolling or jumping cutthroat, check the direction of your drift. Set your boat up so that you will drift toward the cutthroat and then shut down the engine. Don't hesitate to drift silently toward the feeding cutthroats from as far as a hundred feet or more away. This admittedly requires patience but will often put you within casting range of a cutthroat that could have been scared off by a noisy approach.

As you drift into range, a few well placed casts into the area where the cutthroat was spotted will almost always bring a strike. If this doesn't work, turn and make a few casts over the deeper water and allow the fly to sink a bit further before beginning your retrieve. Remember, as previously noted, that deeper cobbled bottoms interspersed with sandy spaces sometimes hold cutthroat that cannot be reached from shore. Since you can cover more water from a boat you might as well take advantage of the opportunity. For this fishing it is a good idea to have two rods strung; one with a floating or intermediate sinking line and a second with a fast sinking head for really getting your fly deep.

Conclusion

For now and into the foreseeable future, fishing for coastal cutthroat trout in salt water is looking pretty good. Fish and Wildlife Department officials are beginning to realize just how important this little fish can be to the salt water fly angler and the sport fishing economy. Through some reaches of its saltwater range the cutthroat's numbers continue to decline. This decline has however been slowed down significantly and in many reversed, thanks in large part to the grass roots efforts of sportsman and conservation groups lobbying for habitat restoration, restricted bag limits and catch-and-release regulations wherever they have been imposed. So, in this writer's opinion, anyone who has not yet cast a fly into the salt in an effort to catch a coastal cutthroat trout should wait no longer. I cannot imagine a better way to test one's light tackle skills. Think about it. With nothing more than your basic trout outfit and a valid fishing license you are casting to a true wild sea trout; a luxury that would cost you and arm and leg in other parts of the world.

If you fish estuaries, even one or two that are within reasonable driving distance, for a period of a few years you will find that every trip brings a new discovery. An estuary will not always give freely of its piscatorial bounty. I have fished for days on an estuary from the low tide turn past high ebb without a strike. Then the next day I may get a strike or two. One more day may bring me superb fishing with perhaps a half-dozen cutthroats brought to hand. This lack of a "sure thing" quality is one of the reasons that estuaries don't appeal to the angling masses who prefer the stacked deck of a hatchery-stuffed lake or river. This is just fine with me because the angling masses have a way of killing estuaries.

Bibliography

California

California Fishing, Tom Sienstra (Avalon Travel)

No-Nonsense Guide to Fly Fishing in Northern California
Ken Hanley (David Communications)

Fly Fishing Northern California Waters, Lilly Wong
(Frank Amato Publications)

Inland Fishes of California, Peter Moyle,
(University of California Press)

Streamside Map: Smith River, George Burdick
(Streamside Maps)

Streamside Map: Klamath River,
George Burdick (Streamside Maps)

California's Smith River, George Burdick (Frank Amato
Publications)

Oregon

Rainland Fly Patterns Tying and Fishing Guide, Rainland
Fly Casters (Frank Amato Publications)

Northwest Fly Fishing; Trout and Beyond, John Shewey
(Frank Amato Publications)

*Sea-Run Cutthroat Trout: Biology, Management, and Future
Conservation*, Oregon Chapter, American Fisheries Society
Corvallis, Oregon

Washington

The Estuary Angler, Steve Raymond
(Frank Amato Publications)

Year of the Trout, Steve Raymond (Simon & Schuster)

Walks & Hikes on the Beaches Around Puget Sound,
Harvey Manning and Penny Manning (The Mountaineers)

Alaska

Fly Patterns of Alaska, Alaska Flyfishers,
(Frank Amato Publications)

British Columbia

Famous British Columbia Fly-Fishing Waters,
Arthur Lingren (Frank Amato Publications)

The Essential Guide to Fly Fishing in British Columbia,
Edited by Robert L. Jones (Blue Ribbon Books)

Fly Patterns of British Columbia, Arthur Lingren
(Frank Amato Publications)

Fraser River, Fish.n.Map Company

Index